The New Pan-Americanism and the Structuring of Inter-American Relations

What is Pan-Americanism? People have been struggling with that problem for over a century. Pan-Americanism is (and has been) an amalgam of diplomatic, political, economic, and cultural projects under the umbrella of hemispheric cooperation and housed institutionally in the Pan-American Union, and later the Organization of American States. *But what made Pan-Americanism exceptional?* The chapters in this volume suggest that Pan-Americanism played a central and lasting role in structuring inter-American relations, because of the ways in which the movement was reinvented over time, and because the actors who shaped it often redefined and redeployed the term. Through the twentieth century, new appropriations of Pan-Americanism structured, restructured, and redefined inter-American relations. Taken together, these chapters underscore two exciting new shifts in how scholars and others have come to understand Pan-Americanism and inter-American relations. First, Pan-Americanism is increasingly understood not simply as a diplomatic, commercial, and economic forum, but a movement that has included cultural exchange. Second, researchers, political leaders, and the media in several countries have traditionally conceived of Pan-Americanism as a mechanism of US expansionism. This volume reimagines Pan-Americanism as a movement built by actors from all corners of the Americas.

Juan Pablo Scarfi is Research Associate at the Argentine National Scientific and Technical Research Council (CONICET) and Lecturer in Global History & International Relations, University of San Andres, Argentina.

David M. K. Sheinin is Professor of History at Trent University.

Routledge Studies in the History of the Americas

Rio de Janeiro in the Global Meat Market, c. 1850 to c. 1930
How Fresh and Salted Meat Arrived at the Carioca Table
Maria-Aparecida Lopes

American Divergences in the Great Recession
Daniele Pompejano

Social and Political Transitions During the Left Turn in Latin America
Edited by Karen Silva-Torres, Carolina Rozo-Higuera and Daniel S. Leon

A New Struggle for Independence in Modern Latin America
Edited by Pablo A. Baisotti

Problems and Alternatives in the Modern Americas
Edited by Pablo A. Baisotti

Setbacks and Advances in the Modern Latin American Economy
Edited by Pablo A. Baisotti

Social, Political, and Religious Movements in the Modern Americas
Edited by Pablo A. Baisotti

The Policy of the Ford Administration Toward Cuba
Carrot and Stick
Håkan Karlsson and Tomás Diez Acosta

The New Pan-Americanism and the Structuring of Inter-American Relations
Edited by Juan Pablo Scarfi and David M. K. Sheinin

For more information about this series, please visit: https://www.routledge.com/Routledge-Studies-in-the-History-of-the-Americas/book-series/RSHAM

The New Pan-Americanism and the Structuring of Inter-American Relations

Edited by
Juan Pablo Scarfi and David M. K. Sheinin

NEW YORK AND LONDON

First published 2022
by Routledge
605 Third Avenue, New York, NY 10158

and by Routledge
2 Park Square, Milton Park, Abingdon, Oxon OX14 4RN

Routledge is an imprint of the Taylor & Francis Group, an informa business

© 2022 selection and editorial matter, Juan Pablo Scarfi and David M. K. Sheinin; individual chapters, the contributors

The right of Juan Pablo Scarfi and David M. K. Sheinin to be identified as the authors of the editorial material, and of the authors for their individual chapters, has been asserted in accordance with sections 77 and 78 of the Copyright, Designs and Patents Act 1988.

All rights reserved. No part of this book may be reprinted or reproduced or utilised in any form or by any electronic, mechanical, or other means, now known or hereafter invented, including photocopying and recording, or in any information storage or retrieval system, without permission in writing from the publishers.

Trademark notice: Product or corporate names may be trademarks or registered trademarks, and are used only for identification and explanation without intent to infringe.

Library of Congress Cataloging-in-Publication Data
Names: Scarfi, Juan Pablo, 1979- editor. | Sheinin, David, editor.
Title: The new Pan-Americanism and the structuring of inter-American relations / edited by Juan Pablo Scarfi and David M. K. Sheinin.
Description: New York, NY : Routledge, [2022] | Series: Routledge studies in the history of the Americas ; 30 | Includes bibliographical references and index.
Identifiers: LCCN 2021045845 (print) | LCCN 2021045846 (ebook) | ISBN 9781032180625 (hardback) | ISBN 9781032180632 (paperback) | ISBN 9781003252672 (ebook) | ISBN 9781000547313 (adobe pdf) | ISBN 9781000547320 (epub)
Subjects: LCSH: Pan-Americanism. | Latin America--Foreign relations--1980- | United States--Foreign relations--1989-
Classification: LCC F1418 .N398 2022 (print) | LCC F1418 (ebook) | DDC 980.03--dc23
LC record available at https://lccn.loc.gov/2021045845
LC ebook record available at https://lccn.loc.gov/2021045846

ISBN: 978-1-032-18062-5 (hbk)
ISBN: 978-1-032-18063-2 (pbk)
ISBN: 978-1-003-25267-2 (ebk)

DOI: 10.4324/9781003252672

Typeset in Sabon
by Taylor & Francis Books

For Kayleigh Hindman and Ricardo D. Salvatore

Contents

Introduction: The Pan-American Shift from Apology for Empire to
Imperial Critique to Latin American Agency   1
JUAN PABLO SCARFI AND DAVID M. K. SHEININ

1   Imperial Pan-Americanism   11
AIDA RODRÍGUEZ

2   Architects, Exchange, and the Consolidation of Pan-American
Cooperation, 1914–40   22
MARK J. PETERSEN

3   Becoming the Third World: Pan-Americanism, South
Americanism, and Liberal Economics in the 1920s   45
TERESA DAVIS

4   Pan-American Intellectual Cooperation: Emergence,
Institutionalization, and Fields of Action   65
JULIETTE DUMONT

5   Popular Pan-Americanism, North and South: International
Relations and the Idea of "American Unity" in Argentina and
the United States, 1939–45   90
LISA UBELAKER

6   The Colombo–Lanusse Doctrine: Cold War Anti-
interventionism and the End of Pan-Americanism   116
DAVID M. K. SHEININ

7   Pan-American Human Rights: The Legacy of Pan-Americanism
and the Intellectual Origins of the Inter-American Human
Rights System   138
JUAN PABLO SCARFI

8 Epilogue: Pan-Americanism and the Changing Nature of US
  Hegemony 163
  RICARDO D. SALVATORE

  Contributors 174
  Index 176

Introduction

The Pan-American Shift from Apology for Empire to Imperial Critique to Latin American Agency

Juan Pablo Scarfi and David M. K. Sheinin

For at least a century and a half, people have been trying to make sense of Pan-Americanism as an unwieldy, changing set of ideals and actions. What *was* Pan-Americanism? There was more agreement in the early twentieth century than at other times. Those writing often saw it as a movement dedicated to a common hemispheric ideal of cooperation and friendly exchange, though not without diplomatic controversies over US military intervention in Latin America. During the Cold War period, many Latin Americans conceived of Pan-Americanism as US-led and a smokescreen for imperialism. At the end of the twentieth century, influenced by a generation of revisionist historians critical of US foreign policy, many US Americans also conceived of Pan-Americanism as the friendly face of US aggression in Latin America. All the while, the agency of Latin Americans in shaping the movement was frequently set aside.

The chapters in this volume reorder our understanding on Pan-Americanism and its legal, diplomatic, political, cultural, and social components. They focus less on the United States and more on Latin American actors, movements, and civic organizations to explain Pan-American initiatives as a hemisphere-wide phenomenon that reflected the interests of Latin American peoples as much as they did those of US Americans. In *Beyond the Ideal: Pan Americanism in Inter-American Affairs* (2000), David M. K. Sheinin provided a succinct definition that signaled the elusiveness of an easy definition of Pan-Americanism. "At its simplest," he argued, "it defines a movement started in the 1880s by diplomats, business leaders, and politicians from many countries. Spearheaded principally by the United States, Pan Americanism was meant to organize the Western Hemisphere republics into an international cooperative body."[1] Sheinin pointed out that it was above all a US-centric movement: "Pan Americanism has always been US led, the friendly face of US dominance in the hemisphere."[2] Pan-Americanism, then, always featured this combination of a movement under US leadership and hegemony, but with continental multilateral prospects and incentives.

In *Cooperation and Hegemony in US–Latin American Relations* (2016), Juan Pablo Scarfi and Andrew Tillman revisited the Western Hemisphere idea, a term coined by Arthur P. Whitaker and associated with the

DOI: 10.4324/9781003252672-1

continental ideal of Pan-America. They also suggested that Pan-Americanism should be seen as a movement of both cooperation and hegemony: The "Western Hemisphere idea—and Pan-Americanism—is a helpful and informative framework of analysis to explore the tensions and contradictions between cooperation and hegemony, intervention and engagement, support and distrust that have characterized the history and politics of US–Latin American relations."[3] According to Whitaker, *The Western Hemisphere Idea* (1954) entailed that "the peoples of this Hemisphere stand in a special relationship to one another which sets them apart from the rest of the world."[4] Whitaker was imagining something larger than the diplomacy of inter-American relations. As a movement, Pan-Americanism forged this idea of continental exceptionalism, according to which the Western Hemisphere was distinct from Europe in the conduct of international affairs and diplomacy, and in existing political, legal and cultural traditions. Driven by the contradictory stimuli of continental cooperation and US hegemony, Pan-Americanism has made of the Americas and inter-American relations an exceptional system of international relations, unusually prone to reinterpretation and reinvention by diplomatic actors and scholarly interpreters.

What else made Pan-Americanism exceptional? Starting with the contributors to *Beyond the Ideal* and *Cooperation and Hegemony*, we have a movement with a multilateral character, with high ideals, distinct from European diplomatic traditions that seemed more rigid to Whitaker and others, and that reflected US hegemony in the Americas. This volume goes one step further in arguing that Pan-Americanism played a central and lasting role in structuring inter-American relations because of the ways the movement was reinvented, and because the actors who shaped it often redefined and redeployed the term. Through the twentieth century, new appropriations of Pan-Americanism structured, restructured, and redefined inter-American relations, particularly following the golden age of the movement in the 1930s when the US Good Neighbor Policy was institutionalized and inter-American multilateralism consolidated.

Two Decades ago, influenced by revisionist historians of US foreign relations like Walter La Feber and Stephen G. Rabe, several contributors to *Beyond the Ideal* were critical of violent US aggression in Latin America, often papered over by the friendly face of Pan-Americanism. In the years since, studies on Pan-Americanism and inter-American relations have reordered the field by focusing less on the United States and more on Latin American actors, movements and civic organizations to explain Pan-American initiatives. The chapters in this volume reflect this transformation of how most scholars now understand Pan-Americanism and inter-American affairs.

Classic studies of Pan-Americanism written in the first half of the twentieth century were often celebratory and at times nostalgic about the genesis of the movement. In one of the first studies devoted to the subject, *Pan-Americanism: Its Beginnings* (1920), Joseph Byrne Lockey regarded the Pan-American Conferences as a lofty morality tale. He stated that, behind the

Pan-American conferences lay "a moral union of American states founded upon a body of principles growing out of the common struggle for independence."[5] Lockey's seven Pan-American tenets were national independence as political autonomy and separation; a community of political ideals; territorial integrity; the rule of law instead of force; non-intervention; equality of peoples; and hemispheric cooperation.[6] In addition, Pan-Americanism was to adopt a robust cultural dimension of intellectual cooperation that Lockey identified ambiguously. A generation later, Samuel Flagg Bemis's *The Latin American Policy of the United States* (1943) celebrated wistful narratives of Pan-Americanism as both hemispheric cooperation and benevolent US policy.[7] This and other examples of pre-Cold War US historiography were often an apologia for US expansionism. In a rejection of Bemis's 1940s triumphalism some liberal history graduate students in the 1960s referred disparagingly to Bemis as "Samuel 'Wave-the-Flagg' Bemis."

During the early Cold War period, Arthur P. Whitaker was one of a handful of historians who professionalized the study of Pan-Americanism in part by placing new emphasis on empirical rigor and archival research. Still, how US scholars understood Pan-Americanism in the United States had not changed substantially since the 1920s. There was some emphasis on Pan-American organizations, including the Pan American Institute of Geography and History. But for the most part, scholars continued to stress the diplomatic functions of Pan-Americanism (and after 1947, the Organization of American States (OAS)) through Pan-American and Inter-American Conferences. Most investigators agreed on sets of touchstones that defined each of the major conferences, while ignoring others, some of which Juan Pablo Scarfi addressed for the first time in *The Hidden History of International Law in the Americas: Empire and Legal Networks* (2017). The First Conference of American States (1889–90), according to traditional interpretations, emphasized broad notions of hemispheric cooperation with projects for the regularization of terms of international trade and investment. The Second and Third Conferences (1901–2 and 1906) produced Latin American criticisms of US intervention in the Caribbean basin. From 1920 to 1946, Leo S. Rowe served as director of the Pan-American Union. He combined a faith in US-led economic development in the Americas with a genuine interest in Pan-Americanism as an opportunity for transnational cultural cooperation that captured the attention of scholars. The Fifth through Seventh Pan-American Conferences drew attention for ongoing Latin American criticisms of US military intervention in the region but beginning with the Eighth Conference (1938), and through the following decade, Pan-Americanism became increasingly focused on inter-American diplomatic and military cooperation in the event of war.

During the early Cold War, anti-Communism emerged as a force in Pan-American meetings and diplomacy. This culminated in the passage of an anti-Communist resolution at the Tenth Inter-American Conference of the OAS (1954) that the US government used to justify its role in the military overthrow of Guatemalan President Jacobo Arbenz. An alliance spearheaded by right-wing authoritarian governments in the Americas and the United States pressed for the OAS to accept a new understanding of Pan-Americanism, identifying international Communism as the principal foreign threat of intervention. That shift prompted a new generation of Latin American scholarship on Pan-Americanism (and the popularization of earlier works) that still focused on US leadership, but unlike Whitaker and Bemis, was harshly critical of US imperialism. The Peruvian, *aprista* lawyer Ezequiel Ramírez Novoa published a remarkable nine editions of *La farsa del panamericanismo y la unidad indoamericana* in 1955. While he began his analysis with the First Conference of American States in 1889–90, Ramírez Novoa's study stressed the 1954 Tenth Inter-American Conference as an almost inevitable endpoint for a half-century of violent US imperialism under the umbrella of Pan-Americanism. Originally published in 1917 to little acclaim, the Mexican diplomat and jurist Carlos Pereyra's *El mito de Monroe* was reissued in 1959 to a much larger readership. With little subtlety (or research), Pereyra traced a direct line from the Monroe Doctrine through to early twentieth-century Pan-Americanism, with stated US policies of purported inter-American cooperation masking an ugly finance-driven search for US dominance in the hemisphere.[8]

Beginning in the 1960s and extending through the end of the century, authors increasingly described inter-American relations and Pan-Americanism as driven by realist hard power politics, hegemony, and US interventionism. Lars Schoultz, Peter Smith, and Brian Loveman, among others, presented US attitudes towards Latin America as less violently hostile than laid out in the analyses of Pereyra and Ramírez Novoa, but all the same, self-interested and motivated by interventionist aspirations.[9] These scholars regarded Pan-Americanism as naive and idealistic, contrasting the Pan-American ideal with crude US interventionist and expansionist policies across the region. This perspective has its origins in the Wisconsin School of historians of US foreign relations (1960s). The approach has been also globally influential and can be found in studies of Pan-Americanism written by dependency theorists of the era. This realist critical approach is epitomized in Alonso Aguilar's influential *El panamericanismo de la Doctrina Monroe a la Doctrina Johnson* (1965).[10]

In the last thirty years, a cultural turn in inter-American relations prompted a number of scholars to focus on Latin American agency in inter-American relations and by extension in Pan-Americanism and the Pan-American movement. They placed special attention on the cultural dimensions of transnational ties, beyond the sphere of hard diplomacy and statecraft.[11] Topics addressed have included cultural and intellectual cooperation, architecture, sports, feminism and gender rights, and the development of modern scholarly disciplines around the Pan-American movement such as Latin American studies and international law.[12]

With the rise of global history, there has been an attendant historiographic shift toward global, hemispheric, and comparative approaches to the study of US–Latin American relations, Pan-Americanism and the international history of the Americas.[13] Most of these explorations have questioned ideas and historical traditions associated with US exceptionalism, highlighting the importance of Latin American actors. These global comparative histories of the United States and Latin America also generated innovative reflections on the extent to which Latin America has influenced and shaped the history of the United States, in addition to the other way around, long the central concern of the historiography of Pan-Americanism. Many new works have focused on the connections between national identities, cultural diplomatic agendas, and Pan-Americanism as a transnational hemispheric movement. This recent historiography has shed new light on the linkages between the local and the global in the evolution of Pan-Americanism and how those linkages shaped the cultural history of international relations and cultural diplomacy in Latin American countries.[14]

Contributors to this book shift the analytical focus even further toward the importance of Latin American actors, agency, and initiatives in the structuring of Pan-Americanism, the Pan-American movement, and inter-American relations in local, national, and transnational settings. On the face of it, Aida Rodríguez's "Imperial Pan-Americanism" may seem closer in analytical emphasis to Pereyra than to more recent scholarship and attendant shifts in the scholarly literature beginning in the 1990s. Rodríguez frames Pan-Americanism in a structuralist analysis of US hegemonic imperialism. But her contribution is far more than a revival of the anti-imperial critique of the movement. In addition to providing a dynamic new analysis of how US imperialism was structured, Rodríguez will prompt readers on two key points. First, her work reflects much of the best scholarly literature in Spain, Germany, and other European countries—as well as in many parts of Latin America—where the best scholarship on Pan-Americanism never abandoned the centrality of US hegemonic imperialism as an analytical framework. Moreover, in a reflection of the profundity of economic, racial, political, and related crises in Latin American countries as essentially modern, many branches of scholarship never underwent the post-modern shifts witnessed in Europe and North America and, as a consequence, continue to some extent to frame the analysis of inter-American relations terms as a function of Lenin's stages of imperial expansion. Second, Rodríguez draws on Robert Alexander González's *Designing Pan-America: US Architectural Visions for the Western Hemisphere* (2011) and other scholarly works unprepared to throw the baby out with the bath water. For González, Rodríguez and others Latin American agency in Pan-Americanism and US hegemonic empire are not mutually exclusive dynamics.

In "Architects, Exchange, and the Consolidation of Pan-American Cooperation, 1914–40," Mark Petersen rejects the reduction of Pan-American cooperation to US hegemonic aspirations. Drawing on the inter-American cooperation of architects, Petersen shows that a broad range of actors from across the Americans drew on a Pan-American framework to advance their particular projects and policies. In so doing, they shaped inter-American relations from all points of the hemisphere. Teresa Davis also rejects Pan-Americanism as an instrument of US hegemony in her chapter, "Becoming Third World: Pan-Americanism, South Americanism, and Liberal Economics in the 1920s." She brings a global backdrop to the problem of Pan-Americanism and finds the issue of US "noxiousness and duplicity" in its efforts to exact economic dominance in the Americas so painfully obvious that they may have dulled scholarly inquiry into Latin American economic agency. Davis argues that Pan-American networks became a forum in which Latin American economists considered and acted upon state intervention in 1920s economies. Moreover, she reasons that regional confrontation of the sort scholars explained in the context of Latin American anti-intervention at Pan American conferences was, in fact, a forerunner of the long-term class of a liberal North and a nationalist South that began to test inter-American ties in the 1930s.

Juliette Dumont's "Pan-American Intellectual Cooperation: Emergence, Institutionalization, and Fields of Action" is the strongest rejection in the volume of the longstanding anti-imperial critique of US-led Pan-Americanism by which Latin America is held up as "the passive recipient of American imperialism." Dumont finds Latin American agency in intellectual cooperation over a broad range of areas within the Pan-American movement, sometimes as a set of projects aimed at asserting distinct Latin American national policies and agendas within the movement. In "Popular Pan-Americanism, North and South: International Relations and the Idea of 'American Unity' in Argentina and the United States, 1939–45," Lisa Ubelaker hones in on how, from 1939 to 1942, forms of everyday Pan-Americanism thrived in cities and towns across the United States in pageants, parades, fashion, cooking, and a range of other celebrations. She explains this brief flourish of popular Pan-Americanism in a larger context of US modernities and popular understandings of the Good Neighbor Policy, but also with reference to popular understandings of Pan-Americanism in Argentina in the period immediately before the start of the Cold War.

The end of Pan-Americanism has sometimes been heralded (and lamented). In "The Colombo–Lanusse Doctrine: Cold War Anti-interventionism and the End of Pan-Americanism," David M. K. Sheinin identifies an end point in the 1960s to much of what shaped diplomatic Pan-Americanism for almost a century. The Colombo–Lanusse doctrine was an Argentine strategic policy initiative to consolidate aspects of the Inter-American Treaty of Reciprocal Assistance (1947) into a militarized Pan-American alliance against Communism. The measure failed to sway other governments and its failure ushered in the most violent period of Latin American military rule. If the twenty years between 1960 and 1980 might be understood as a period of breakdown of Pan-American diplomacy, it also signaled the emerging importance of what, by the mid-1980s, may well have marked the emergence of the most significant and dynamic area of a new Pan-Americanism, the inter-American human rights system. In "Pan-American Human Rights: The Legacy of Pan-Americanism and the Intellectual Origins of the Inter-American Human Rights System," Juan Pablo Scarfi shows that human rights loomed large in Pan-Americanism in the search for a body of legal principles for the Americas. Human rights were bound up in the efforts of those who sought to create a body of Pan-American international law. In that search, Pan-American international legal norms on human rights helped define global human rights laws.

Notes

1 David Sheinin, "Rethinking Pan Americanism: An Introduction," *Beyond the Ideal: Pan Americanism in Inter-American Affairs*, ed. David Sheinin (Westport: Praeger, 2000), 1.
2 Sheinin, "Rethinking Pan Americanism," 1.
3 Juan Pablo Scarfi and Andrew R. Tillman, "Cooperation and Hegemony in US–Latin American Relations: An Introduction," *Cooperation and Hegemony in US-Latin American Relations: Revisiting the Western Hemisphere Idea*, ed. Juan Pablo Scarfi and Andrew Tillman (New York: Palgrave Macmillan, 2016), 2.
4 Arthur P. Whitaker, *The Western Hemisphere Idea: Its Rise and Decline* (Ithaca: Cornell University Press, 1954), 1.
5 Joseph Byrne Lockey, *Pan-Americanism: Its Beginnings* (New York: Macmillan, 1920), 33.
6 Lockey, *Pan-Americanism*, 33–5.
7 Samuel Flagg Bemis, *The Latin American Policy of the United States* (New York: Harcourt, Brace and Company, 1943), 262.
8 Carlos Pereyra, *El mito de Monroe* (Buenos Aires: Ediciones del Buho, 1959); E. Ramírez Novoa, *La farsa del panamericanismo y la unidad indoamericana* (Buenos Aires: Editorial Indoamericana, 1955).
9 Lars Schoultz, *Beneath the United States: A History of US Policy toward Latin America* (Cambridge: Harvard University Press, 1998), Peter Smith, *Talons of the Eagle: Dynamics of US-Latin American Relations* (New York: Oxford University Press, 2000); Brian Loveman, *No Higher Law: American Foreign Policy and the Western Hemisphere since 1776* (Chapel Hill: University of North Carolina Press, 2010).
10 Alonso Aguilar, *El panamericanismo de la Doctrina Monroe a la Doctrina Johnson* (México: Cuadernos Americanos, 1965); Lloyd C. Gardner and Thomas C. McCormick, "Walter LaFeber: The Making of a Wisconsin School Revisionist," *Diplomatic History* 28, no. 5 (2004): 613–24.
11 Max Paul Friedman, "Retiring the Puppets, Bringing Latin America Back in: Recent Scholarship on United States-Latin American Relations," *Diplomatic History* 27, no. 5 (2003): 621–36. See also, Gilbert M. Joseph, Catherine C. LeGrand, and Ricardo D. Salvatore, eds., *Close Encounters of Empire: Writing the Cultural History of US–Latin American Relations* (Durham: Duke University Press, 1998), David Sheinin, *Searching for Authority: Pan Americanism, Diplomacy and Politics in United States-Argentine Relations,1910–1930* (New Orleans: University Press of the South, 1998), Ricardo Salvatore, *Imágenes de un imperio: Estados Unidos y las formas de representación de América Latina* (Buenos Aires: Editorial Sudamericana, 2006).
12 Richard Cándida Smith, *Improvised Continent: Pan-Americanism and Cultural Exchange* (Philadelphia: University of Pennsylvania Press, 2017); Mark Petersen,

"The 'Vanguard of Pan-Americanism': Chile and Inter-American Multilateralism in the Early Twentieth Century," *Cooperation and Hegemony in US-Latin American Relations: Revisiting the Western Hemisphere Idea*, ed. Juan Pablo Scarfi and Andrew Tillman (New York: Palgrave Macmillan, 2016), 111–37; Petersen, "Argentine and Chilean Approaches to Modern Pan-Americanism, 1888–1930" (PhD diss., University of Oxford, 2014); Juliette Dumont, *Diplomaties culturelles et fabrique des identités: Argentine, Brésil, Chili (1919–1946)* (Rennes: Presses Universitaires de Rennes, 2018); Robert Alexander González, *Designing Pan-America: US Architectural Visions for the Western Hemisphere* (Austin: University of Texas Press, 2011); Cesar R. Torres and Bruce Kidd, "Introduction: The History and Relevance of the Pan-American Games," *International Journal of the History of Sport* 33, nos. 1–2 (2016): 1–5; David M. K. Sheinin, "The 1971 Pan-American Games and the Search for Colombian Modernities," *International Journal of the History of Sport* 33, nos. 1–2 (2016): 147–63; Megan Threlkeld, *Pan American Women: US Internationalists and Revolutionary Mexico* Charles A. Jones, *American Civilization* (London: Institute for the Study of the Americas, 2007), (Philadelphia: University of Pennsylvania Press, 2014); Katherine M. Marino, *Feminism for the Americas: The Making of an International Human Rights Movement* (Chapel Hill: University of North Carolina Press, 2019); Ricardo D. Salvatore, *Disciplinary Conquest: US Scholars in South America, 1900–1945* (Durham: Duke University Press, 2016); Juan Pablo Scarfi, *The Hidden History of International Law in the Americas: Empire and Legal Networks* (New York: Oxford University Press. 2017).

13 See for example, Charles A. Jones, *American Civilization* (London: Institute for the Study of the Americas, 2007), Felipe Fernández-Armesto, *The Americas: The History of a Hemisphere* (London: Phoenix, 2003), James Dunkerley, *Americana: The Americas in the World around 1850* (London: Verso, 2000), and Lester D. Langley, *The Americas in the Modern Age* (New Haven: Yale University Press, 2003).

14 Leandro Morgenfeld, *Vecinos en conflicto: Argentina y Estados Unidos en las conferencias panamericanas (1889–1955)* (Buenos Aires: Continente, 2011); Pablo Ortemberg, "Dossier: Panamericanismo, hispanoamericanismo y nacionalismo en los festejos identitarios de América Latina, 1880–1920. Performances y encrucijadas de diplomáticos e intelectuales," *Anuario IEHS* 32, no. 1 (2017): 99–110; Nathalia Henrich and Luciano Aronne de Abreu eds., "Dossiê: Pan-Americanismo: novos olhares sobre as relações continentais," *Estudos Ibero-Americanos* 46, no. 3 (2020): 1–3; Perla Zusman, "Negociando representacionalmente el panamericanismo. Estados Unidos y Argentina en la Exposición Universal de Búfalo (1901)," *Espaço e Cultura* 29 (2011): 22–34.

Bibliography

Aguilar, Alonso. *El panamericanismo de la Doctrina Monroe a la Doctrina Johnson*. Mexico City: Cuadernos Americanos, 1965.

Bemis, Samuel Flagg. *The Latin American Policy of the United States*. New York: Harcourt, Brace and Company, 1943.

Cándida Smith, Richard. *Improvised Continent: Pan-Americanism and Cultural Exchange*. Philadelphia: University of Pennsylvania Press, 2017.

Dumont, Juliette. *Diplomaties culturelles et fabrique des identités: Argentine, Brésil, Chili (1919–1946)*. Rennes: Presses Universitaires de Rennes, 2018.

Dunkerley, James. *Americana: The Americas in the World around 1850*. London: Verso, 2000.

Fernández-Armesto, Felipe. *The Americas: The History of a Hemisphere*. London: Phoenix, 2003.
Friedman, Max Paul. "Retiring the Puppets, Bringing Latin America Back in: Recent Scholarship on United States-Latin American Relations." *Diplomatic History* 27, no. 5 (2003): 621–636.
Gardner, Lloyd C. and Thomas C. McCormick. "Walter LaFeber: The Making of a Wisconsin School Revisionist." *Diplomatic History* 28, no. 5 (2004): 613–624.
González, Robert Alexander. *Designing Pan-America: US Architectural Visions for the Western Hemisphere*. Austin: University of Texas Press, 2011.
Henrich, Nathalia and Luciano Aronne de Abreu eds. "Dossiê: Pan-Americanismo: novos olhares sobre as relações continentais." *Estudos Ibero-Americanos* 46, no. 3 (2020): e38464. (doi:doi:10.15448/1980-864X.2020.3.38464)
Jones, Charles A. *American Civilization*. London: Institute for the Study of the Americas, 2007.
Joseph, Gilbert M., Catherine C. LeGrand, and Ricardo D. Salvatore, eds. *Close Encounters of Empire: Writing the Cultural History of US–Latin American Relations*. Durham: Duke University Press, 1998.
Langley, Lester D. *The Americas in the Modern Age*. New Haven: Yale University Press, 2003.
Lockey, Joseph Byrne. *Pan-Americanism: Its Beginnings*. New York: Macmillan, 1920.
Loveman, Brian. *No Higher Law: American Foreign Policy and the Western Hemisphere since 1776*. Chapel Hill: University of North Carolina Press, 2010.
Marino, Katherine M. *Feminism for the Americas: The Making of an International Human Rights Movement*. Chapel Hill: University of North Carolina Press, 2019.
Morgenfeld, Leandro. *Vecinos en conflicto: Argentina y Estados Unidos en las conferencias panamericanas (1889–1955)*. Buenos Aires: Continente, 2011.
Ortemberg, Pablo. "Dossier: Panamericanismo, hispanoamericanismo y nacionalismo en los festejos identitarios de América Latina, 1880–1920. Performances y encrucijadas de diplomáticos e intelectuales." *Anuario IEHS* 32, no. 1 (2017): 99–110.
Pereyra, Carlos. *El mito de Monroe*. Buenos Aires: Ediciones del Buho, 1959.
Petersen, Mark. "Argentine and Chilean Approaches to Modern Pan-Americanism, 1888–1930." PhD diss., University of Oxford, 2014.
Petersen, Mark. "The 'Vanguard of Pan-Americanism': Chile and Inter-American Multilateralism in the Early Twentieth Century." In *Cooperation and Hegemony in US–Latin American Relations: Revisiting the Western Hemisphere Idea*, edited by Juan Pablo Scarfi and Andrew Tillman, 111–137. New York: Palgrave Macmillan, 2016.
Ramírez Novoa, E. *La farsa del panamericanismo y la unidad indoamericana*. Buenos Aires: Editorial Indoamericana, 1955.
Salvatore, Ricardo D. *Disciplinary Conquest: US Scholars in South America, 1900–1945*. Durham: Duke University Press, 2016.
Salvatore, Ricardo D. *Imágenes de un imperio: Estados Unidos y las formas de representación de América Latina*. Buenos Aires: Editorial Sudamericana, 2006.
Scarfi, Juan Pablo. *The Hidden History of International Law in the Americas: Empire and Legal Networks*. New York: Oxford University Press. 2017.
Scarfi, Juan Pablo and Andrew R. Tillman. "Cooperation and Hegemony in US–Latin American Relations: An Introduction." In *Cooperation and Hegemony in US–Latin American Relations: Revisiting the Western Hemisphere Idea*, edited by Juan Pablo Scarfi and Andrew Tillman, 1–32. New York: Palgrave Macmillan, 2016.

Schoultz, Lars. *Beneath the United States: A History of US Policy toward Latin America*. Cambridge: Harvard University Press, 1998.

Sheinin, David M. K. "The 1971 Pan-American Games and the Search for Colombian Modernities." *International Journal of the History of Sport* 33, nos. 1–2 (2016): 147–163.

Sheinin, David, ed. *Beyond the Ideal: Pan Americanism in Inter-American Affairs*. Westport: Praeger, 2000.

Sheinin, David. "Rethinking Pan Americanism: An Introduction." In *Beyond the Ideal: Pan Americanism in Inter-American Affairs*, edited by David Sheinin, 1–8. Westport: Praeger, 2000.

Sheinin, David. *Searching for Authority: Pan Americanism, Diplomacy and Politics in United States-Argentine Relations,1910–1930*. New Orleans: University Press of the South, 1998.

Smith, Peter. *Talons of the Eagle: Dynamics of US–Latin American Relations*. New York: Oxford University Press, 2000.

Threlkeld, Megan. *Pan American Women: US Internationalists and Revolutionary Mexico*. Philadelphia: University of Pennsylvania Press, 2014.

Torres, Cesar R. and Bruce Kidd. "Introduction: The History and Relevance of the Pan-American Games." *International Journal of the History of Sport* 33, nos. 1–2 (2016): 1–5.

Whitaker, Arthur P. *The Western Hemisphere Idea: Its Rise and Decline*. Ithaca: Cornell University Press, 1954.

Zusman, Perla. "Negociando representacionalmente el panamericanismo: Estados Unidos y Argentina en la Exposición Universal de Búfalo (1901)." *Espaço e Cultura* 29 (2011): 22–34.

1 Imperial Pan-Americanism

Aida Rodríguez

There are two ways of looking at Pan-Americanism as informal imperial expansion. Pan-Americanism and its attendant objectives of commercial and financial investment advancement can be seen as a US response to late nineteenth-century overproduction in the US industrial sector and an imperative to ship surplus production overseas. In addition, Pan-Americanism underscored a predominant US racial and cultural discourse. The putative inferiority of Latin Americans stood as a basis in the United States for US hegemony in the hemisphere, with Pan-Americanism as an organizing framework for an ordered inter-American system.[1] After 1889, Washington promoted hegemonic Pan-Americanism as a weapon of realpolitik to reaffirm its positions as a local, regional, hemispheric, and global power. By contrast, a radical Pan-Americanism emerged in the Americas to counter the US hegemonic narrative, rooted in the history of anti-colonial struggle that opposed the US attempts to undermine Latin American sovereignty. Drawing on a common Latin American history of US exploitation, radical Pan-Americanism focused on greater economic, cultural, political and infrastructural cooperation that might overcome inequality and political oppression.[2] That version of the movement held little sway.

In 1823, responding to Venezuelan independence leader Simón Bolívar's initiatives to establish a union of newly independent countries in the Americas, the US presented itself unilaterally as the guarantor of independence and integrity in the Americas. US political leaders launched a narrative of shared struggle from North to South America against European colonialism. They often adopted Bolívar as a symbol of early Pan-Americanism,[3] with particular reference to his *Jamaica Letter* (1815) asserting that those in the Americas were different from Europeans and should free themselves from the absolutism of the Old World.[4] A congress of nations was held in Panama in 1826 to consolidate a stable confederation of states in the hemisphere and to eliminate the threat of former colonial powers reasserting control in the region.[5] Participant states were limited at first to the new Spanish-American republics.[6] But Francisco de Paula Santander, vice-president of Gran Colombia, subsequently invited the United States to send delegates. Congress of Panama attendees agreed that their governments would continue meeting every two

DOI: 10.4324/9781003252672-2

years to maintain good international ties, promote peace and conciliation, and consolidate treaties, where useful. Tangible results from this moment of Pan-American enthusiasm were almost nil, though the Congress of Panama functioned as a historical and mythological foundational episode for Pan-Americanism.

As elites and national governments consolidated power domestically in many countries, the movement languished for decades. After the US Civil War, US business, military, and political leaders began to link Pan-Americanism to opportunities stemming from exponential industrial growth in the United States and an anticipated opportunity to convince Latin American countries to align themselves with US interests.[7] After 1880, the term "Pan-American" was always controversial, and associated by many with US imperialism. In fact, the evolution of formal conference nomenclature reflected that legacy. A series of inter-American meetings held by South American countries between 1847 and 1888 were called "American Conferences." Those initiated by the US in 1889—the flagship enterprise of the Pan-American movement—were officially called "International Conferences of American States." But this nomenclature soon became interchangeable with the popular term "Pan-American Conferences." The term "Inter-American Conference" was introduced in the 1930s,[8] as an antidote to the word "Pan-American," increasingly associated with US imperialism. New York City business and political leaders played an important role in promoting this imagined Pan-American community, fashioning the city a Pan-American trade center in order to attract Latin American industry, naming Sixth Avenue as the Avenue of the Americas, and planning for (but never completing) the construction of twenty-one skyscrapers, one for each Latin American country.[9]

The journalist William E. Curtis, a director of the Bureau of American Republics, saw US interests as linked to the First Pan-American Conference (or First International Conference of American States, which he co-organized).[10] Curtis promoted an image of Latin America as backward but with the potential to modernize. This and other manifestations of imperial Pan-Americanism developed a hemispheric civilizing mission based on a putative Latin American inferiority and a US potential for civilizing uplift in the Americas.[11] The combination of US superiority notions and the supposed equality of all the hemispheric countries quickly became an ongoing Pan-American paradox. The word "Pan-Americanism" was first used in the *New York Evening Post* on September 7, 1889.[12] It heralded an ambiguous solidarity and a community of hemispheric interests conditioned by geography and a supposedly unique cultural community. The US assigned itself the leading role in inter-American affairs.

The First International Conference of American States (Washington, DC, 1889–90) aimed to promote peace and trade. The main driving force was US Secretary of State James G. Blaine, who called for trust, respect, friendship, and equality under the banner of "America for the Americans." At the conference, US delegates won agreement on an arbitration treaty that remained unratified. The delegations tried to create a customs union, but it was blocked by Argentina over doubts about a loss of national sovereignty, and protectionism in the US Congress.[13] The key success was the formation of the International Bureau of American Republics, on which the US Secretary of State would sit a permanent, influence wielding board member. Delegates also proposed building a library dedicated to gathering historical, geographical, and literary works, as well as official government documents pertaining to the history of the Americas. At the First Conference, varied positions on regional unity became evident. US Americans linked international cooperation to burgeoning US economic predominance and to creating a structure to arbitrate potential trade and financial disputes. In Latin America, however, there was a commitment to continental cooperation, minus the leadership of the United States or any nation.[14]

The Second Pan-American Conference (Mexico City, 1902) came in a context of the rapid advance of US military interventionism in the Caribbean. In 1902, the Argentine jurist and foreign minister, Luis María Drago, formulated the Drago Doctrine,[15] following a US refusal to intervene against a European naval blockade of Venezuelan ports over unpaid Venezuelan government debt. To Drago and others, this seemed a US abrogation of the Monroe Doctrine and Washington's failure to express hemispheric solidarity against European powers. The Drago Doctrine asserted that the use of military force for debt collection was illicit until after an effort at arbitration had been made and unless the debtor nation had made resolution of the conflict unattainable.[16] The Doctrine called for a treaty that would establish the right of countries to non-intervention by a foreign power. Several Latin American governments tried to include this principle in Pan-American agreements; the precept had little echo in the United States, which blocked its advance. At the Second Pan-American Meeting, the US delegates agreed that the use of force should be eliminated in debt collection, save when debtor countries refused to submit to international arbitration. There was a first effort at the Second Conference to codify international law in the Americas and measures were put in place for the arbitration of financial claims. Delegates expanded the economic functions of the Bureau of American Republics and the word "commercial" was removed from the title of the organization, which became "The International Bureau of American Republics."[17]

By the Third Pan-American Conference (Rio de Janeiro, 1906) it was clear to many that the greatest threat to the independence of Latin American countries came not from Europe, but from the US, which had established protectorates in Cuba and Panama and had incorporated Puerto Rico after the Spanish–American-Cuban War (1898). Reacting to the Drago Doctrine, in 1904 US President Theodore Roosevelt formulated the Roosevelt Corollary to the Monroe Doctrine; if a Latin American or Caribbean country in what Roosevelt considered the US strategic sphere of influence threatened the rights or property of US citizens or businesses, the US government would be obliged to intervene in the internal affairs of the "errant" country. This new and aggressive foreign policy applied not only to the former Spanish possessions; between 1900 and 1917 the US army intervened militarily in Cuba, Panama, the Dominican Republic, Mexico, Nicaragua, and Haiti.[18]

The United States reserved for itself the role of a continental police force, legitimizing military intervention on the pretext of preventing European incursions into the hemisphere and presupposing the inability of Latin American nations to manage their own affairs. In the years prior to World War I, the United States violently expanded its interests throughout the Caribbean and Central America. In 1905, the US took over the financial control of the Dominican Republic to guarantee the regular payment of the foreign debt to creditors and to achieve strategic advantage in the region.[19] So-called "Dollar Diplomacy" became an element of informal US imperialism, non-negotiable within the Pan-American movement.[20] The Third Pan-American Conference was held at the Palácio do Brasil, renamed at the time the "Palácio Monroe" in honor of the US[21] The building was a remodeled version of the Brazilian pavilion at the Louisiana Purchase Exposition (Saint Louis, 1904) and underscored both the friendly ties between Brazil and the United States and influence of the US within Pan-Americanism. Faced with possible Latin American challenges to US military interventions in the Caribbean basin, US Secretary of State Elihu Root offered a conciliatory but inaccurate tone in his opening remarks: "We the younger nation of the North salute you of the older civilization of the South ... We neither claim nor desire any rights, or privileges, or powers that we do not freely concede to every American Republic."[22] At the Fourth Pan-American Conference (Buenos Aires, 1910), the Brazilian Ambassador to the US, Joaquim Nabuco, proposed a resolution affirming that the Monroe Doctrine had been beneficial to all hemispheric countries. In a first significant diplomatic challenge to US imperialism under the umbrella of Pan-Americanism, Chilean delegates dissent. This prompted US delegates to urge that Nabuco to withdraw his resolution for fear it might ignite diplomatic conflict at the meeting.[23] As it did on other occasions, the US dodged possible infighting among conference delegates.

Shortly before the Fourth Pan-American Conference, the newly renamed Pan-American Union (PAU) inaugurated a new home building on the Mall in Washington, DC, designed by the architects Paul Philippe Cret and Albert Kelse. Financing was provided by the steel industrialist Andrew Carnegie and from each of the Latin American republics, whose funding quotas were based on their populations.[24] The new building and the name change were intended to express a new Pan-American spirit. Pan-American Union director John Barrett described the situation as one of "children in their father's house."[25] It was an ominous literal and figurative description. The building façade was meant to represent the cultural differences between the North and the South and, as such, marked a cultural component of US imperial thought. Two female statues, each with a child in their arms, flanked the entrance to the building, marking North and South America. The features of each child were meant to suggest typical, racially defined characteristics. The "northern" child showed the energetic and active face of an "awakened" North American, while the southern child exhibited a softer and more sensual quality that was closer, according to Barrett's description, to the tropical and lustful South.[26]

There was a Spanish-style patio in the center of the building that included an "Aztec Fountain," the work of artist Gertrude Vanderbilt Whitney. Here, Aztec, Maya and Inca designs were combined, reaffirming a tripartite Indigenous genealogy of the Americas and the antiquity of the continent. These and other building facets boasted an imperial iconography of Pan-American themes that included a once-glorious (but now concluded) indigenous past; the "discovery" of the New World by Christopher Columbus; the Spanish colonial heritage; the independence of the New World; and the imagined landscape of the tropics.[27] According to the Pan-American Union Bulletin, the building would "be devoted to signifying and perpetuating the *entente cordiale* among all the American nations."[28]

Through the 1920s, US military interventions in Central America and the Caribbean continued apace. Latin American cultural and political anti-imperialism reached a peak at the end of the 1920s. At that time, alarm over US military intervention in Nicaragua brought together disparate anti-imperial actors and associations in Latin America and the United States to confront US imperial policy.[29] Meanwhile, at the Fifth Pan-American Conference (Santiago de Chile, 1923) Mexico had no representation because the Mexican revolutionary government had not been recognized by the US, and therefore, was permitted no members on the Pan-American Union Board of Directors.[30] The Costa Rican delegation, headed by Alejandro Alvarado Quirós, proposed an end to this overlap of the PAU and US foreign policy imperatives; the delegation called for an end to the circumstance whereby a nation's break in relations with the United States would lead to *de facto* expulsion from the PAU. The Costa Ricans wanted to end to the practice where Latin American countries were represented on the PAU Board of Directors by their same diplomats accredited in Washington to the US government. As always, the US government controlled the conference agenda, giving priority to problems it sought to resolve and setting aside potentially controversial themes. This time, Latin American delegations fought back, trying to alter the US hegemonic position on conference themes and PAU board membership. The US delegation countered the Costa Rican proposal by suggesting that governments without representation in Washington could, with the consent of the majority of the PAU membership, have a representative on the board; the US Americans knew that most Latin American countries would back the United States on the exclusion of revolutionary Mexico.[31] In the end, a resolution was approved allowing countries without diplomatic representation in the US to have a special representative to the PAU. At the same time, the resolution established the principle of elections for the president and vice-president of the PAU Board of Directors.[32] Small as they were, these changes marked a break in US Pan-American authority.

At the same time, Baltasar Brum, president of Uruguay, proposed the creation of an alternative to the PAU—an American society of nations based on the equality of member states, and where all disputes arising between countries would be submitted to arbitration. The proposed organization would intensify inter-American friendships, improve friendly relations with other countries of the world, and block future colonization efforts by one hemispheric nation over another.[33] Predictably, the proposal failed in the face of US resistance to what seemed an assault on the Monroe Doctrine, other components of US foreign policy, and the suggested multilateralization of their precepts.[34] The Sixth Pan-American Conference (Havana, 1928) fell in the midst of a military confrontation in Nicaragua between the guerrilla forces of Augusto César Sandino and the US Marines.[35] The meeting venue itself was controversial, as Cuba was under the dictatorship of President Gerardo Machado, an ally of the US government who gave the inaugural conference speech lauding US President Calvin Coolidge.[36] With tensions in the hemisphere rising over the US military presence in Central America, Latin American delegates pressed for a Pan-American solution to ending US intervention and to democratizing the PAU.[37]

In Havana, delegates also sought agreement on immigration policy, customs duties, and the arbitration of international disputes. The Mexican delegation proposed that the PAU be led by a president who would rotate out of office annually, and by a director general. The US blocked the proposal.[38] However, delegates passed a resolution establishing the American Code of Private International Law, known as the Bustamante Code.[39] In 1927 a commission of jurists had written a draft code on the rights and obligations of states, which included a clause declaring that "no state has the right to intervene in the internal affairs of another." Yet the agreed upon code did not explicitly condemn intervention, which was unsatisfactory to Latin American delegations. During a plenary session of the Havana meeting the delegation of El Salvador proposed the specific adoption of a new non-intervention motion.[40] The US opposed the measure, claiming that it restricted its right to protect its citizens in a foreign country while US Secretary of State Charles E. Hughes insisted that the US government had no interest in dominating any country in the Americas.[41]

Meanwhile, the head of the Argentine delegation to the meeting, Honorio Pueyrredón, pressed for an end to excessive US-imposed tariff barriers in inter-American trade. Once again, the US delegation fought back while Pueyrredón managed only weak backing from most delegations. At the same time, he incurred the wrath of the Argentine government for fear of spoiling Argentine diplomatic ties with the US Pueyrredón resigned his post before the meeting was over.[42] In the end, for all but the United States, the conference was a failure. The US remained in control of the PAU. Several Latin American governments opposed the strengthening of the PAU out of concern that a stronger PAU would mean greater US influence over Latin America. And Latin American nations remained divided on most key issues at hand.[43]

In ways that could not have been predicted in Havana, and that were influenced by US economic retrenchment as a consequence of the Great Depression, the 1930s Good Neighbor Policy of the Franklin D. Roosevelt US presidential administration transformed inter-American relations. The United States renounced intervention in Latin America and the use of military force. This radical shift had an impact on the Seventh Pan-American Conference (Montevideo, 1933). The Monroe Doctrine was not invoked and for the first time, all parties were willing to consider significant tariff reform.[44] For the United States, the Pan-American movement became a central forum for its new emphasis on economic force and diplomatic persuasion, over military force and intervention in the Americas.[45]

The agenda of the Eighth Pan-American Conference (Lima, 1938) was shaped in considerable measure by the rise of the Axis powers and the decline of the League of Nations. Delegates agreed to a declaration in defense of democracy in the Americas which can be understood as a new continentalization of the Monroe Doctrine to negate new threats of European incursion.[46] Signaling the shift of the Pan-American movement toward a Cold War inter-American alliance, the Ninth Pan-American Conference (Bogotá, 1948) changed the name of the Pan-American Union to the Organization of American States (OAS). Good will generated fifteen years earlier in Montevideo dissipated as some Latin American delegates revived animosity toward US economic and strategic dominance, while others shared US concerns over international communism.[47] Tensions escalated still further at the Tenth Pan-American Conference (Caracas, 1954). Led by US Secretary of State John Foster Dulles, the US delegation pressed for a reinterpretation of the Monroe Doctrine as a defense against radical tendencies of non-American origin—meaning communism—and justified their eradication through force. Pan-Americanism became an anti-communist instrument.[48]

Jacobo Arbenz, president of Guatemala, promoted modernizing his country through land redistribution, controls on foreign capital, and other leftist programs. The US-based United Fruit Company, which owned port facilities, railroads, and thousands of acres of arable land, huddled with the administration of US President Dwight D. Eisenhower to block Arbenz's reforms. The US government designated Arbenz a Soviet-backed communist and worked to reorganize Pan-Americanism to assign multilateral backing for its position.[49] In June 1954, US-backed opponents of Arbenz invaded Guatemala. Without success, Arbenz sought the help of the United Nations and Pan-American anti-intervention resolutions. While some right-leaning Latin American governments applauded the ouster of Arbenz, many Latin Americans revived their antipathy for US intervention in the region. To counter what some US leaders considered an unreasonable and unfounded anti-Americanism in the hemisphere,[50] within the Pan American movement the United States sought to build what it called Pan-American citizenship. April 14 was "Pan-American Day," "a commemorative symbol of the sovereignty of the American nations and the voluntary union of all in one continental community" fostered in schools throughout the hemisphere.[51]

Pan-American Day built on a longer tradition of intellectual cooperation, particularly through a proposed Pan-American University to have been built in Panama. A constructed Pan-American identity that never took hold was based on the idea of an imagined state in which all the peoples of the Western Hemisphere might peacefully co-exist. In Orientalist terms, it was rooted in the curiosity generated by the desire to have access to the Other.[52]

In theory, Pan-Americanism through the early Cold War was based on cooperation and friendship but largely motivated by US economic objectives. US leaders built the movement on myths that included the idea that the US contributed significantly to Latin American independence and that Simon Bolivar was the father of Pan-Americanism. Meanwhile, until the Good Neighbor Policy, the US exercised tight control over Pan-American conferences and did its best to sidestep potential controversies in the movement, including its military interventions in the region. The Pan-American Union presented as a space for what appeared to be the democratic, egalitarian discussion of hemispheric problems. However, at the periodic Pan-American Conferences, while Latin American delegates resisted and protested US influence in a variety of ways, the United States found a way to maximize its economic, political, and strategic influence in the hemisphere culminating in its firm control over the Tenth Pan-American Conference and the toppling of the Guatemalan government.

Notes

1 Benjamin Coates, "The Pan-American Lobbyist: William Eleroy Curtis and US Empire, 1884–1899," *Diplomatic History* 38, no. 1 (2014): 24–5.
2 Andrea McCarthy-Jones and Alastair Greig, "Somos hijos de Sandino y Bolívar: Radical Pan-American Traditions in Historical and Cultural Context," *Journal of Iberian and Latin American Research* 17, no. 2 (2011): 231–48. See also A. N. Glinkin, *El latinoamericanismo contra el panamericanismo: desde Simón Bolívar hasta nuestros días* (Moscow: Progreso, 1984); David Sheinin, ed., *Beyond the Ideal: Pan Americanism in Inter-American Affairs* (Westport: Greenwood Publishing, 2000); Sebastiaan Faber, "Learning from the Latins: Waldo Frank's Progressive Pan-Americanism," *The New Centennial Review* 3, no.1 (2003): 257–95.
3 Stephen M. Park, *The Pan-American Imagination: Contested Visions of the Hemispheric in Twentieth-Century Literature* (Charlottesville: University of Virginia Press, 2014), 57.
4 Simón Bolívar, Contestación *de un Americano Meridional á un Caballero de ésta Ysla* (Venezuela: Comisión Presidencial para la Conmemoración del Bicentenario de la Carta de Jamaica, 2015).
5 John E. Fagg, *Pan-Americanism* (Malabar: Robert E. Krieger, 1982), 15; Stefan Rinke, *América Latina y Estados Unidos. Una historia entre espacios desde la época colonial hasta hoy* (Madrid: Marcial Pons, 2015), 52.
6 McCarthy-Jones and Greig, "Somos hijos," 234.
7 Pedro Ortega Díaz, *El congreso de Panamá y la unidad latinoamericana* (Caracas: Ministerio de Comunicación e Información, 2006), 54.
8 Samuel G. Inman, *Inter-American Conferences, 1826–1954* (Seattle: Washington University Press, 1965), 257.
9 González, *Designing Pan-America*, 153–4.

10 Coates, "Pan-American Lobbyist," 25.
11 Ibid., 33–8.
12 Juan Carlos Morales Manzur, "La doctrina Monroe y el Panamericanismo: dos propuestas y un mismo fin continental," *Frónesis* 9, no. 3 (2002): 54.
13 Rinke, *América Latina*, 88.
14 José Briceño Ruiz, "Del Panamericanismo al ALCA: la difícil senda de las propuestas de una comunidad de intereses en el continente americano (I)," *Anuario Latinoamericano de Ciencias Políticas y Relaciones Internacionales* 3 (2016): 154.
15 See Luis M. Drago, *Cobro coercitivo de deudas públicas* (Buenos Aires, Coni Hermanos, 1906).
16 Luis Suárez Salazar and Tania García Lorenzo, *Las relaciones interamericanas. Continuidades y cambios* (Buenos Aires: CLACSO Libros, 2008), 63.
17 Inman, *Inter-American Conferences*, 59.
18 Carmen de la Guardia, *Historia de Estados Unidos*, (Madrid: Sílex, 2010), 263.
19 Peter H. Smith, *Estados Unidos y América Latina: hegemonía y resistencia* (Valencia: PUV, 2010), 99.
20 Rinke, *América Latina*, 105–6.
21 Tereza Maria Spyer Dulci, "As Conferências Pan-Americanas: identidades, união aduaneira e arbitragem (1889 a 1928)" (Master diss., Universidade de Sao Paulo, 2008), 30.
22 *Report of Delegates of the United States to the Third International Conference of the American States* (Washington, DC: Government Printing Office, 1907), 39–40.
23 Alexandra Pita González, "Panamericanismo y nación. La perspectiva de Samuel G. Inman," *Anuario IEHS* 32, no.1 (2017): 151–2.
24 Gordon Connell-Smith, *Los Estados Unidos y América Latina* (Mexico City: Fondo de Cultura Económica, 1977), 69–73.
25 Ibid., 10.
26 John Barrett, *The Pan-American Union: Peace, Friendship, Commerce*, (Washington, DC: The Pan-American Union, 1911): 108–10.
27 González, *Designing Pan-America*, 69.
28 "New Pan-American Building," *Bulletin of the Bureau of American Republics* 25, no. 166–71 (1907): 386.
29 Roberto Deras, "Una mirada al antiimperialismo latinoamericano desde la invasión norteamericana de Nicaragua y la fundación de la Liga Anti-imperialista de San Salvador," *Realidad: Revista de Ciencias Sociales y Humanidades* 136 (2013): 281.
30 Inman, *Inter-American Conferences*, 93.
31 Notes from the US delegation, April 10, 1923. National Archives Record Administration (NARA), RG (Record Group) 43/133, box 2.
32 Glinkin, *Latinoamericanismo*, 72.
33 US Government Correspondence with Embassy in Santiago de Chile, Februrary 23, 1923. NARA, 43/133, box 2.
34 Fagg, *Pan-Americanism*, 39.
35 Ibid., 41.
36 Inman, *Inter-American Conferences*, 109.
37 *Imparcial*, November 26, 1928. NARA, RG 43/152, box 1.
38 Fagg, *Pan-Americanism*, 42.
39 Spyer Dulci, "Conferências Pan-Americanas," 33.
40 Connell-Smith, *Estados Unidos*, 86–94.
41 Foreign Policy Association, Information Service, vol. IV, nº 4, April 27, 1928, "The Sixth Pan-American Conference, Part I," Archivo General de la Administración (AGA) 10–54/08289, leg. 1404.
42 Connell-Smith, *Estados Unidos*, 92.

43 Report from the Foreign Policy Association, Information Service, vol. IV, no. 4, April 27, 1928. "The Sixth Pan-American Conference, Part I," AGA 10–54/08289, leg. 1404.
44 Inman, *Inter-American Conferences* 143–50.
45 Smith, *Estados Unidos*, 126.
46 Inman, *Inter-American Conferences*, 194.
47 Ibid., 236–47.
48 McCarthy-Jones and Greig, "Somos hijos," 237.
49 Graziano Palamara, "Entre panamericanismo y macartismo: la X Conferencia Interamericana de Caracas en el juicio de la diplomacia italiana," *Cuadernos Americanos* 149 (2014): 113.
50 Aida Rodríguez Campesino, "¿Antiamericanismo o antiimperialismo? Encuentros y conflictos en el panamericanismo del siglo XX," *Resistiendo al imperio: nuevas aproximaciones al antiamericanismo desde el siglo XX hasta la actualidad*, ed. Misael Arturo López Zapico and Irina Feldman (Madrid: Sílex, 2019), 23–42.
51 "Pan-American Day," *Bulletin of the Bureau of American Republics* 65, no. 1–12 (1931): 684.
52 González, *Designing Pan-America*, 11.

Bibliography

Barrett, John. *The Pan-American Union: Peace, Friendship, Commerce*. Washington, DC: The Pan-American Union, 1911.
Bolívar, Simón. *Contestación de un Americano Meridional á un Caballero de ésta Ysla*. Venezuela: Comisión Presidencial para la Conmemoración del Bicentenario de la Carta de Jamaica, 2015.
Briceño Ruiz, José. "Del Panamericanismo al ALCA: la difícil senda de las propuestas de una comunidad de intereses en el continente americano (I)." *Anuario Latinoamericano de Ciencias Políticas y Relaciones Internacionales* 3 (2016): 154.
Coates, Benjamin. "The Pan-American Lobbyist: William Eleroy Curtis and US Empire, 1884–1899." *Diplomatic History* 38, no. 1 (2014): 24–25.
Connell-Smith, Gordon. *Los Estados Unidos y América Latina*. Mexico City: Fondo de Cultura Económica, 1977.
De la Guardia, Carmen. *Historia de Estados Unidos*. Madrid: Sílex, 2010.
Deras, Roberto. "Una mirada al antiimperialismo latinoamericano desde la invasión norteamericana de Nicaragua y la fundación de la Liga Anti-imperialista de San Salvador." *Realidad: Revista de Ciencias Sociales y Humanidades* 136 (2013): 281–328.
Drago, Luis M. *Cobro coercitivo de deudas públicas*. Buenos Aires: Coni Hermanos, 1906.
Faber, Sebastiaan. "Learning from the Latins: Waldo Frank's Progressive Pan-Americanism," *The New Centennial Review* 3, no. 1 (2003): 257–295.
Fagg, John E. *Pan-Americanism*. Malabar: Robert E. Krieger, 1982.
Glinkin, A. N. *El latinoamericanismo contra el panamericanismo: desde Simón Bolívar hasta nuestros días*. Moscow: Progreso, 1984.
Inman, Samuel G. *Inter-American Conferences, 1826–1954*. Seattle: Washington University Press, 1965.
McCarthy-Jones, Andrea and Alastair Greig. "Somos hijos de Sandino y Bolívar: Radical Pan-American Traditions in Historical and Cultural Context." *Journal of Iberian and Latin American Research* 17, no. 2 (2011): 231–248.

Morales Manzur, Juan Carlos. "La doctrina Monroe y el Panamericanismo: dos propuestas y un mismo fin continental." *Frónesis* 9, no. 3 (2002): 54.

Ortega Díaz, Pedro. *El congreso de Panamá y la unidad latinoamericana*. Caracas: Ministerio de Comunicación e Información, 2006.

Palamara, Graziano. "Entre panamericanismo y macartismo: la X Conferencia Interamericana de Caracas en el juicio de la diplomacia italiana." *Cuadernos Americanos* 149 (2014): 113.

Park, Stephen M. *The Pan-American Imagination: Contested Visions of the Hemispheric in Twentieth-Century Literature*. Charlottesville: University of Virginia Press, 2014.

Pita González, Alexandra. "Panamericanismo y nación. La perspectiva de Samuel G. Inman." *Anuario IEHS* 32, no. 1 (2017): 151–152.

Rinke, Stefan. *América Latina y Estados Unidos. Una historia entre espacios desde la época colonial hasta hoy*. Madrid: Marcial Pons, 2015.

Rodríguez Campesino, Aida. "¿Antiamericanismo o antiimperialismo? Encuentros y conflictos en el panamericanismo del siglo XX." *Resistiendo al imperio: nuevas aproximaciones al antiamericanismo desde el siglo XX hasta la actualidad*, edited by Misael Arturo López Zapico and Irina Feldman, 23–42. Madrid: Sílex, 2019.

Sheinin, David, ed. *Beyond the Ideal: Pan Americanism in Inter-American Affairs*. Westport: Greenwood Publishing, 2000.

Smith, Peter H. *Estados Unidos y América Latina: hegemonía y resistencia*. Valencia: PUV, 2010.

Spyer Dulci, Tereza Maria. "As Conferências Pan-Americanas: identidades, união aduaneira e arbitragem (1889 a 1928)." Master diss., Universidade de Sao Paulo, 2008.

Suárez Salazar, Luis and Tania García Lorenzo. *Las relaciones interamericanas. Continuidades y cambios*. Buenos Aires: CLACSO Libros, 2008.

2 Architects, Exchange, and the Consolidation of Pan-American Cooperation, 1914–40

Mark J. Petersen

In its initial decade, Pan-American cooperation rested on uncertain foundations. After the contentious First International Conference of American States in 1889–90, Latin American governments displayed little enthusiasm for US-led hemispheric cooperation. The Commercial Bureau of American Republics, established in 1890 to foster inter-American trade, languished; by 1896, several countries had stopped participating. Progress on the proposed Pan-American Railroad stalled as governments were unwilling to divert resources to a logistically and politically challenging project. In 1898, the United States' intervention in Cuba inspired anti-US sentiment in many parts of Latin America, imperiling Pan-Americanism as a concept. While events at the turn of the century, especially a second International Conference of American States in 1901–2, suggested some hope for Pan-Americanism, many observers doubted its sustainability. Argentina's delegate to the 1901–2 Conference, Lorenzo Anadón, was blunt in his assessment. "Pan-Americanism," he suggested, "is destined to disappear in short order."[1]

Anadón was wrong, of course. Pan-Americanism not only survived; it became a major form of regional cooperation in the Western Hemisphere. By the 1920s, it boasted a growing institutional framework and scope of activity. Historians of Pan-Americanism have offered several reasons for this outcome. Prominent among them are Washington's persistence and the expansion of US imperialism. Pan-Americanism became a means of softening US hegemonic aspirations, increased military intervention, and dollar diplomacy.[2] The United States' growing political and economic clout in the circum-Caribbean made engagement with the Pan-American project necessary for many governments. Others, even those that had strongly opposed Pan-Americanism in the 1880s and 1890s, came to see it as useful for managing relations with the emerging Colossus of the North, attracting its capital outflows, and even competing with US influence.[3]

While these explanations are important, they are not fully satisfactory. A growing corpus of scholarship has demonstrated that Pan-American cooperation was neither merely a matter of geopolitics and economic integration nor was it always led by the United States. Instead, it transcended the realms of diplomacy and foreign policy in the first decades of the twentieth century

DOI: 10.4324/9781003252672-3

in ways similar to contemporaneous cultural internationalism.[4] Proponents of Pan-American cooperation in both North and South America extolled its potential to bring people together and foster mutual familiarity. As they predicted, a range of non-state groups employed the Pan-American label to expand pre-existing transnational networks and build new ones in the Western Hemisphere. Multiple efforts to construct Pan-American communities thus emerged, a phenomenon that one observer in the 1920s called "cultural Pan-Americanism" and another called the "larger" or "constructive" aspects of Pan-Americanism.[5]

One of the earliest non-state groups to embrace the Pan-American label was the American Medical Association (AMA), which convened a Pan-American Medical Congress in Washington, DC in 1893. The effort demonstrated significant patterns that others repeated in coming decades. Although the congress participants invoked the ideal of hemispheric harmony, their main objectives were more mundane: to exchange information, develop professional networks, discuss common challenges, and set professional standards.[6] They used the Pan-American label and platform to legitimize certain approaches in their field and further the process of professionalization. While the AMA was a non-state organization, it partnered with the state to accrue the legitimacy of state sanction and gain access to state resources and institutions. Thus, they received funding from the US Congress, help from the US State Department in inviting foreign delegates, and the participation of governmental representatives. These strategies were repeated by groups of scientists, social reformers, women's rights activists, journalists, educators, missionaries, students, and architects.

The impact of such Pan-American cooperation on the field of hemispheric affairs is difficult to measure. The fact that many Pan-American meetings and initiatives failed to produce clear results in terms of state policymaking exposes cultural Pan-Americanism to accusations of boondoggle, veneer, or distraction. Latin American assessments from the early days of Pan-Americanism also make the non-state initiatives appear as mere sideshows to US foreign policy or tools of US imperialism. Sardonic commentary on bloviating Pan-Americanists in Washington and warnings of "hegemonic pretensions" of the United States color the historic record.[7] Nonetheless, non-state initiatives played a role in keeping Pan-Americanism on the regional agenda.[8] In general, they were easier for governments to support. They were less logistically cumbersome, explicitly political, and obviously linked to US pretensions. Most participants in cultural Pan-Americanism avoided thorny geopolitical controversies. Governments could, therefore, lend their support to such initiatives and the ideal of hemispheric harmony with less concern for compromising other foreign policy objectives. That many leaders of cultural Pan-Americanism were Latin American also mitigated the perception of US influence and imperialism in Pan-American cooperation overall. These features did not eliminate US imperialism as a factor in cultural Pan-Americanism, as recent works on non-state Pan-Americanism have clearly shown.[9] Yet, the political implications of cultural Pan-Americanism were more ambiguous and less threatening than other Pan-Americanisms.

24 Mark J. Petersen

To gain a better understanding for the development and significance of non-state, cultural Pan-American cooperation, this chapter will closely examine one case: the Pan-American Congress of Architects (PCA), which met five times before the Second World War. The chapter will first consider the PCA's origins, in which a dense, transnational network of Southern Cone architects redefined architecture's relationship to Pan-Americanism. Following sections will explore why architects choose Pan-American cooperation and why their project became attractive to Southern Cone governments. The case thus offers an opportunity to reflect on the intersecting efforts and motives that sustained Pan-American cooperation in the early twentieth century.

Laying the Foundations for Architectural Cooperation

As Robert González notes, architecture played a role in Pan-Americanism as early as the 1880s.[10] Initially, architecture served as a medium to project an ideal of hemispheric peace and progress through commerce and cooperation. Early examples of such efforts included the world fairs in New Orleans in 1884 and Chicago in 1893, the 1901 Pan-American Exposition at Buffalo, and the Pan-American Union (PAU) Building completed in Washington, DC in 1910. These initiatives demonstrated the potential for collaboration between architects and government officials. In the Buffalo Exposition, a team of US architects led by John M. Carrère worked with a local Pan American Exposition Company and the US government to give structure to the Pan-American vision. The Exposition aimed to display the products and achievements of the Americas to raise awareness of the hemisphere's potential and encourage further commercial ties. The architectural team thus developed an eclectic design scheme arranged on perpendicular axes, highlighting unity within hemispheric multiplicity.[11] The main axis, with a north-south orientation, channeled visitors toward a tower covered in electrical lights, dazzling the observer and dispelling any doubts over hemispheric promise. The PAU building—sponsored by the US government, funded by philanthropist Andrew Carnegie, and designed by US-based architects Paul P. Cret and Albert Kelsey—similarly sought to unify a diverse array of national symbols and styles in a single scheme. The Beaux-Arts exterior combined Spanish and French Renaissance Revival elements, Maya hieroglyphs, and statues representing both North and South America. The interior organized the national iconography from all PAU members around a central patio.

Like the Pan-American ideal that inspired them, such architectural designs reflected US hegemonic aspirations in the hemisphere. Both employed a form of Mission or Spanish Renaissance Revival, styles tied directly to US imperial expansion. The former was produced as the US incorporated Mexican territories into its cultural narrative, while the latter drew inspiration from colonial acquisitions in the circum-Caribbean.[12] At the Pan-American Exposition, the

US government buildings sat imposingly on a major secondary axis, while the Latin American pavilions were placed among those of US states. The temporary structures that lined the main axis displayed the wonders of US-defined modernization, suggesting the transfer of technology and civil engineering techniques between the Americas that Ricardo Salvatore has described as the "mechanics of empire."[13] Cret and Kelsey's PAU Building, meanwhile, situated the institutional center of Pan-American cooperation between the White House and the US State Department, at the heart of Washington's foreign policy-making network. The building's design meant to inspire awe in the diplomats and dignitaries that entered its doors and crossed through the central patio.[14]

The allusions to US hegemony in these designs did not repulse Latin American observers and policymakers, however. Governments throughout the region participated in the Pan-American Exposition, eager to seek markets for their country's products and investment for national development. The Exposition also provided an opportunity for Latin American governments to affirm their place within the universe of civilized nations. Chile's government, for example, hoped to market the country's major export, nitrates, and demonstrate the country's cultural achievements, authorizing around $170,000 for a pavilion.[15] Other countries, including Mexico and Argentina, also spent considerable sums on exhibitions at the fair.[16] Reactions to the PAU Building in 1910 were generally positive. Reviews in newspapers that had, a decade before, disparaged Pan-Americanism—such as *El Mercurio* in Chile and *La Nación* in Argentina—praised the architecture while also applauding Pan-American ideals: commerce, friendship, and peace.[17]

While US-based architects were first to use architecture to reflect an ideal of Pan-American harmony, their Latin American counterparts were first to suggest Pan-American cooperation among architects. The idea appeared in 1914 as the initiative of the recently established Architectural Society of Uruguay (Sociedad de Arquitectos del Uruguay, or SAU). Alfredo Campos, an architect, military engineer, and founding member of the SAU, initially proposed a "*congreso americano*," which the SAU later renamed the Pan-American Congress of Architects.[18] The SAU clearly viewed Montevideo as a focal point of architectural innovation in the early-twentieth-century Americas, a position that counterparts in Buenos Aires also claimed.[19] Their prowess in architecture was the product of intersecting trends: rapid population growth through European immigration and internal migration, the influx of new ideas and architects via that immigration, and government support for modernizing urban infrastructure.[20] The region eventually attracted the attention of international architectural celebrities; when Swiss architect and urban planner, Le Corbusier, first visited the Americas in 1929, his tour included Rio de Janeiro, Buenos Aires, and Montevideo.[21]

The impulse toward internationalism in Southern Cone architects coincided with debates over the direction of Latin American architecture. As interest shifted away from French-inspired, academic formalism, new "anti-academic" alternatives such as Art Nouveau, Art Deco, and, eventually, modernism gained adherents.[22] Although many architects remained committed to European traditions, others—such as Argentina's Martín Noel, Chile's Pedro Prado, and Uruguay's Elzeario Boix—explored regional aesthetics and wished to place their architecture within an authentic, legitimate tradition distinct from contemporary European styles. Interest in national aesthetics also emerged as a correlation to nationalist political and cultural projects throughout Latin America. Recent centenary celebrations of independence, literary cultural nationalism, and the intellectual effervescence of Mexico's Revolution of 1910 all fueled these developments.[23]

In general, these new American architectures focused on the mixture of indigenous and Iberian traditions.[24] One of the most audacious early visions came from Argentina's Hector Greslebin and Ángel Pascual in 1920. Their plan for an American Mausoleum claimed to combine multiple indigenous influences—from Tenochtitlán to Tiahuanaco—in a modern framework. Modernity was key to the new styles; rather than an atavistic reproduction of ancient design, these architects used modern techniques of construction and spatial organization to re-invent indigenous traditions and thus offer an alternative to modernity defined by Europe or the United States. Their effort thus ran parallel to and existed in conversation with broader intellectual movements for "alternative modernities" in Latin America.[25] As in literature, the push for an authentic modernity frequently crossed the blurred lines between regional and national identities. Platine neocolonial architecture, for example, incorporated Hispano-Incan architecture from Peru yet still claimed to be an organic product of each nation's history.

The SAU's plan for a congress was also part of a broader expansion of transnational architecture networks in the Southern Cone that included the circulation of specialized architecture journals. *Arquitectura* of Montevideo (established in 1914), the *Revista de Arquitectura* of Buenos Aires (established in 1915), *Arquitectura y Arte Decorativo* of Santiago (established in 1930), among others, reprinted articles from regional counterparts and discussed projects throughout the Americas. These publications spread ideas, designs, and awareness of common challenges. Correspondence between members of national architectural societies, the occasional exchange of envoys between architectural societies and schools, and government-sponsored fact-finding missions furthered the transnational connections. The results can be seen in architects' growing list of foreign affiliations. For example, the Dean of Montevideo's Architecture Faculty, Horacio Acosta y Lara, held honorary memberships in societies in Havana, Buenos Aires, Santiago, and Rio de Janeiro; corresponding memberships in societies in Mexico, Peru, Portugal, and the United States; and relationships with a handful of universities and faculties.

As Acosta y Lara's list suggests, connections to US-based architects and institutions expanded in the 1910s, especially after the outbreak of war limited travel to Europe. In 1917, Fernando Capurro—a member of the

PCA's organizing committee—traveled to the United States on a state-sponsored trip to study architectural education. A year later, Montevideo's Architecture Faculty sponsored one outstanding graduate, Mauricio Cravotto, to undertake an educational tour of eleven countries in the Americas and Europe, including the United States. The trip brought Cravotto into direct contact with Pan-Americanism in 1919 when he met with the Assistant Director of the PAU, Francisco Yáñes.[26] That same year, the "father" of the PCA, Alfredo Campos, also visited the United States. While financed to study military construction by the Ministry of War and Navy, Campos also conducted studies for the Architecture Faculty.[27] Like Cravotto before him, Campos made connections with the PAU while in Washington. Overall, Campos left the United States with mixed impressions. Quoting another architect earlier sent to the United States, Campos noted "without chauvinism but with patriotic satisfaction" that Montevideo's architecture school was superior to most US counterparts.[28] Campos was not alone in this sentiment toward the United States. Attitudes among Southern Cone architects occasionally veered toward disdain; one newspaper article, published in a Chilean newspaper in 1923 and reprinted in Argentina's *Revista de Arquitectura*, noted true art and good taste had only recently come to US architecture.[29] Other architects, however, desired greater engagement with the United States. Argentina's Alejandro Christophersen, for example, believed the Mission Style was a potential model for developing an "Argentine" architecture.[30]

By 1919, after a delay for the First World War, the PCA organizing committee was prepared to issue their invitations. The Uruguayan Foreign Ministry functioned as a conduit for this non-state internationalism through official diplomatic correspondence, asking governments to forward the invitation to appropriate entities. The organizers invited the PAU and thirty US universities. The SAU made little effort to assure US participation, however. US-based institutions, meanwhile, demonstrated limited enthusiasm for the effort. Ultimately, the American Institute of Architecture named one representative to attend: Thomas Newberry, a US-born architect based in Buenos Aires. By the time of the Congress, an Argentine-born architect and alumnus of the University of Pennsylvania became a second US representative.

With scant US participation, this congress changed architecture's relationship to Pan-Americanism, transforming it into a subject for Latin-American-led cultural Pan-Americanism. The Washington-based PAU recognized the congress as a Pan-American effort but offered minimal support beyond publishing notices in the monthly *Bulletin*. The decisively Latin American nature of this Pan-American cooperation became clear in the opening session of the congress when the congregated participants toasted the memory of José Enrique Rodó and proposed a monument to the Uruguayan author in Montevideo.[31] Rodó, in fact, embodied the architects' approach to the United States and inter-American exchange: they admired US achievements and were willing to engage with the United States but also maintained a commitment to cultural distinction and Latin American equality (and, perhaps, superiority). The Latin American dominance of this strand of Pan-Americanism continued in the PCAs that followed at Santiago, Chile in 1923, Buenos Aires in 1927, Rio de Janeiro in 1930, and Montevideo in 1940. Southern Cone architects also controlled the Permanent Committee of the Pan-American Congress of Architects, established in 1920 to organize cooperation.

Pan-Americanism, in the hands of South American architects, was more inclusive than the US-led PAU. In 1927, the organizers of the Buenos Aires congress invited Canadian architects to participate. Canada was not entirely outside of the realm of Pan-American cooperation before this; the architecture of the PAU Building had incorporated Canadian symbols and Canadian representatives had participated in hemispheric sanitation efforts. Yet the US government generally kept Canada at a distance from Pan-American affairs, partly to keep Britain out of the project. The organizers of the 1930 congress in Rio de Janeiro went a step further by inviting representatives from Britain, France, and Portugal.

Choosing a Pan-American Blueprint

The architects could have chosen another banner for their internationalism. Many alternatives existed, from Campos's original suggestion of "americano," which recalled older traditions of Latin American regionalism, to "latinoamericano," which had enjoyed a surge of popularity after Argentina's Manuel Ugarte toured the continent in 1911–13 to foster Latin American cooperation and resistance to US intervention. The Pan-American label had troubling political implications. In 1916, the year that the SAU renamed its project, US President Woodrow Wilson's government used the Second Pan-American Scientific Congress as a platform to launch a vision for a revived Pan-Americanism under US leadership. This decision led several Latin American observers to question the ramifications of cultural Pan-Americanism. Argentina's Dr. Emilio Coni, for example, warned his colleagues that the United States, "being the richest, the most powerful [country] ... would take for themselves, as the saying goes, the lion's share" of any potential benefits.[32] The SAU, however, seemed unfazed. So, too, did subsequent architects who pursued Pan-American cooperation throughout the 1920s, a decade of heightened Latin American opposition to US intervention. Pan-American cooperation, despite its political connotations, appealed to these architects as a viable model of internationalism. With war raging in Europe in the 1910s, the Americas seemed the true arena for internationalism based on a common culture of peace and democracy; this sentiment fueled enthusiasm for Pan-American idealism and minimized considerations of hegemony. Moreover, Pan-American architectural congresses allowed architects to engage the United States on their own terms.

Pan-American idealism undoubtedly attracted architects to cooperation. Some believed, for example, that cooperation could guide continental architecture toward greater artistic heights. Rather than mimicking the "Pan-American" architecture of the Buffalo Exhibition or PAU Building, however, the South American architects took their cues from local developments and encouraged national aesthetics. The 1920 congress recommended emphasizing national traditions in architectural history curricula, though it also approved lessons in other American traditions of indigenous and colonial design, including the non-Iberian traditions of Dutch and English colonialism.[33] The 1923 congress in Santiago affirmed the national preference, calling for the greater use of local materials. Following conferences, in 1927 and 1930, dedicated committees to "the Spiritual Orientation of American Architecture." This was less a swell of Pan-American spirit and more a reaction to the growing influence of European modernist schools. The European ideas prioritized engineering over ornamentation, relied on new industrial construction materials, and proposed that style was universal or international. New lines were thus drawn in the debate between regional and universal approaches, dividing Southern Cone architects.[34] Some argued that European modernism provided models for growing Latin American societies. Others disagreed and held firmly to a desire for more "organic" or authentic expression in design. Ultimately, compromises emerged. In 1927, the architects agreed that no one school of thought should define American architecture; three years later, at Rio de Janeiro, the architects' resolution fell back on the national framework, suggesting that each nation should develop its own mixture of traditionalist, regionalist, and internationalist approaches.

Discussions of a hemispheric aesthetic initially marginalized the United States, though interest in US architecture gradually grew among South American architects. The "organicism" of Frank Lloyd Wright, for example, gained a following by the late 1920s.[35] While some South American architects derided US skyscrapers for their emphasis of size over style, others celebrated their imagination and engineering. The PCA encouraged engaging the United States. The SAU lamented the neglect of the United States in "spiritual orientation" debates as a "source of division and weakness."[36] In 1927, the Pan-American Architecture Exposition—which ran alongside the PCA—awarded US architect Charles Z. Klauder the Grand Prix in the Architects' section for his design of a Gothic Revival skyscraper for the University of Pittsburgh. Three years later, organizers of the 1930 Rio de Janeiro congress added "the hygienic, economic, social, and aesthetic" aspects of skyscrapers to the agenda.[37] The Pan-American congresses thus provided an opportunity to engage with US ideas of modernity and modern architecture, but on Latin American terms. Rather than creating a template for a common hemispheric modernity under US tutelage, Pan-American architects upheld the value of diverse traditions and national identities.

Many of the participants in the PCA also saw a bigger purpose for their meetings: furthering hemispheric harmony, progress, and cooperation in the face of common challenges. Speeches at the opening and closing of each PCA heralded the common cause of American fraternity. While some orators limited their scope to the architectural community, others offered more comprehensive continental visions. At the 1920 Montevideo Congress, Acosta y Lara declared that the architects contributed to an "American harmony" that pushed humanity towards progress.[38] The president of the 1923 Congress in Santiago called on the "dreamers and revolutionaries of Art" to strive for the "just aspirations within American fraternity."[39] Argentine architect Fernando Valdivieso Barros hailed the architects' efforts at cooperation in 1923 as a "link in the great chain of Pan-Americanism."[40] Reflecting on the 1930 Rio de Janeiro congress, Brazilian engineer—and one of Latin America's first female urban planners—Carmen Velsaco Portinho noted that "of all the movements of cordiality between nations and peoples, none is of more import than the Pan-American movements."[41]

These sentiments found expression outside of the Congresses, too. When a major inter-American diplomatic conference met in Montevideo in 1933, the country's architects reiterated their commitment to solidarity, intellectual exchange, and "the consolidation of the most intimate cordiality between the American peoples."[42] A year later, the history of inter-American cooperation convinced Argentina's *Revista de Arquitectura* that the "near cosmic" American soil inoculated the hemisphere from the passions that "poison European spirit and there maintain ... the tragic 'error' of nationalist hatred."[43] Considering the fact that Bolivia and Paraguay were in the midst of the Chaco War (1932–5), this article's declaration was a remarkable example of Pan-American utopianism divorced from reality.

The extent to which the architects believed their rhetoric and sought to build relationships with other Pan-American groups with similar aims was limited, however. The PCA ignored another major Pan-American architectural project: a monumental lighthouse to celebrate Columbus's arrival in the Americas couched in the ideals of hemispheric civilization and cooperation. First proposed by the Dominican Republic's government in the 1880s, the project gained approval from the Fifth International Conference of American States in 1923. The PAU eventually took up the project in 1927 and organized a competition—initially hemispheric, later global—for the design, with a winner chosen in 1932.[44] South American architects were aware of the competition; Acosta y Lara joined the judging committee, many others submitted designs, and regional architectural journals offered updates and reproduced the winning submissions. The project appeared an obvious topic for the PCA, yet no official discussion occurred there. Despite their talk of regional style and Pan-American ideals, the architects that participated in the PCA had other matters on their mind.

By invoking Pan-Americanism and appealing to grander ideals, nonetheless, the architects attracted the attention of the press, the PAU, the US State Department, and governments around the region, helping publicize the effort and securing the attendance of delegates. This served more pragmatic purposes: information exchange, discussion of common problems, and the process of professionalization. The range of topics covered included historical preservation, the standardization of training, city planning, logistics of public and private competitions, professional regulations and exchange, construction materials, and affordable housing. By 1930, separate sections for students and architectural institutions appeared. Daily sessions in each congress involved the presentation of papers and designs, followed by general discussion. Participants then considered resolutions for recommended further action. Those unable to attend in person could submit material for presentation *in absentia*. The concurrent Pan-American Expositions of Architecture celebrated the hemisphere's brightest talents, facilitated the spread of design ideas, and—after 1930—presented information on industrial techniques and construction materials. After the congress adjourned, the transactions found a wider audience through publication in individual volumes (as in the case of the First, Third, and Fifth Congresses) and in architecture magazines.

Among the various topics discussed, urbanism was of special interest. The term, invented at the turn of the twentieth century, described an emerging episteme of urban design and city planning.[45] The rapid growth of cities in the Southern Cone in the early twentieth century, a process which strained existing social and political structures, gave urban planning added urgency. Although European schools of urbanism profoundly influenced South American architects, many of those architects also recognized that cities of the Americas had characteristics and challenges different to those in Europe. As Argentine architect A. E. Coppola noted in a presentation in 1927, European cities had emerged from collective mentalities while "American cities [were] the products of an individual's point of view."[46] Hence, the organizers of the First PCA proposed discussion of the "transformation, development, and beautification of the typical American City." Hemispheric discussions on urbanism appealed to South American architects who saw value in the progressive reforms of US cities, especially the within the "City Beautiful" movement.[47] The transfer of ideas and models were hardly one-sided, however. As one US architect at the 1927 Congress in Buenos Aires noted, "there is a deep-seated feeling that we Americans of the United States have perhaps much more to learn from our brothers of the South than we have to teach them."[48]

Congress organizers hoped their discussions would help find solutions for common social problems. This objective continued long-standing traditions of perfecting society through design and the organization of space.[49] In the late nineteenth century, many Latin American architects and politicians sought to civilize their societies through the introduction and adaptation of European architecture and urban beautification. Their early-twentieth-century counterparts hoped to resolve the challenges and tensions of modern societies through proper organization of space. This effort was a reaction to the "social question," a broad set of social ills—including poverty, disease, crime, and labor-capital conflict—that had gained new dimensions with industrialization, urbanization, and immigration. Many architects of the 1910s and 1920s believed better city planning and greater access to sanitary housing offered a solution. In this, the architect had an important role. Architecture, according to one Chilean delegate from 1923, could improve class relations by bringing comfort and dignity to all housing.[50]

Starting with the First PCA, working-class housing and healthy urban design were staples on congress agendas. Architects discussed efficient construction, suggestions on healthy public recreation space, and advice on securing funds for working-class housing. Their resolutions called for greater state intervention in urban development and demanded the elimination of taxes and tariffs on construction materials destined for affordable housing. At the 1927 congress in Buenos Aires, the architects declared that the state had a "moral obligation" to channel private enterprise toward better public housing. They also suggested that architects act as arbiters during conflicts between capital and labor on construction projects.[51] By the late 1930s, the question of affordable and sanitary housing—for both working and middle classes—had become a priority in Pan-American architectural cooperation, as seen in the 1939 Pan-American Congress on Popular Housing in Buenos Aires and the 1940 Fifth PCA in Montevideo.

The architects invoked Pan-Americanism also to enhance the prestige, professionalization, and political importance of their field. Launching a Pan-American initiative brought attention to architectural societies and gave their members a platform with pre-existing international clout. The architects clearly understood the opportunity. The SAU's call for international cooperation promised to "secure for the Architect ... the position that he legitimately deserves for his eminently educational labor and for his work in social improvement."[52] The *Revista de Arquitectura* in Buenos Aires applauded the invitation for demonstrating "the importance that the profession ... has throughout America."[53] Eugenio Baroffio, a founding member of the SAU, later confirmed their initial goal: "a harmonious joining of forces aimed at dignifying the profession."[54] Post-congress assessments dwelled on the point. The magazine *Arquitectura* applauded the Second PCA in 1923 for claiming "for the profession of Architecture all the consideration that it deserves."[55] One review of the Buenos Aires congress in 1927 cheered the "legitimate and effective propaganda that the profession has obtained among the ruling classes of the country."[56] Acosta y Lara noted in an article on the 1930 Congress that Pan-American cooperation had helped secure architecture's reputation for professionalism, rigorous standards, and importance to "the march of progress" and "the general order of things."[57] He urged his fellow architects to continue "demonstrating that their collaboration was indispensable" to governments.

This desire for recognition went beyond mere vanity. In an era of positivism, progressivism, export-led development, and evolving ideas of modernity, architects felt pressure to prove their field was more than mere ornamentation. As states across Latin America began to regulate and fund urban development, the financial future of architecture was at stake and architects sought to capture state institutions.[58] The growing range of fields in modern urbanism increased the possibilities for collaboration across expertise, but also heightened instability and competition for resources among the professionals in each field.[59] Rivalry between architecture and engineering was particularly acute. In Montevideo, the rivalry between professions gained new dimension with the formation of an independent Architecture Faculty in 1915, officially separating the training of architects and engineers.[60] Across the Río de la Plata, the decision to elevate an engineer to the Director General of Architecture in 1916 indicated a worrying trend. To combat stereotypes and ensure standards, architects pushed for better training in engineering, economics, history, and sociology. They defined architecture as a "*saber del estado,*" a field of expertise recognized and regulated by state institutions.[61] By the 1930s, as economic crisis and political disruption upended established institutions throughout the continent, *Arquitectura* of Montevideo called on architects to politicize their profession.[62]

Architects used Pan-American congresses to protect their professional interests and open a new front in their battle for relevance to modern society. In panels, they discussed barriers for entry into the profession and regulation of professional standards. In the daily sessions and subsequent congress publications, architects proved and legitimized their expertise with papers and presentations. They gathered knowledge of urban planning issues, from hygiene regulation and public park maintenance to zoning laws and traffic patterns. Some participants suggested that architects with national certification should receive preference in deciding commissions for public buildings and monuments, though this failed to achieve approval. Greater consensus was found on the need for architects in devising urban development plans. Efficiency and safety were not sufficient; balance and beauty were fundamental for true order within diverse populations. Only architects could claim mastery of both the efficient and the aesthetic, the material and the spiritual. Resolutions thus urged governments to create architect-led urban planning committees. At the fourth congress in 1930, Brazilian architect José Marianno made the argument more bluntly. He declared that urbanism "belongs principally to the culture of architecture," prompting applause from the architects and protests from the engineers in attendance.[63]

Overall, architects pursued generally pragmatic, and specifically professional, objectives under the banner of idealism and hemispheric good. In choosing Pan-Americanism, they furthered the circulation of people and ideas and won international and domestic recognition for their efforts. They attracted the attention not only of the PAU and Washington, but also of local and national governments: the very authorities with the power to implement their ideas, recognize their prestige, and secure their professional and social position. Their professional campaign appeared to bear fruit by the mid-1920s. Starting in 1925, governments throughout Latin America commissioned and adopted plans for the reorganization of their capital cities.[64] Planning committees appeared in Buenos Aires, Santiago,

Rio de Janeiro, and Montevideo by 1930. All included architects. How important the Pan-American congresses were to this trend is difficult to measure; nonetheless, the architects believed that such international cooperation was consequential.

Bringing in the State

Their multiple motivations, especially the desire to tackle social issues and the need for professional legitimacy, led the architects to incorporate state actors in their Pan-American project. From the beginning, the architecture congresses included local government officials, delegates representing foreign governments, and the diplomatic corps. While the inclusion of the state was meant to further the architects' goals, it also provided an opportunity for state actors to advance their own agendas. Overall, the process drew non-state actors into the state and state actors further into Pan-American cooperation, contributing to the perpetuation of Pan-Americanism overall.

Like other non-state Pan-Americanists, the First PCA's organizing committee appealed to the state for funds and help in attracting foreign delegates. Pre-existing connections between SAU members and state officials helped their cause. SAU President Acosta y Lara, for example, was well-known by Montevideo's municipal authorities through his work on the city's Junta Económico-Administrativa in the 1900s. Others had established relationships with the Ministry of Public Instruction and the Foreign Ministry through government-sponsored travel in the late 1910s. The state officials they approached saw potential benefit in their cooperation. The Chamber of Representatives' Budget Commission, which authorized the funding requests, highlighted both the honor the event would bring to the nation and the "undeniable benefits" of discussions on public hygiene, affordable housing, and urban growth.[65] The Minister of Public Instruction, Rodolfo Mezzera, believed congress deliberations could help address "the demands of modern life."[66] Mezzera clearly embraced the idealism of post-war internationalism. The Americas, where "almost everything is under construction," provided the ideal environment to reconstruct both urban life and international relations. The Foreign Ministry agreed that the time was ripe for internationalism. It situated the architects' proposal within the broader international context after the peace of Versailles, "a brilliant era ... for the American Continent."[67]

The SAU's appeal to Pan-Americanism aligned with the priorities of the Foreign Ministry under the influence of Baltasar Brum, who served as Foreign Minister from 1916 to 1919 and President of the Republic from 1919 to 1923. Brum supported pro-active hemispheric cooperation to prevent European intervention, consolidate legal norms in inter-American relations, and give new shape to global affairs.[68] By the early 1920s, Montevideo proposed a radical vision of Pan-American cooperation: transforming the PAU into a permanent and political League of American Nations. The "Brum Doctrine," as the idea became known, invoked the Monroe Doctrine but was not blind deference to the United States. In fact, Uruguay's proposal appropriated the framework for US hegemony and granted Latin American governments more power within it. Washington, unsurprisingly, opposed the idea as a potential restraint to its freedom of action.[69] In this context, the architects' use of Pan-Americanism offered the government another platform to further its vision of hemispheric cooperation. Brum's support for the initiative was evident: he presided over the PCA's opening ceremony with four executive ministers and a representative of the National Administrative Council. Mezzera offered the government's official welcome, heralding modernity in American architecture as the force that would "open to the whole world the promising routes to renovating human civilization ... such is our ideal of continental concord, fraternity, and love."[70]

The Uruguayan government's support for the first congress helped secure state support for subsequent conferences by elevating the congress to a matter of national honor. The ABC powers (Argentina, Brazil, and Chile) were loath to allow Uruguay to outdo them, especially in terms of cultural leadership. When each hosted a PCA, their governments offered considerable support, exhibiting a similar mixture of Montevideo's practicality and idealism. The Chilean government, busy hosting Fifth International Conference of American States in 1923, was initially slow to extend official sanction to the 1923 PCA.[71]

Once secured, the government's financial and moral support was significant. The Chilean President, Arturo Alessandri (1920–25), welcomed the delegations during a presidential audience and attended the opening ceremony. His Minister of Public Instruction addressed the opening ceremonies, drawing a direct connection between the architecture congress and the diplomatic one earlier in 1923. Like his Uruguayan counterpart in 1920, the Chilean minister used the platform to reiterate his government's commitment to regional cooperation and to resolving the social question.[72] In Buenos Aires three years later, the Minister of Public Works Roberto M. Ortiz and the Director General of Architecture—and attendee at the 1920 PCA—Sebastián Ghigliazza helped secure funding and a suitable meeting space for the congress. At the opening ceremony, Foreign Minister Ángel Gallardo congratulated the architects for discussing matters of public health and welfare.[73] The Brazilian Minister of Justice and Public Instruction, welcoming delegates to the 1930 congress in Rio de Janeiro, chose to emphasize his country's honor and cultural achievement: "Architecture represents and signifies the pinnacle of civilization of a people; and Brazil is on the path, surely, toward this end."[74]

None of the ABC powers supported a Pan-Americanism as strident as Uruguay's—in fact, all three opposed Brum's idea—yet all had reason to support this Pan-American cooperation. It was practical in terms of both geopolitics and domestic matters. Technical Pan-American cooperation offered a means to maintain each country's place within the emerging hemispheric system and navigate relations with the United States—increasingly important in terms of economic investment—without compromising their freedom of action. They used the PCA to demonstrate commitment to hemispheric cooperation while also staking a claim to leadership in continental modernization. The weak US presence meant lesser risk of endorsing U. hegemony. By avoiding geopolitical questions, the congresses offered the Southern Cone powers an opportunity to shape the regional agenda without other governments embarrassing or cajoling them into unsavory commitments. Partly for these reasons, Argentine and Chilean officials repeatedly expressed their preference for the "practical usefulness" of technical cooperation.[75]

Argentina's Foreign Ministry even suggested abandoning general conferences for more specialized, technical meetings in the mid-1920s.[76] The congresses also placed their countries on par with Europe, which had hosted architecture congresses since the 1860s.

By the 1920s, the range of issues addressed in Pan-American congresses increasingly overlapped with the domestic agendas of Southern Cone states. Among the topics discussed were telecommunications, aviation, and targeted responses to diseases such as tuberculosis. Southern Cone governments also recognized that the PCA's discussions touched on pressing social policy issues. At the time, political elites in the Southern Cone were under pressure from labor, tenant, and Catholic Action groups to resolve the urban housing crisis.[77]

Labor militancy spiked in the late 1910s and early 1920s, leading to state repression and shocking violence, such as the *Semana Trágica* in Buenos Aires in 1919 and the massacre at Marusia in Chile in 1925, both of which left hundreds dead. Members of the upper and emerging middle classes demanded that national governments prevent threats to social order without seriously challenging the broader social structures at the heart of the problem.[78] The solutions offered by architects, themselves generally members of the upper or upper-middle classes, responded to these demands. Beyond the social question, other topics also matched shifting government agendas. Architects' discussion on national styles and the value of historical conservation, for example, fit into the increasingly nationalist rhetoric of governments in the 1920s and 1930s.

In supporting non-state Pan-American cooperation, however, governments did not relinquish control over their policy agenda. Governments used the architects' work when it seemed valuable. As governments in the Southern Cone moved to increase state intervention in society in the 1920s and 1930s, they found sympathetic voices in the architect's calls for state-led reform. In Chile, for instance, the 1923 PCA in Santiago shaped government reforms to professional training curricula, artistic property rights, historical conservation, and public housing funding.[79] Yet, in practice, governments felt no obligation to heed the architects' recommendations. By 1927, the SAU lamented the minimal influence that their Pan-American discussions had on public policy.[80] The architects occasionally struggled to have their ideas heard by state actors at all; when the SAU submitted a proposal for a permanent Pan-American Institute of Housing to the Seventh International Conference of American States (Montevideo, 1933), the organizers of the conference dismissed it on a technicality. As with geopolitics, international cooperation was a means for state actors to demonstrate their responsiveness to public pressures and emerging social challenges while still maintaining their freedom of action.[81]

Conclusions

Pan-American cooperation survived its turbulent beginnings for several reasons, including the participation of non-state actors. Groups from around the hemisphere saw in Pan-American cooperation a framework to advance personal, professional, national, and international goals. Architects provide a good example. Architecture initially served to project an image of hemispheric harmony as defined by the United States. Through the intervention of Southern Cone architects, however, it became a subject of non-state Pan-American cooperation. These architects constructed a different vision of Pan-American cooperation that was definitively Latin American in articulation and participation, challenging the image of the United States as progenitor of modernization models. US ideas spread through this Pan-American channel, but in a way that emphasized the limits of US hegemony. US models of urbanism entered the South American debate but struggled to compete against European schools.[82] Uruguay's Mauricio Cravotto, for example, marveled at the "civic center" designs in the United States during his trip in 1919 but still preferred the work of French urban planners such as Léon Jaussely. These preferences carried into his work in Montevideo's Architecture Faculty and its Institute of Urbanism (established in 1936).[83] Meanwhile, all but one of the urban development committees created by Southern Cone governments in the 1920s and 1930s adopted plans led by European architects. The exception was Montevideo, where Cravotto led the design team.

As in other forms of cultural Pan-Americanism, architectural cooperation fostered collaboration between state and non-state actors. For the architects, this collaboration assured the success of their project and furthered a major objective: to secure their financial and social position by gaining state recognition and capturing state institutions. For governments, the congresses became a platform for their own agendas. Ultimately, this encouraged Southern Cone participation in Pan-American cooperation and contributed to the validity, desirability, and diversity of Pan-Americanism as an internationalist framework. In the 1920s, a decade shaped by radical Latin-Americanism, opposition to continued US intervention in the circum-Caribbean, and competing globalist ideas of cooperation in the League of Nations, this support for Pan-Americanism was not to be taken for granted.

The architects' accomplishments through Pan-American cooperation were limited. Many of their recommendations failed to have an impact. Greater familiarity and awareness flourished in the Southern Cone but had less success farther afield. When the New York Museum of Modern Art hosted an influential exhibition on international modern architecture in 1932, for example, it included no mention of Latin America. The architects' commitment to Pan-American cooperation itself seemed to falter after the 1930 PCA. When plans for a fifth congress at Havana, Cuba fell through in 1933 due to political upheaval in the country, no alternative plans emerged until the SAU revived the idea at the end of the decade. Nonetheless, the cooperation of the 1920s set the stage for developments of the following decades. Historians and architects, such as Jorge Nudelman Blejwas and Cecilia Parera, agree that Southern Cone architects' "professional assertiveness" helped them to capture state institutions and redefine architecture as a *saber del estado* in the 1930s.[84] The results were most striking in Uruguay, where architects came to occupy several important political posts by the end of the decade, including the presidency with Alfredo Baldomir (1938–43). The regional cooperation designed by these architects also helped to lay the foundations for expanding cultural Pan-Americanism in the Good Neighbor era and architectural exchange that has persisted into the new millennium.

Notes

1 Lorenzo Anadón, "Informe confidencial, presentado al Exmo. Señor Ministerio de Relaciones Exteriores, Dr. Luis M Drago, con ocasión del Congreso de Méjico y sobre cuestiones de política americana," 1903, Archivo Histórico del Ministerio de Relaciones Exteriores y Culto (Buenos Aires) [AMRECIC] Series 25 Box 2:III, pp. 35–36 and 43.
2 David Sheinin, "Rethinking Pan Americanism: An Introduction," *Beyond the Ideal: Pan-Americanism in Inter-American Affairs*, edited by David Sheinin (Westport: Praeger, 2000), 1.
3 See, for example, David Sheinin, *Searching for Authority: Pan-Americanism, Diplomacy, and Politics in United States–Argentine Relations, 1910–1930* (New Orleans: University Press of the South, 1998) and Max Paul Friedman and Tom Long, "Soft Balancing in the Americas: Latin American Opposition to US Intervention, 1898–1936" *International Security* 40, no. 1 (Summer 2015): 120–56.
4 See, for an example of this literature, Richard Cándida Smith, *Improvised Continent: Pan-Americanism and Cultural Exchange* (Philadelphia: University of Pennsylvania Press, 2017).
5 Juan Senillosa, *Panamericanismo cultural* (Buenos Aires: Pedemonte, 1924), and Leo S. Rowe, "The Significance of Pan-Americanism," speech to academic conference presented August 7, 1925, Columbus Memorial Library Leo S. Rowe Papers Box 12.
6 The full transactions can be found in American Medical Association, *Transactions of the First Pan-American Medical Congress Held in the City of Washington, DC, USA, September 5, 6, 7, and 8, AD 1893*, 3 volumes (Washington: Government Printing Office, 1895).
7 This was the assessment of one Chilean diplomat, for example, in Envoy in Japan to Foreign Minister, 12 February 1910, Archivo Nacional Histórico (Santiago, Chile), Fondo Varias 280.

8 I have argued elsewhere that the cultural and social dimension of Pan-Americanism was crucial to political Pan-Americanism's viability; see Mark Petersen, "'Vanguard of Pan-Americanism': Chile and Inter-American Multilateralism in the Early Twentieth Century," *Cooperation and Hegemony in US–Latin American Relations:*
Revisiting the Western Hemisphere Idea, eds. Juan Pablo Scarfi and Andrew Tillman (London: Palgrave Macmillan, 2016), 111–37.
9 This theme is present in works such as Alex Bryne, "The Potential of Flight: US Aviation and Pan-Americanism during the Early Twentieth Century," *Journal of the Gilded Age and Progressive Era* 19 (2020): 48–76; Cándida Smith, *Improvised Continent*; Katherine Marino, *Feminism for the Americas: The Making of an International Human Rights Movement* (Chapel Hill: University of North Carolina Press, 2019); and Megan Threlkeld, *Pan American Women: US Internationalists and Revolutionary Mexico* (Philadelphia: University of Pennsylvania Press, 2014).
10 Robert Alexander González, *Designing Pan-America: US Architectural Visions for the Western Hemisphere* (Austin: University of Texas Press, 2011).
11 For further description of the architectural plan, see González, *Designing Pan-America*, 49–63.
12 On Mission and Spanish Revivalism, see Roberto Ramón Lint Sagarena, *Aztlán and Arcadia: Religion, Ethnicity, and the Creation of Place* (New York: New York University Press, 2014).
13 Ricardo D. Salvatore, "Imperial Mechanics: South America's Hemispheric Integration in the Machine Age," *Americas Quarterly* 58:3 (2006): 662–91.
14 González, *Designing Pan-America*, especially ch. 2.
15 J. Tadeo Laso, *La exhibición chilena en la Exposición Pan-americana de Buffalo, E.U. 1901* (Santiago: Imprenta y Encuadernación Barcelona, 1902), 51.
16 For more on the various Latin American countries represented, see *Official Catalogue and Guide Book to the Pan American Exposition with Maps of Exposition and Illustrations, Buffalo, NY, USA, May 1st to Nov. 1st, 1901* (Buffalo: Charles Ahrhart, 1901), 31–4.
17 "Palacio de las Repúblicas Americanas," *El Mercurio* (Santiago), May 23, 1910; and "La Oficina Internacional de las Repúblicas Americanas: El nuevo edificio," *La Nación*, May 16, 1910.
18 The history of the Congress can be found in several sources. The most definitive overview can be found in Ramón Gutiérrez, Jorge Tartarini, and Rubens Stagno, *Congresos Panamericanos de Arquitectos, 1920–2000: Aportes para su historia* (Buenos Aires: CEDODAL, 2007). The official account is given in the transactions of the congress: Comité Ejecutivo del Congreso, *Primer Congreso Pan-Americano de Arquitectos: Montevideo, Marzo 1 al 7 de 1920: Actas y Trabajos* (Montevideo: Imprenta y Casa Editorial "Renacimiento," 1921). See also articles on the later congresses from the period; for example, "El origen de los Congresos y sus conclusiones" *Arquitectura* (Montevideo) [hereafter, *Arquitectura*] XVI No. 151 (June 1930): 126–48.
19 For more on the history of Montevideo's architecture, see Hugo Baracchini and Carlos Altezor, *Historia urbanística de la ciudad de Montevideo: Desde sus orígenes colonials a nuestros días* (Montevideo: Ediciones Trilce, 2010).
20 For an overview of these trends, see Arturo Almandoz, *Modernization, Urbanization and Development in Latin America, 1900s–2000s* (London: Routledge, 2014).
21 Ramón Gutiérrez, ed., *Le Corbusier en el Río de la Plata, 1929* (Montevideo: CEDODAL and FADU, 2009).
22 See Ramón Gutiérrez, *Arquitectura y urbanismo en Iberoamérica* (Madrid: Ediciones Catedra, 1983), ch. 20; and Damián Bayón, "Latin American Architecture, c. 1920–c. 1980," *The Cambridge History of Latin America, Volume X: Latin America*

Since 1930: Ideas, Culture, and Society, ed. Leslie Bethell (Cambridge: Cambridge University Press, 1995).
23 Gutierrez, *Arquitectura y urbanismo*, 554–67.
24 Noel wrote an influential article on Hispanic-American architecture in 1915: "Nacimiento de la Arquitectura Hispana-Americana," *Revista de Arquitectura* 1, no. 1 (1915): 8–12.
25 On alternative modernities and twentieth-century intellectuals, see Nicola Miller, *Reinventing Modernity in Latin America: Intellectuals Imagine the Future, 1900–1930* (New York: Palgrave Macmillan, 2008) and Rebecca Earle, *The Return of the Native: Indians and Myth-Making in Spanish America, 1810–1930* (Durham: Duke University Press, 2007).
26 Information about Cravotto's 1919 visit to the United States can be found in the Archivo del Ministerio de Relaciones Exteriores del Uruguay [AMREU] 66: Fondo Legación del Uruguay en Washington, DC, fol. 359: Misiones de estudio a los Estados Unidos, 1919, exp. "Misión de Mauricio Cravotto, arquitecto, confiado en misión oficial de la Facultad de Arquitectura de Montevideo."
27 Information on Campos's trip can be found in AMREU 66 359, Exp. 7: "Misión de Estudios Militares de Teniente Coronel Alfredo R. Campos."
28 Campos to Hugo de la Peña (Uruguayan Chargé d'Affaires in Washington), August 25, 1919, in AMREU 66 fol. 359, Exp. 7: "Misión de Estudios Militares de Teniente Coronel Alfredo R. Campos."
29 Article cited in "Crónica del Segundo Congreso Panamericano de Arquitectos," *Revista de Arquitectura* IX No. 35 (November 1923), 104–7.
30 Gutiérrez et al., *Arquitectura*, 560.
31 SAU, *Primer Congreso*, 56.
32 Emilio Coni, "Los congresos científicos y médicos latino-americanos," *Revista de Derecho, Historia y Letras* LVI (March 1917): 214.
33 SAU, *Actas y trabajo*, 105–6. Gutierrez et al focus on the debate between national, regional, and international approaches in *Congresos panamericanos*.
34 Gutierrez et al, *Los congresos*, 12–16. See also Mauro Guillen, "Modernism Without Modernity: The Rise of Modernist Architecture in Mexico, Brazil, and Argentina, 1890–1940," *Latin American Research Review* 39, no. 2 (2004): 6–34.
35 Alberto Sartori, "Wright and South America" in *Frank Lloyd Wright: Europe and Beyond*, edited by Anthony Alofsin (Berkeley: University of California Press, 1999)
36 "Al Margen del Congreso: La orientación espiritual de la arquitectura americana" *Arquitectura*, 13, no. 120 (November 1927): 318.
37 "El origen de los congresos y sus conclusiones," *Revista de Arquitectura* 16, no. 151 (June 1930): 144–6.
38 SAU, *Primer Congreso*, 65.
39 "Crónica del Segundo Congreso Panamericano de Arquitectos," *Revista de Arquitectura* 9, no. 34 (October 1923): 80.
40 "Crónica del Segundo Congreso Panamericano de Arquitectos" *Revista de Arquitectura* 9, no. 35 (November 1923): 104.
41 Carmen Velasco Portinho, "La señorita Carmen Velasco Portinho, Ingeniero Civil" *Revista de Arquitectura* 16, no. 117 (September 1930), 541.
42 "Conferencia I. Americana: Palabras Liminares," *Arquitectura* 20, no. 181 (1934): 1.
43 "Fin de año," *Revista de Arquitectura*, 20, no. 168 (December 1934): 506.
44 See González, *Designing Pan America*, ch. 3.
45 See Gutiérrez, *Arquitectura y urbanismo*; Clare Cardinal-Plett, *A History of Architecture and Urbanism in the Americas* (New York: Routledge, 2010); and Ana María Rigotti, *Las invenciones del urbanismo en Argentina (1900–1960): Inestabilidad de sus representaciones científicas y dificultades para su profesionalización* (Rosario: Editorial de la Universidad de Rosario Facultad de Arquitectura, Planeamiento y Diseño, A&P, 2014).

46 Tercer Congreso Panamericano de Arquitectos, *Actas y Trabajos* (Buenos Aires: Les Congres, 1927), 225.
47 Jeffrey Cody discusses the importance of US models in city planning in *Exporting American Architecture, 1870–2000* (New York: Routledge, 2002), 87–99. See also Mauricio Cravotto, "Sobre urbanización: Centros cívicos en los Estados Unidos" *Arquitectura* VII No. 47 (October 1921), 132–4.
48 Tercer Congreso Panamericano, *Actas y Trabajos*, 237.
49 See Luis Carranza and Fernando Luis Lara, *Modern Architecture in Latin America: Art, Technology, and Utopia* (Austin: University of Texas Press, 2014) and Jean François Lejeune, "Dreams of Order: Utopia, Cruelty, and Modernity," *Cruelty and Utopia: Cities and Landscapes of Latin America*, ed. Jean François Lejeune (Princeton: Princeton Architectural Press, 2006), 30–50.
50 "Crónica del Segundo Congreso Panamericano de Arquitectos," *Revista de Arquitectura*, 9, no. 35 (November 1923): 105.
51 Francisco Squirru, "III Congreso Panamericano de Arquitectos: Un balance favorable," *Revista de Arquitectura*, 13, no. 80 (August 1927): 315–16.
52 SAU, *Primer Congreso*, 4.
53 "Primer Congreso Pan-Americano de Arquitectos," *Revista de Arquitectura* 5, no. 23 (October 1919): 3.
54 Eugenio Baroffio, "Resultados de los cuatro primeros Congresos Panamericanos de Arquitectura," in V Congreso Panamericano de Arquitectos, *Actas y Trabajos* (Montevideo: Talleres Gráficos Urta y Curbelo, 1940), 650.
55 "Segundo Congreso Panamericano," *Arquitectura* 9, no. 71 (1923), 222.
56 Squirru, "III Congreso Panamericano de Arquitectos," 312.
57 Horacio Acosta y Lara, "Frutos de los Congresos," *Arquitectura* 16, no. 151 (June 1930): 123.
58 Cecilia Parera, "Arquitectura pública y técnicos estatales: la consolidación de la arquitectura como saber de Estado en la Argentina, 1930–1943," *Anales del IAA* 42, no. 2, November 20, 2014.
59 Rigotti, *Las invenciones*, 6–7.
60 Nudelman, "Corbusians," 54.
61 Parera, "Arquitectura pública y técnicos estatales."
62 Juan Scasso, "Urbanismo y política," *Arquitectura* 18, no. 171 (February 1932).
63 "IV Congreso Pan Americano de Arquitectos realizado en Rio de Janeiro, Brasil," *Revista de Arquitectura* 16, no. 116 (August 1930): 498.
64 For more on this trend, see Almodoz, *Planning Latin American Capital Cities*.
65 A copy of the congressional debate from March 1920 (Folder 86 [1920] Issue 14) can be found in Archivo General de la Nación del Uruguay [AGNU] Fondo Ministerio de Instrucción Pública Box 166 Fol. 2912.
66 Ministry of Public Instruction, Resolution written for the Consejo Nacional de Administración, AGNU Fondo Ministerio de Instrucción Pública Box 166 Fol. 2912.
67 Ministry of Foreign Relations to Minister of Public Instruction, August 8, 1919, AGNU Fondo Ministerio de Instrucción Pública Box 166 Fol. 2912.
68 See James C. Knarr, *Uruguay and the United States, 1903–1929: Diplomacy in the Progressive Era* (Kent, OH: Kent State University Press, 2012), especially ch. 4 and 5.
69 Brum's idea was neither the first nor last Latin American attempt to appropriate the Monroe Doctrine—see the Drago Doctrine, for example.
70 SAU, *Primer Congreso*, 63.
71 This delay caused considerable anxiety amongst the architectural societies in Uruguay and Argentina; see "II Congreso Pan Americano de Arquitectos: Actas del Comité Argentino," *Revista de Arquitectura* (Buenos Aires) 8, no. 32 (August 1923): 33.
72 "Crónica Segundo Congreso Panamericano de Arquitectos," *Revista de Arquitectura* (Buenos Aires) 9, no. 34 (October 1923): 76–82.

73 Tercer Congreso Panamericano de Arquitectos, *Actas*, 467.
74 "IV Congreso Panamericano de Arquitectos en Rio de Janeiro, Brasil," *Revista de Arquitectura*, 16, no. 116 (August 1930): 478.
75 "Minutes of the Governing Body of the Pan American Union, 5 May 1926," Library of Congress Frank Kellogg Papers Roll 22.
76 Isidoro Ruiz Moreno, "Memorandum sobre la lista de temas para la Sexta Conferencia Pan Americana," August 24, 1926, AMRECIC, Series 25 Box 26:I.
77 Ronn Pineo and James Baer eds., *Cities of Hope: People, Protests, and Progress in Urbanizing Latin America, 1870–1930* (Boulder: Westview Press, 1998).
78 Much has been written about the "social question" and the responses to it. For an introduction to the topic in the Southern Cone, see James O. Morris, *Elites, Intellectuals, and Consensus: A Study of the Social Question and the Industrial Labor Relations System in Chile* (Ithaca: Cornell University Press, 1966) and Juan Suriano, ed. *La cuestión social en Argentina, 1870–1943* (Buenos Aires: La Colmena, 2000).
79 Chilean architect Ricardo González Cortés discussed this at the Third Pan American Congress of Architects; see Tercer Congreso, *Actas*, 472.
80 "Los Congresos Pan-Americanos de Arquitectos," *Arquitectura* 13, no. 111 (February 1927): 26–8.
81 Carsten-Andreas Schulz and I have developed this argument more fully about Latin American regionalism since the 1820s in "Setting the Regional Agenda: A Critique of Posthegemonic Regionalism," *Latin American Politics and Society* 60, no. 1 (2018): 102–27.
82 Arturo Almandoz, "Urbanization and Urbanism in Latin America: From Haussmann to CIAM," in *Planning Latin America's Capital Cities, 1850–1950*, ed. Arturo Almandoz (New York: Routledge, 2002), 23.
83 Jorge Nudelman Blejwas, "'Corbusians' in Uruguay: A Contradictory Report," in *Latin American Modern Architectures: Ambiguous Territories*, ed. Patricio del Real and Helen Gyger (New York: Routledge, 2013), 53–74.
84 Nudelman, "Corbusians," 54, and Parera, "Arquitectura pública."

Bibliography

Almandoz, Arturo. *Modernization, Urbanization and Development in Latin America, 1900s–2000s*. London: Routledge, 2014.

Almandoz, Arturo. "Urbanization and Urbanism in Latin America: From Haussmann to CIAM." In *Planning Latin America's Capital Cities, 1850–1950*, edited by Arturo Almandoz, 20–36. New York: Routledge, 2002.

Baracchini, Hugo and Carlos Altezor. *Historia urbanística de la ciudad de Montevideo: Desde sus orígenes coloniales a nuestros días*. Montevideo: Ediciones Trilce, 2010.

Bayón, Damián. "Latin American Architecture, c. 1920–c. 1980." In *The Cambridge History of Latin America, Volume X: Latin America Since 1930: Ideas, Culture, and Society*, edited by Leslie Bethell, 231–257. Cambridge: Cambridge University Press, 1995.

Bryne, Alex. "The Potential of Flight: US Aviation and Pan-Americanism during the Early Twentieth Century." *Journal of the Gilded Age and Progressive Era* 19 (2020): 48–76.

Cándida Smith, Richard. *Improvised Continent: Pan-Americanism and Cultural Exchange*. Philadelphia: University of Pennsylvania Press, 2017.

Cardinal-Plett, Clare. *A History of Architecture and Urbanism in the Americas*. New York: Routledge, 2010.
Carranza, Luis and Fernando Luis Lara. *Modern Architecture in Latin America: Art, Technology, and Utopia*. Austin: University of Texas Press, 2014.
Cody, Jeffrey. *Exporting American Architecture, 1870–2000*. New York: Routledge, 2002.
Earle, Rebecca. *The Return of the Native: Indians and Myth-Making in Spanish America, 1810–1930*. Durham: Duke University Press, 2007.
Friedman, Max Paul and Tom Long. "Soft Balancing in the Americas: Latin American Opposition to US Intervention, 1898–1936." *International Security* 40, no. 1 (Summer 2015): 120–156.
González, Robert Alexander. *Designing Pan-America: US Architectural Visions for the Western Hemisphere*. Austin: University of Texas Press, 2011.
Gutiérrez, Ramón. *Arquitectura y urbanismo en Iberoamérica*. Madrid: Ediciones Catedra, 1983.
Gutiérrez, Ramón, ed., *Le Corbusier en el Río de la Plata, 1929*. Montevideo: CEDODAL and FADU, 2009.
Gutiérrez, Ramón, Jorge Tartarini, and Rubens Stagno. *Congresos Panamericanos de Arquitectos, 1920–2000: Aportes para su historia*. Buenos Aires: CEDODAL, 2007.
Knarr, James C. *Uruguay and the United States, 1903–1929: Diplomacy in the Progressive Era*. Kent, OH: Kent State University Press, 2012.
Lejeune, Jean François. "Dreams of Order: Utopia, Cruelty, and Modernity," In *Cruelty and Utopia: Cities and Landscapes of Latin America*, ed. Jean François Lejeune, 30–50. Princeton: Princeton Architectural Press, 2006.
Lint Sagarena, Roberto Ramón. *Aztlán and Arcadia: Religion, Ethnicity, and the Creation of Place*. New York: New York University Press, 2014.
Marino, Katherine. *Feminism for the Americas: The Making of an International Human Rights Movement*. Chapel Hill: University of North Carolina Press, 2019.
Miller, Nicola. *Reinventing Modernity in Latin America: Intellectuals Imagine the Future, 1900–1930*. New York: Palgrave Macmillan, 2008.
Morris, James O. *Elites, Intellectuals, and Consensus: A Study of the Social Question and the Industrial Labor Relations System in Chile*. Ithaca: Cornell University Press, 1966.
Nudelman Blejwas, Jorge. "'Corbusians' in Uruguay: A Contradictory Report." In *Latin American Modern Architectures: Ambiguous Territories*, edited by Patricio del Real and Helen Gyger, 53–74. New York: Routledge, 2013.
Petersen, Mark. "'Vanguard of Pan-Americanism': Chile and Inter-American Multilateralism in the Early Twentieth Century." In *Cooperation and Hegemony in US–Latin American Relations: Revisiting the Western Hemisphere Idea*, edited by Juan Pablo Scarfi and Andrew Tillman, 111–137. London: Palgrave Macmillan, 2016.
Petersen, Mark and Carsten-Andreas Schulz. "Setting the Regional Agenda: A Critique of Posthegemonic Regionalism." *Latin American Politics and Society* 60, no. 1 (2018): 102–127.
Pineo, Ronn and James Baer, eds. *Cities of Hope: People, Protests, and Progress in Urbanizing Latin America, 1870–1930*. Boulder: Westview Press, 1998.
Rigotti, Ana María. *Las invenciones del urbanismo en Argentina (1900–1960): Inestabilidad de sus representaciones científicas y dificultades para su profesionalización*. Rosario: Editorial de la Universidad de Rosario Facultad de Arquitectura, Planeamiento y Diseño, A&P, 2014.

Salvatore, Ricardo D. "Imperial Mechanics: South America's Hemispheric Integration in the Machine Age." *Americas Quarterly* 58, no. 3 (2006): 662–691.
Sartori, Alberto. "Wright and South America" in *Frank Lloyd Wright: Europe and Beyond*, edited by Anthony Alofsin. Berkeley: University of California Press, 1999.
Senillosa, Juan *Panamericanismo cultural*. Buenos Aires: Pedemonte, 1924.
Sheinin, David. "Rethinking Pan Americanism: An Introduction." In *Beyond the Ideal: Pan Americanism in Inter-American Affairs*, edited by David Sheinin, 1–8. Westport: Praeger, 2000.
Sheinin, David. *Searching for Authority: Pan-Americanism, Diplomacy, and Politics in United States-Argentine Relations, 1910–1930*. New Orleans: University Press of the South, 1998.
Suriano, Juan, ed. *La cuestión social en Argentina, 1870–1943*. Buenos Aires: La Colmena, 2000.
Threlkeld, Megan. *Pan American Women: US Internationalists and Revolutionary Mexico*. Philadelphia: University of Pennsylvania Press, 2014.

3 Becoming the Third World

Pan-Americanism, South Americanism, and Liberal Economics in the 1920s

Teresa Davis

> [T]he best solution lies not in subtle theory, but rather in the growth in taxable material, in effective wealth, in the economic autonomy that is at the root of political and international autonomy.
> —Carlos Saavedra Lamas[1]

Pan-Americanism has often been understood as an instrument of hegemony, through which the United States sought to impose both its will and a set of ideas, institutions, and values that, in one way or another, bolstered US power. More than anything else, commitments to free trade and broader liberal economic programs are understood as the central tenets of an ideology that flowed in one direction—North to South. The noxiousness and duplicity of US advocacy for open economic borders in the Americas seems so obvious in retrospect that we rarely stop to ask how Latin American governments, experts and publics thought about the matter. As a result, the economic side of Pan-Americanism is dismissed as its least interesting aspect: there was little room for cooperation or contestation in an arena so obviously dominated by US self-interest. In this chapter I wish to re-center the place of conversations about the economy in our understanding of the history of Pan-Americanism. I show, instead, that Pan-American networks were one of the central arenas in which new ideas about state intervention in the economy in the 1920s were debated and put into practice.

Years ago, Robert Neal Seidel recognized that the Pan-American space constituted a field in which US government officials and economists re-imagined the role of the state in the economy. In the era of growing Hooverite experiments with a "managerial" state, individuals like Julius Klein, Paul Warburg, and Hoover himself saw Latin America as an arena in which to try out a significantly expanded government role in facilitating and channeling foreign trade. These efforts were not an abandonment of free trade, but rather a liberal departure from orthodox nineteenth-century views that all exchange must be voluntary and self-directed. Global economic relations were taking place on such a massive scale that some form of government coordination had become an urgent necessity for avoiding dangerous crises. In this chapter I extend Seidel's insights to the remainder of

DOI: 10.4324/9781003252672-4

the continent, and particularly to Argentina and Chile. I show that, as economists in those two countries sought to increase the state's capacity to manage the national economy, they too looked to Pan-American networks of ideas. At the same time, they tentatively embraced the Pan-American space as an area into which a newly activist state might channel foreign trade.

The punchline of this story is a paradox. The 1920s constituted a period of extraordinary Pan-American agreement on the contours of the international economy. Economics appeared to be replacing law as a new, decisively neutral arena of scientific management within which experts in North and South could collaboratively manage economic affairs at a distance from politics. Nevertheless, as economists debated the inter-American economy, *Pan*-America came to seem an increasingly unviable economic space. The result was a decisive internal blow to the Pan-American project. Abandoning earlier belief in a natural affinity between independent democracies, economists re-imagined solidarity through the lens of regional markets. Drawing upon recent theorizing about European union, economists in South America argued that their nations' development could only succeed through the intelligent construction of regional markets based on "natural" complementarities.

Growing regional confrontation between North and South America evidenced a clash *within* liberalism rather than a precursor to confrontation between a liberal North and a nationalist South. Put differently, the Pan-American debate over the economy in the 1920s was not a debate between liberalism and its critics, but rather one in which liberals in South America contested a vision of liberal progress that exclusively benefited the North. Finally, this chapter suggests that a key legacy of Pan-Americanism lies, paradoxically, in the ways in which Pan-Americanism pushed South American states down the path to becoming the Third World. Pan-Americanism dramatized in a particularly stark form the non-universality of liberalism. While the United States prospered, Latin Americans who themselves lauded the US model found their own efforts to emulate it thwarted by an unrelenting mixture of internal and external pressures.

In this sense, Pan-Americanism was most important in the *gap* it created between intellectual cooperation and continental politics. One problem with approaches that view intellectual cooperation as exclusively the handmaiden of hegemony is their tendency to overlook the complex interplay between the aspirations of intellectuals and the pragmatism of politics. In the case under study here, it was this interplay—and disillusionment with the gap— that led prominent lawyers and economists in Latin America to look away from the United States and toward what would become the Third World. Pan-American cooperation enabled the hegemony of liberal ideas but, in the end, it could not control their consequences.

Lawyers and Pan-American Liberalism to 1920

The transformation of Pan-American understandings of economic space paralleled a broader disciplinary transformation which saw the demotion of lawyers from their long-held position as the arbiters of the international. In this first section I travel backwards, exploring how the predominance of lawyers, especially international lawyers, in managing international affairs before 1920 intersected with broad continental commitments to the principle of free trade, even as conflict over specific national policies persisted. I argue here that it was domestic and disciplinary factors—more than dynamics internal to law—that led to the demise of international law as the primary arena of Pan-American contestation.[2]

Across the globe, lawyers promoted and defended the expansion and transformation of global capitalism that took place between 1870 and 1930. Law professionals wrote codes governing everything from international copyright to port legislation. They drew up international standards for ship manifests and fought for neutrality laws protecting commerce from conflict on the high seas. At the same time, lawyers were at the forefront of a process of intellectual globalization. They served within international law associations such as the *Institut de Droit International* and, on the American continent, in the *American Institute of International Law*. Lawyers bolstered European empires by providing legal justification for the expansion of European principles of individual freedom, private property, and free enterprise to uncivilized peoples, depicting empires as the agents of a new universalism. Lawyers were also at the forefront of the late nineteenth-century expansion of US empire.[3] They wrote the codes governing the Philippines and inserted special clauses allowing for US intervention into Cuba's first post-independence constitution. They litigated cases at the US Supreme Court that enabled the United States to govern Puerto Rico without any promise of statehood. US lawyers served on corporate boards and traveled to Latin America and East Asia to argue for their individual and corporate clients.

This was the context in which Pan-Americanism emerged, and it is unsurprising that the early decades of Pan-American cooperation were concerned primarily with debate over the legalist project. Legalism in the United States was tied to a group of (largely Republican) lawyers, most prominently Elihu Root, who argued that the United States ought to base its foreign power on the advocacy of arbitration, neutrality, and the promotion of international peace. The core tenets of the legalist program were rooted, first, in an exceptionalist understanding of the perfection of US institutions. Second, the legalist project was linked to the view that the United States was a primarily commercial power, whose aims were best served by law as opposed to force. What is striking about the legalist moment is the degree to which these ideas were shared by the Latin American elites who participated in the Pan-American process. In North and South, parallel ideologies of Americanism developed, each rooted in the understanding of the Americas as a space of *doux commerce* and anti-colonialism.[4] At the First Pan-American Conference (Washington, 1890), US Secretary of State James G. Blaine proposed the creation of an inter-American *Zollverein* (the customs union that preceded the formation of the German state). He argued for his project by claiming that such a union would solidify bonds between nations committed to free trade and republicanism. The implicit opposite was Europe, mired in imperialism and alleged mercantilism. When the Argentine delegate and future president Roque Saénz Peña arose to oppose the project, he did not argue from nationalist protection, but rather in the name of a more expansive understanding of trade freedom. The Americas must not close in on themselves, but rather serve as the beacon for free trade worldwide, opening their commercial doors to the nations of the globe. He closed his speech with a rousing, and now famous, *"¡Que sea América para la humanidad!"*[5]

Far more than has been acknowledged by scholars of international law traditions in the Americas, the development of a distinctive approach to international law on the American continent stemmed from the effort to create more propitious conditions for international trade. Latin American international lawyers at the end of the nineteenth century—from Carlos Calvo to Alejandro Álvarez—saw the law as an instrument for both facilitating and controlling the arrival of foreign capital and immigration in Latin America.[6] When countries intervened to protect misbehaving corporations and individuals it perturbed the free functioning of the market and created artificial advantages in favor of those who wielded the most force. Latin American international lawyers envisioned a vast process of legal codification that would ensure, as much as possible, equality of legal protections across the variegated national spaces of the global economy. The rules they developed were in part designed to protect weak nations from depredations by the strong. But they also responded to an almost utopian faith in the free market. These authors conceived them as key measures for stimulating and perfecting free trade, and for enabling the human mobility so fundamental to economic globalism.

In this sense, in the period before 1920, the law appeared to provide a neutral arena within which commercial conversations could be freed from the rivalries and tiresome meddling of politics. Though significant differences existed (such as those between lawyers who argued for the domiciling of capital and those who defended diplomatic intervention), the common language of law enabled interests to be harmonized and contestation muted. At the same time, law and lawyers served a second function in the construction of an ostensibly neutral trade sphere in the Americas. As the United States expanded into Latin American markets in the years after 1910, lawyers became key players in the process. They served the obvious function of litigating disputes and sitting on claims commissions, but they also acted as personal emissaries from particular countries. Lawyerly expertise ensured significant social capital, and enabled lawyers to speak before important audiences of businessmen and fellow lawyers in the United States, arguing that their country's institutions were stable and ready to accept foreign investment.[7] A set of non-political, technical Pan-American conferences served as key networking venues, and enabled the advancement of codification. As late as 1916, lawyers like Alejandro Álvarez believed that the construction of an International High Commission to manage everything from currency exchange to tariff laws could easily resolve the deep conflicts generated by the spread of the US capital into Latin America.

The effort by lawyers to manage the inter-American economy came under attack from various sectors simultaneously. First came the global crisis of international law that followed the First World War. Germany's rapid advance through Belgium inaugurated a series of events that made international law appear at best ineffective, and at worst complicit, while the war had seen massive violations of the laws of war. Local factors were at work as well: in South America, lawyerly claims to neutral economic management had been met with suspicion since they emerged at the end of the nineteenth century. Estanislao Zeballos, Argentina's foreign minister, wrote of Carlos Calvo that, though he had achieved great international renown, "Mr. Calvo never employed his pen in the service of the Argentine Republic."[8] Zeballos thus depicted Calvo's internationalism as anathema to the particular problems and interests of the Argentine nation. Even individuals who were themselves lawyers, like Luis María Drago, recognized the perils of legal codification. Laws could always be interpreted in favor of the strong, often serving paradoxically to justify the very behaviors they sought to outlaw. He argued that his Drago Doctrine (which opposed intervention for the collection of public debt) must be understood as a political principle much like the Monroe Doctrine: this meant that it would remain up to the Latin American states (especially Argentina) and not a potentially partisan international court, to determine when a violation had taken place.

An even more robust attack on law's neutrality arrived during the war, when democratic-populist presidents such as Hipólito Yrigoyen in Argentina and Woodrow Wilson in the United States took aim at the entire legalist project, calling instead for a political understanding of sovereignty rooted in collective self-determination and, in Yrigoyen's case, economic autonomy. Wilson explicitly declared that he did not want the League of Nations pact written by lawyers. Yrigoyen derided the new institution for proclaiming formal-juridical equality while leaving political decision-making to a restricted council of great powers.[9] Finally, and perhaps most decisively, lawyers' importance as international mediators diminished due to the emergence of a rival discipline with its own claims on neutrality and objectivity. In part in response to the appearance of new forms of popular politics and increasing social unrest, economists began to replace lawyers as the most important intellectuals of state and as the central brokers of the international.

From Law to Economy, From Market to State: Transformations of Pan-American Expertise

In the early twentieth century, a new movement began to stir within South American law schools. In the case of Argentina, for instance, signs of the shift could be seen at the University of Buenos Aires, where law professors began increasingly to deliver systematic lectures on economic matters. In 1912, for instance, a year before the inauguration of the Economics Department at the University of Buenos Aires, the lawyer Carlos Saavedra Lamas gave a course entitled "The Monetary Question." In reporting on the course for the Law School bulletin he outlined both a new thematic emphasis and, relatedly, a new methodological and pedagogical approach. He proclaimed that his courses were designed to avoid "the focus on minute matters that come from book learning," instead asking students to think expansively and draw connections between subject matters traditionally separated by disciplinary boundaries. Saavedra Lamas decried anachronistic practices, such as assigning a single official text for a course covering complex social matters, and forcing students to take a single final exam.[10] Despite the emphasis on collective over heroic knowledge, elitism persisted. Through the intensive study of money, Saavedra declared, students could hone their professional sight by resisting the "prejudices of peoples, who take paper money as a pretext for converting every object into money, resisting the return to convertibility."[11]

Many of Saavedra Lamas's generation exalted an empiricist practicality derived from the investigation of reality not philosophical reflection. This pragmatic approach opened the door for a revision of liberal economic orthodoxies, and the arrival of the economics discipline accompanied by a re-valorization of the role of states and experts in managing economic affairs.[12] In the portrait painted of him by his biographer Saavedra Lamas appears as a liberal through and through, committed to free trade and to Argentina's traditional relationship to Great Britain. As a matter of practicality, however, he believed that a degree of protectionism was necessary to ensure that countries in the process of developing their resources not be squashed by uneven competition from abroad. During his time in the Argentine Chamber of Deputies, for instance, he became an ardent defender of the Tucumán sugar industry, pushing for tariff protections and for investment in technical improvements for the industry.[13]

Though calls for protectionism had been floated as early as the 1880s and 1890s, it was the First World War that gave the greatest impulse to industrialization in countries like Argentina, where young economists now joined older voices—such as Luis Colombo, head of the Rosario stock exchange and future director of the *Unión Industrial Argentina*—in calling for government policies to promote industrialization. In 1916, as Argentina prepared to celebrate the hundred-year anniversary of the Congress of Tucumán declaration that severed ties with the Spanish monarchy, the government organized a commemorative Congress of the Social Sciences to be held in San Miguel de Tucumán. Saavedra Lamas presided over the meeting as the special envoy of the administration of Argentine president Victorino de la Plaza. Also in attendance were an array of figures from the social sciences, from military engineers like Luis Dellepiane, to criminologists like Eusebio Gómez (a student of the Italian socialist Enrico Ferri), to the two Bunge brothers (Carlos Octavio and Alejandro, the first an historian and philosopher, the second an engineer and, later, an economist). In his inaugural address, Saavedra Lamas outlined a new role for social scientists, as the shepherds of a newly complex social entity and as advisors to a state whose responsibilities were rapidly expanding. At the same time he redefined sovereignty: if liberal sovereignty had previously been a creature of law, it must now be understood additionally as a function of "economic autonomy."[14]

In the same years, policymakers and intellectuals began to take a more active role in rethinking the bases of Argentine foreign trade. In 1912, for instance, the Argentine lawyer Isidoro Ruiz Moreno published an extensively researched article in the *Revista Argentina de Ciencias Politicas* in which he declared that Argentina must urgently expand its commercial presence on the American continent. Relying on recent commercial statistics published by the Argentine government and by the Pan-American Union, he argued that Argentina would be well served by dramatically expanding its trade relations with the other American Republics. He decried the absurd situation created by the hegemony of the Atlantic trade, in which Argentina purchased numerous raw materials from other American countries via Europe: coffee, rubber, tobacco, cacao, mercury, asphalt, wax and honey, cotton and various textiles, vanilla, wood, fruit and medicinal plants.[15]

Further, as would occur more frequently as the first generation of economists came of age, Ruiz Moreno challenged the reliance of the Argentine economy on agricultural exports, particularly on the sale of frozen and chilled beef to Great Britain. He pointed to reports by the Smithfield Argentine Meat Company indicating that recent advances in the speed and regularity of Atlantic shipping, coupled with the growth of the United States as a major exporter of beef, had pushed British markets to capacity, causing a dramatic dip in prices.[16] Anticipating by several decades the crisis that would erupt as, in the wake of the Great Depression, Britain proclaimed that it would only purchase agricultural products from its dominions, Ruiz Moreno noted the startling appearance of new beef producers, from New Zealand to Morocco. Even in Costa Rica in recent years, the government had taken to providing subsidies for the development of new agricultural facilities which, Ruiz Moreno argued, were not far off from being able to compete with those of Argentina.[17]

Though no full-scale transformation of Argentina's economy took place, these calls did not go unheeded. The period saw a significant rapprochement between the "ABC" countries (Argentina, Brazil, and Chile), premised on the belief that, together, the three countries constituted the vanguards of Latin American social and economic progress. Perhaps more surprisingly, beginning in 1910, the traditionally antagonistic Argentina engaged in a concerted effort to woo US financiers and to explore expanded trade with the United States and with Latin America more broadly. At the forefront of

Argentina's process of rapprochement from the South was Rómulo S. Naón. The Argentine representative (and later ambassador) in Washington was a key figure in the negotiation of expanding trade relations, as well as in the meetings that led to the creation of the first US foreign branch bank in Buenos Aires in 1915.[18] Naón was also a staunch advocate of Pan-Americanism who, during the First World War, lobbied incessantly for the creation of an organization of Pan-American neutrals tasked with cordoning off an American zone of free commerce from the obstructive effects of the war.

The growth of economics and an increased interest in foreign trade within Argentina mirrored a broader continental trend that shifted the conduct of transnational relationships into the hand of experts (many of them economists) and businessmen, and away from the lawyers who had been the primary agents of globalization up to that moment. In his dissertation, focused exclusively on the United States, Seidel situated Pan-Americanism within the politics and intellectual universe of the US Progressive Era. If a new generation of engineers, economists and bureaucrats was reshaping the state from within, "Progressive Pan-Americanism" was a movement both within and outside the US government which aimed to instantiate new US American principles of economic governance at a continental level. Pan-American advocacy intersected with a broader movement that pushed for the rationalization and scientific management of foreign trade. There were precedents: in 1908, for instance, at the First Pan-American Scientific Congress, PAU Director General Leo S. Rowe spoke of a new era of cooperation between labor and management, and between countries reliant on foreign trade. Such cooperation would enable commerce to proceed by means other than the bald competition that had dominated in the late nineteenth century.[19] Rowe's predecessor as PAU director, John Barrett, had advanced what he called practical Pan-Americanism that likewise sought to draw apart economic and political questions and to subject the former to science through meetings of businessmen and lawyers, standardization, and the information-gathering function of the Pan-American Union.

Nevertheless, it was only with the advent of new disciplines and a culture of expertise that a formal effort to transform US foreign policy got under way. Under Wilson, officials at the Commerce and Treasury Departments began to collect data on foreign trade, sending expeditions to Latin America and East Asia to deliver reports on infrastructure, natural resources, and potential new markets. In 1913, the Federal Reserve Act for the first time allowed banks to establish foreign branches. Over the course of the war a raft of new legislation sought to promote foreign trade and finance through means ranging from corporate legislation making it easier for companies to do business abroad, to incentives for shipping companies to create new lines. From within the Woodrow Wilson presidential administration and its Republican successors, state officials such as Julius Klein, Herbert Hoover, Paul Warburg, and "private" Pan-American advocates like Guillermo Sherwell and the Princeton economist Edwin Kemmerer, sought to develop the science of foreign trade. They eschewed state-level multilateralism in favor of cooperation between academics, bureaucrats and enlightened businessmen from across the continent. This was to be a vast project of knowledge acquisition that required the mobilization of experts within Latin American countries themselves. In practice, US officials focused primarily on cultivating reform-minded figures from the more economically advanced—"progressive" they sometimes called them—nations of South America. They sought academics—lawyers and economists, primarily—but also Latin American businessmen and bankers. They thus aimed to replicate at the international level what they believed to be a highly fruitful model of public–private collaboration in national governance. Knowledge and policy were to be shaped in collaboration between the science of experts and the know-how and sectoral interests of corporations and banks (the third corporate body, trade unions, occupied a separate and less central place in the progressive pantheon). By the 1920s progressive advocates of Pan-Americanism unabashedly called for a continent-wide associationism.[20] Julius Klein, who served as an assistant to US President Herbert Hoover, wrote that the primary objective of Pan-Americanism was to avoid all (by then potentially inflammatory) political questions. It was best, he thought, to "work quietly and efficiently with the best Latin American minds."[21]

Latin America, however, was more than a laboratory. Following on the heels of early developments in the economics discipline, the experimental mood of progressive political economy became a continental phenomenon, driven in large part by the shared economic shock of the First World War. The war shredded the sinews of transatlantic trade linking the American continent to Europe. European conflict thus catalyzed economic inventiveness and economic thinking across the American continent. Argentina closed its *Caja de Conversión* in 1914, subsisting essentially on paper currency until the *Caja* reopened in 1927. The earliest generation of economics professors was shaped by the war, with many of Latin America's first economics departments being founded during or immediately after the war. Protectionism had been a mainstay of political economy in both North and South since at least the 1890s. But the first generation of professional economists took state intervention in the economy much further. Marked by the experience of wartime vulnerability, they sought to diversify their countries' export-oriented economies and to prevent the catastrophic effects of collapsing transatlantic markets on laborers. They were at the head of the movement to establish price indices, which they viewed as essential for working class standards of living. Like figures such as Herbert Hoover in the United States, they argued for government and private initiatives to promote the modernization of mining and agriculture and for new models of cooperation between labor and management in setting wages and prices. Most controversially, they sought to "scientifically" manage tariffs to promote economic diversification and protect nascent industry.

Not only did crisis generate parallel responses in North and South, then, it also brought continental economists and entrepreneurs together. Few studies of Pan-Americanism have sufficiently underscored the profound mobilizing effect of the First World War. Indeed, scholars have often viewed the First World War as a sort of hiatus, seeing the suspension of official conferences during the war as a sign that Pan-American networks ceased to function. The opposite was in fact the case: under the aegis of a brief Wilsonian foray into Pan-Americanism, two crucial conferences were held: the First Pan-American Financial Conference (1915) and the Second Pan-American Scientific Conference (1915–16). These conferences were large and well publicized events (the second drew over a thousand participants). Just as important, they served as clearing houses for the ideas and networks that would dominate Pan-Americanism in the post-First World War era. The Second Pan American Scientific Conference played a crucial role in bringing together members of the economics discipline from North and South America. Sessions of the section on transportation, commerce, taxation, and finance were held jointly with the American Economics Association. Attendees from the United States included leading economists Jacob Hollander, Jeremiah Jenks, Edwin Kemmerer, and John Bates Clark. The conference was also attended by Latin American economic pioneers such as the Mexican economist-diplomat Joaquín D. Casasús and the architect of the Central Bank of Chile, Guillermo Subercaseaux. The Subercaseaux–Kemmerer meeting at the conference, where the two debated the benefits of a continental monetary union, would reverberate in Chilean economics for nearly two decades: Subercaseaux would be instrumental in inviting Kemmerer to Chile in 1925 to help construct Chile's Central Bank and he was briefly the head of the bank in the early 1930s.[22]

The meetings inaugurated at the Second Pan-American Scientific Conference grew into a set of robust networks in the ensuing years. The wartime crisis accelerated the South American reception of US economists such as Edwin Seligman—a staunch proponent of the universal income tax—and Irving Fisher, who had pioneered new statistical methods for studying prices. Subercaseaux's Argentine colleague and interlocutor Alejandro Bunge played a central role in disseminating Fisher's *Purchasing Power of Money*, which was available in Argentina starting in 1915. By the Second Pan-American Financial Conference (1920), American economists had begun to speak of a common mission uniting economic experts across the continent. Seligman declared:

> The Second Pan-American Financial Conference recommends a study of the practicability, in all the American Republics, of the plan to stabilize the money unit as set forth by Professor Irving Fisher of the United States, and of the project to establish the index of money correction as set forth by Professor Alexander E. Bunge, of Argentina.[23]

Even as common problems came to be debated through shared lenses, other avenues of intellectual networking emerged. The Carnegie Endowment for International Peace (CEIP) and the Social Sciences Research Council (SSRC) began funding research not only in international law, but also in economics and other nascent social sciences. CEIP, for instance, funded a joint study by Subercaseaux and David Kinley on monetary and banking policy in Chile, as well as various pieces by Alejandro Bunge over the course of the 1920s.[24]

The First World War also saw the consolidation of a parallel group of North–South ties. Less publicized and much smaller than the Second Scientific Congress, the First Pan-American Financial Conference (1915) represented the apex of US Secretary of the Treasury William G. McAdoo's brand of Pan-American trade activism. It brought together finance ministers, jurists, diplomats, and representatives from chambers of commerce from Buenos Aires to New York. The meeting was meant to enact what McAdoo and other Progressives sought to instantiate locally: a coordinating mechanism capable of illuminating shared problems in shipping, banking, infrastructure, and commercial law. US officials at the conference emphasized a spirit of cooperation and knowledge sharing. To great applause, the Argentine businessman and conference delegate Samuel Hale Pearson hoped that, "we shall not be obliged to create a new interdependence among the American Republics such as formerly existed with Europe, but that the immediate and permanent result will be the stimulation of inter-American reciprocity in the field of commerce and finance."[25]

The networks generated over the course of the First World War continued to be vital to the inter-American economic conversation well into the 1920s, even as official Pan-Americanism languished and new US administrations soured on the notion of North–South cooperation. In 1919, for instance, Alejandro Bunge and several of his collaborators founded the *Revista de Economía Argentina* (REA). Like other journals, such as the *Revista de Ciencias Económicas*, founded just a few years earlier, the REA was the immediate product of the emergence of the economics discipline in Argentina.[26] The REA was Bunge's brainchild, and it was there that, in the years after 1919, Bunge began publishing regular reports on the price movements of basic goods. The journal also served, however, to enhance the networks that had developed over the course of the war. Subercaseaux was a regular contributor to the journal, writing primarily on monetary policy. The journal also frequently translated and published the writings of North American economists and administrators, from Seligman to Hoover. Just as important, the REA functioned as a meeting point for the various corporate bodies at the heart of the new science of economic administration. Luis Colombo, head of the *Unión Industrial Argentina* (UIA) wrote regularly for the journal, advocating for protections for nascent Argentine industry and contributing analyzes of the present state of industrial machinery and labor. Another frequent contributor was the banker and businessman Carlos Alfredo Tornquist. Tonrquist's father, Ernesto Tornquist, had been intimately involved in the creation of the *Banco de la Nación Argentina* in the 1890s, and had founded his own banking venture, Ernesto Tornquist y Cía, which the younger Tornquist helped manage.[27] In addition to serving as an intellectual conduit, the REA's networks generated practical effects: it was in part Hoover's personal closeness with REA contributors which made Argentina a privileged site of US investment in the 1920s.[28]

The REA spent the period between 1919 and 1930 predicting the imminent arrival of a phase of massive industrial development in Argentina along the lines of what had taken place in the United States and, more recently, in Canada.[29] For the participants in the REA, facilitating this process meant a degree of economic nationalism *after the model of the United States*. Unlike nationalist measures in the 1930s, REA participants advocated surgically precise government interventions in favor of nascent industries. They often worried about the creation of unwieldy state bureaucracies, and they argued that true protectionism must be limited and temporary.[30] Bunge thus worked to distinguish his ideas from some of the policies of the Argentine government, actively criticizing, for instance, the 1922 law nationalizing the petroleum sector.[31]

The salience of the US model—and of Herbert Hoover's ideas in particular—were on full display in late 1928, when the then US president-elect visited Argentina in person. In the wake of the visit, the *Review of the River Plate* declared:

> Our feelings towards Mr. Hoover reach far beyond the scope of mere admiration. He in fact, appeals to us irresistibly as by far the most inspiring individual personality of our time. In our deliberately reasoned concepts of what Hoover stands for, we constantly find ourselves bordering upon that exuberance of expression which, in a schoolboy, we should be constrained to regard as the outcome of a fit of hero worship.[32]

Bunge met Hoover upon his arrival and escorted him throughout much of his trip, conducting an extensive interview with the future president which was published in *La Nación* and reproduced in the REA and the *Review of the River Plate*. In the interview, Hoover meditated on what he saw as the lessons of United States development for Argentina. He "declared that America had lost any illusions she ever possessed regarding State administration of industrial and commercial undertakings," leaving a "very definite hint to Argentina that this country would do well to profit by such mistakes." At the same time, however, he emphasized the "right of a country to engineer its economic arrangements with a view to the common wellbeing and a generally high standard of living amongst its people, Mr. Hoover's case for tariff protection, both for the urban worker and for the agricultural producer, was almost unanswerable."[33] Hoover also spoke optimistically of future trade reciprocity between the two countries, arguing that within a space of three years Argentina was likely to become a major supplier of meat and grain to the United States.[34] Indeed, the editors of the *Review of the River Plate* crowed that the visit itself furthered this process by drawing the interest of Hoover's "fellow country men—bankers, businessmen, manufacturers and investors—more than ever intently upon this country."[35] Some economic experts believed, then, that it would be possible for the collective management of rational, scientific protectionism to generate even greater economic interpenetration, by preventing crisis of overproduction and the collapse of foreign national markets upon which even the United States depended.

As they lauded Hoover, however, a number of voices in South America began to express increasing doubts about the role the United States and other foreign powers played in shaping Latin American economies. In a piece for the *Revista de Ciencias Económicas* (RCE), the economist Italo Luis Grassi spoke of "the second immigration"—that of foreign capital—that had shaped the Argentine economy.[36] Foreign capital had been essential to the construction of Argentina's infrastructure, yet it posed particular dangers for national sovereignty. Unlike human immigrants, Grassi wrote, "capital does not assimilate," remaining tied to the interests and loyalties of foreigners.[37] Grassi wondered about the new conditions that would prevail once European capital flows returned to the continent.

> Will they [capital flows] be as large as before? What conditions will be imposed on investments in railways, ports, public works and extraction, etc. ...? The Spanish-American countries earned their political independence at great sacrifice: their economic independence is yet to be achieved, and will not be gained without the same sacrifices.[38]

In 1918, an editorial published in both the RCE and the *Boletín de Fomento Urbano* accused the United States of practicing financial imperialism, which the editors now contrasted to regular commerce, noting that many northern entrepreneurs sought to place capital abroad in order to extract exorbitant and unjust profits. The article also pointed to the case of Mexico where, its authors argued, the weight of petroleum interests had been behind the ascent of President Victoriano Huerta, whose leadership had in turn engendered even more radical forms of revolution.[39] What was needed, Grassi thought, was the "nationalization of the economy,"[40] enabling the formation of local capital ostensibly more aligned with national interests. Suspicions thus arose not about the model of moderate, "scientific" interventionism, but rather about the willingness of the United States to allow Latin American states sufficient autonomy to guide their own economic futures.

From Pan-Americanism to Regionalism: The Economists and the Reconfiguration of Continental Space

While significant consensus existed on the nature of the US American economic model, increasing doubts emerged over the possibility of enacting that model through Pan-American cooperation. The 1920s were a global era of internationalist creativity, despite the emergence of parallel strains of nationalism and isolation in the United States. In speeches in 1929 and 1930, for instance, French foreign minister Aristide Briand for the first time called for an economic and defense union amongst the industrial powers of Europe. Alejandro Álvarez's French colleague and collaborator Georges Scelle had long argued that regions constituted the natural locus of evolving global solidarity, and that areas with similar economic interests, such as France and Germany, had particularly strong cause to federate.[41] In South America too, the logic of the new economic administration increasingly pointed towards some kind of market federation.

The impossibility of creating an open tariff union with the United States had been evident since the first Pan-American conference, when James G. Blaine's American *Zollverein* was roundly defeated by Latin American resistance. The economies of the United States and especially of the agro-exporting countries of temperate South America produced essentially the same goods. Bunge believed that, over time, the two economies might arrive at greater complementarity. But for now, the United States remained an inadequate market for Argentina's primary exports, simply because both countries produced (and protected) many of the same things. Looking to the United States itself, he argued that the key to prosperity lay not only in creating new industries, but also in generating expanding markets for manufactured goods. In the United States, the western territories and territorial possessions outside of the mainland United States served as important outlets for the country's industrial capacity.[42] This was not yet the case in the South American countries. Subercaseaux went further, arguing that protectionism itself would be ineffective without some effort at creating a viable consumer market. Bunge and Subercaseaux's shared obsession with working-class standards of living stemmed in large part from the belief that, without generating an internal society of consumers, Argentine and Chilean industry would remain stunted, unable to compete with already established manufacturers abroad.

Behind such arguments was an understanding of the model of the United States as an economic *space*, a territorial behemoth providing not only its own markets but also its own primary goods. In 1928, Bunge wrote an article entitled, "The Greatness of the United States is the mirror of our future." In it, the Argentine economist marveled at the geographical and climatological diversity of the United States, which contains within its political borders such a [territorial] expanse, variety of climates, fertile lands, navigable rivers, hydraulic force, richness of forests, livestock, minerals, which, in their totality, as a result of their variety and suitedness to the progress of the white race, constitute what might unequivocally be called an economic unit.[43]

The idea of economic units—self-enclosed, though not autarchic systems that contained both industry and abundant sources of primary materials—obsessed Bunge, who saw in Argentina's vast expanses, abundant resources, and primarily European population a potential parallel to the United States. Both countries also belonged to the temperate zones of the world, suited to the production of agricultural commodities like wheat. Yet both Bunge and Subercaseaux worried that their countries would not be able to construct markets rapidly enough to support short-term economic growth on the level of more advanced industrial countries. Further, Bunge especially worried about the effects of disparate international productive capacity on nascent industries: he railed against dumping—the practice by which manufacturers offloaded their excess production on foreign markets, flooding them and depressing prices. It was clear to both economists that, in the short term, the countries of the Americas needed a solution that would provide secure markets for industrial goods while also ensuring a modicum of political protection against such damaging economic practices. It was this hope for greater market share and firmer political protection which led both economists to contemplate the possibility of a South American tariff union.

Pan-American ties, Subercaseaux wrote, "cannot in the present be so close in the economic realm that they create free commerce between all of the American Republics." Such an intimate union would not account for the different circumstances of the South American countries, which needed to protect certain industries before they would be fully capable of competing with the United States. Instead, Subercaseaux suggested, what was needed were "a second kind of, more intimate, economic union," at the sub-regional level.[44] In 1909, Bunge had proposed the creation of a South American monetary and tariff union. But the initiative only got under way after the First World War, as South American economists contemplated the emergence of economic cooperation in postwar Europe. By 1928, both were calling for a Customs Union of the South, and they began to promote the idea in the academic and popular presses. Their efforts included a series of meetings in Santiago, as well as the publication of numerous editorials in leading journals and newspapers. In Chile, they enlisted the support of liberal jurist, politician, and newspaperman Eliodoro Yáñez, who had served as president of the Chilean Senate and founded the Chilean newspaper *La Nación* which published supportive editorials and hosted meetings between economists and bankers sympathetic to the idea.

The South American customs union was to include Argentina, Chile, Uruguay, Paraguay, and Bolivia. These countries, Bunge wrote, "would together have the same population—in its majority white—that the United States of the North have today."⁴⁵ Built on an imagined European demographic foundation, the union would also be modeled economically after the United States: internal barriers would be abolished, creating a market far larger than any single member country could provide on its own. At the same time, political unity between the member countries would enable the union to protect against dumping and other deleterious economic practices. In all, Bunge noted, the *Unión Aduanera del Sud* would possess an extraordinary share of some of the world's most coveted agricultural and mining products:

> In agriculture, this "Union" possesses sodium nitrate, which cannot be found in any other part of the world. The production of flax in the "Union of the South" presently stands at 56% of global production, and in the future it is very likely that this figure will increase. At the present time 23% of global tin and 17% of copper is produced in the "Customs Union of the South," and this last percentage will increase due to the expansion of the mines at Chuquicamato [sic] in Northern Chile, which are the largest mines in the world.⁴⁶

The list continued to include other mining products, livestock, and railways. In his defense of the *Unión Aduanera del Sud* in the REA, Bunge included a map in which he inverted South America, to place the Union alongside other economic unions (the United States and, rather prematurely, Europe). He pointed to greater longitudinal size of the Southern Union. This would grant it even wider climatic variety and, as a result, a more diverse set of natural resources.

Internal tariff barriers would be completely removed between member countries, with the exception of specific and temporary protections for developing industries. Such an agreement could, the two economists thought, be easily carried out through an international conference of the member states that would establish conventions to be ratified by the respective national congresses. Conventions would create:

> 1. A single customs tax vis à vis the exterior and between the signatory countries; 2. A reduction of those duties by 20% annually between the five member nations, such that in five years they disappear entirely; 3. A duration of 20 years, which may be extended if so convened.⁴⁷

Like their Pan-American counterparts in the United States, advocates of economic union in South America envisioned a world in which capital and labor would increasingly transcend the bounds of the nation-state, thus requiring the coordination of markets well outside of the territorial limits of the state. Yet they also took their cue from the experience of already industrialized nations. Above all they noted that—declarations of global free trade aside—prosperity in those countries was by no means the product of a

Cobdenite utopia; the abolition of global barriers must not occur radically, they surmised, but rather through partial unifications carefully planned to enable the protection of developing countries.

Conclusion

This effort at managed development from the Third World never came to fruition. Most important, the Great Depression hit, leading to regime change across the continent and turning countries in upon themselves as they struggled with the crisis. At the same time, the economic arena turned out, much like law before it, to not be immune to politics. Over the course of the 1930s it became increasingly difficult for experts in South America to implement what they viewed as scientifically sound economic administration without being accused of Soviet-style statism. Even as the United States and Europe shored up their own economic protections, the space to maneuver in Latin America grew smaller. US- and German-led missions to fix banking systems were deemed permissible, while tariff protectionism and state control of natural resources (and even utilities), were ruled out. Over the course of the 1930s, anti-imperialists and early dependency theorists increasingly abandoned cooperation with the United States in favor of an approach centered on the South more broadly. This North–South schism would ultimately be enshrined in the fight between the *dependentistas* and the modernization theorists in the 1960s and 70s. Yet it was not inevitable. The break was preceded by an era in which economic experts—however beset by elitism and anti-popular suspicions—advocated for broad Pan-American interests against domination by the United States. That this project failed is in large part the result of United States refusal to accept for others the modifications to liberal orthodoxy that had enabled its own development—and not the inevitable outgrowth of Latin America's illiberal pathology.

Notes

1 Carlos Saavedra Lamas, "Por la paz de las Américas," Address to the American Congress of the Social Sciences, Tucumán, Argentina, 1916.
2 In *The Hidden History of International Law in the Americas,* Juan Pablo Scarfi argues that the American international law tradition died out in part because of its inability to confront a challenge to US unilateralism by Latin American jurists at the Seventh Pan American Conference, held at Montevideo in 1933. This is in part true, and Montevideo was certainly an important turning point in continental relations. Yet by the time the United States proclaimed solemnly that it would not intervene in Latin America international law had already ceded a great deal of its role as a continental organizing principle to the economists. Juan Pablo Scarfi, *The Hidden History of International Law in the Americas: Empire and Legal Networks* (New York: Oxford University Press, 2017).
3 Benjamin Allen Coates, *Legalist Empire: International Law and American Foreign Relations in the Early Twentieth Century* (New York: Oxford University Press, 2016).

4 On the hemispheric adoption of the Monroe Doctrine, see Juan Pablo Scarfi, "In the Name of the Americas: The Pan-American Redefinition of the Monroe Doctrine and the Emerging Language of American International Law in the Western Hemisphere, 1898–1933," *Diplomatic History* 40, no. 2 (2016): 189–218.
5 Roque Saénz Peña and Miguel Cané, *Derecho público americano: escritos y discursos* (Buenos Aires: Talleres Gráficos de la Penetenciaria Nacional, 1905), 1–58.
6 See, Carlos Calvo, *Étude sur l'émigration et la colonisation; réponse à la première des questions du groupe v, soumises au Congrès international des sciences géographiques de 1875* (Paris: A. Durand et Pedone-Laurìel, 1875); Carlos Saavedra Lamas, *Economía colonial: fundamentos de la convención diplomática y proyecto de Ley de Colonización presentado á la Cámara de Diputados* (Paris: J. Lajouane, 1910); Alejandro Álvarez, *La nationalité dans le droit international américain* (Paris: Pedone, 1907).
7 See, for instance, Rómulo S. Naón, Argentine Constitutional Ideas: Address Delivered before the American Bar Association, 63d Congress, 2d Session (1914), Document no. 618.
8 Vicente Quesada, "Reclamaciones diplomáticas durante mi misión a Estados Unidos," *Anales de la Facultad de Derecho y Ciencias Sociales* 9 (Serie 2) (1914): 245.
9 On the Argentine government's diplomacy at the League see, Juan Archibaldo Lanus, *Aquel Apogeo: Politica Internacional Argentina, 1910–1939* (Buenos Aires: Emece Editores, 2001); Lucio Manuel Moreno Quintana, *La diplomacia de Yrigoyen* (Buenos Aires: Editorial Inca, 1928).
10 Carlos Saavedra Lamas, "Caracter de los Cursos Intensivos," *Crónica de la Facultad de Derecho* (1912): 710.
11 Ibid., 725.
12 On the economics profession and the state, see, Jimena Caravaca and Mariano Ben Plotkin, "Crisis, ciencias sociales y elites estatales: La constitución del campo de los economistas estatales en la Argentina, 1910–1935," *Desarrollo Económico* 47, no. 187 (2007): 401–28. On expertise and the state more broadly, see, Federico Neiburg and Mariano Plotkin, eds., *Intelectuales y expertos: La constitucion del conocimiento social en la Argentina* (Buenos Aires: Ediciones Paidos Iberica, 2004).
13 Teresa Fernández Bengoechea, *Carlos Saavedra Lamas: Un Obrero de La Paz* (Buenos Aires: Dunken, 2007).
14 Carlos Saavedra Lamas, "Discurso de apertura del congreso americano de ciencias sociales," *Anales de la Facultad de Derecho y Ciencias Sociales* 1, no. 1, Serie 3 (1916): 497.
15 Isidoro Ruiz Moreno, "Propaganda Argentina en América," *Revista Argentina de Ciencias Políticas* 4 (1912): 43.
16 Ibid., 44–5.
17 Ibid., 46.
18 See Mark T. Gilderhus, *Pan American Visions: Woodrow Wilson in the Western Hemisphere, 1913–1921* (Tucson: University of Arizona Press, 1986), 15.
19 Leo S. Rowe, "Address to the Pan American Scientific Congress at Santiago de Chile," December 25, 1908, cited in Robert Neal Seidel, "Progressive Pan Americanism: development and United States policy toward South America, 1906–1931" (PhD diss., Cornell University, 1973), 36.
20 See William J. Barber, *From New Era to New Deal: Herbert Hoover, the Economists, and American Economic Policy, 1921–1933*, revised edition (Cambridge: Cambridge University Press, 1989).
21 Julius Klein, "The Coming Competition with Europe," cited in Seidel, "Progressive Pan Americanism," 246.
22 Kemmerer Papers, Boxes 90 and 91.

23 Florencia Sember, "The Reception of Irving Fisher in Argentina: Alejandro Bunge and Raúl Prebisch," *The European Journal of the History of Economic Thought* 20, no. 2 (2013): 377.
24 In 1928, for instance, Bunge published an extensive survey of immigration to Argentina which was funded by the SSRC. REA, "Setenta Años de Immigración."
25 Ibid., 92.
26 For an account of the development of the economics discipline (and of state economics) in Argentina, see, Jimena Caravaca and Mariano Ben Plotkin, "Crisis, ciencias sociales y elites estatales: la constitución del campo de los economistas estatales en la Argentina, 1910–1935," *Desarrollo Económico* 47, no. 187 (2007): 401–28; Hernán González Bollo, *La teodicea estadística de Alejandro E. Bunge, 1880–1943* (Buenos Aires: Universidad Católica Argentina, 2012).
27 Tornquist's biography in the "Who's Who" of Latin America (1940) shows the extent of his involvement in banking and business enterprises, as well as in the negotiation of the international economy in the 1920s: "Member of the League of the Finance Committee of the League of Nations; head of the banking house of Ernesto Tornquist y Cia, founded by his father; member of the boards of directors (and in many cases also president) of the following companies: Crédito Ferrocarrilero Argentino SA, Compañía Introductora de Buenos Aires, Compañía Argentina de Electricidad SA, Refinería Argentina, SA, Talleres Metalúrgicos SA, Banque de Commerce of Antwerp, Société Immobiliaire Franco Argentine of Paris, Banque Belge de Prêt Foncier of Antwerp, Société Anonyme Pastorale Belge Sud Américaine, and more than 30 others." Tornquist was also a member of the most important social clubs in Buenos Aires and had received decorations from the Légion d'Honneur, the Order of Leopold of Belgium and the Order of Isabella the Catholic of Spain. *Who's Who in Latin America: A Biographical Dictionary of the Outstanding Living Men and Women of Spanish America and Brazil* (Stanford: Stanford University Press, 1940), 399.
28 Seidel, "Progressive Pan Americanism," 322.
29 Bunge himself somewhat wryly noted the regularity with which the journal had predicted the arrival of a new cycle of growth in the years after 1919. In 1928, just months before the effects of the global depression began to be felt in earnest, Bunge once again declared that this was the real one. See, Alejandro Bunge, "Nueva etapa en el progreso nacional," *REA*, March 1928.
30 Colombo, "Protección a las industrias propias," *REA*, February 1929.
31 See Bunge, "La legislación del petroleo," *REA*, October 1928.
32 "Notes on News," *Review of the River Plate*, March 1933, 6. Kemmerer Papers, Box 74.
33 Ibid., 7.
34 Ibid., 7.
35 Ibid., 7.
36 Italo Luis Grassi, "Problemas económicos sudamericanos," *Revista de Ciencias Económicas*, March 1918, 215.
37 Ibid., 212.
38 Ibid., 210.
39 *RCE*, Unsigned Editorial, March 1918, 22.
40 Ibid., 21.
41 Georges Scelle, *Essai relatif à l'Union européenne* (Paris: A. Pedone, 1931).
42 See Daniel Immerwahr, "The Greater United States: Territory and Empire in US History," *Diplomatic History* 40, no. 3 (2016): 373–91.
43 Alejandro Bunge, "La grandeza de Estados Unidos es el espejo de nuestro futuro," *REA*, April 1928.
44 Guillermo Subercaseaux, "El panamericanismo en su aspecto económico," *REA*, November 1928.

45 Alejandro Bunge, "Union aduanera del Sud," *REA* (1929): 186.
46 Ibid., 184.
47 Ibid., 196.

Bibliography

Barber, William J. *From New Era to New Deal: Herbert Hoover, the Economists, and American Economic Policy, 1921–1933*, revised edition. Cambridge: Cambridge University Press, 1989.

Caravaca, Jimena and Mariano Ben Plotkin. "Crisis, ciencias sociales y elites estatales: La constitución del campo de los economistas estatales en la Argentina,1910–1935." *Desarrollo Económico* 47, no. 187 (2007): 401–428.

Fernández Bengoechea, Teresa. *Carlos Saavedra Lamas: Un Obrero de La Paz.* Buenos Aires: Dunken, 2007.

Gilderhus, Mark T. *Pan American Visions: Woodrow Wilson in the Western Hemisphere, 1913–1921.* Tucson: University of Arizona Press, 1986.

González Bollo, Hernán. *La teodicea estadística de Alejandro E. Bunge, 1880–1943.* Buenos Aires: Universidad Católica Argentina, 2012.

Immerwahr, Daniel. "The Greater United States: Territory and Empire in US History." *Diplomatic History* 40, no. 3 (2016): 373–391.

Neiburg, Federico and Mariano Plotkin, eds. *Intelectuales y expertos: La constitucion del conocimiento social en la Argentina.* Buenos Aires: Ediciones Paidos Iberica, 2004.

Scarfi, Juan Pablo. *The Hidden History of International Law in the Americas: Empire and Legal Networks.* New York: Oxford University Press, 2017.

Scarfi, Juan Pablo. "In the Name of the Americas: The Pan-American Redefinition of the Monroe Doctrine and the Emerging Language of American International Law in the Western Hemisphere, 1898–1933." *Diplomatic History* 40, no. 2 (2016): 189–218.

Sember, Florencia. "The Reception of Irving Fisher in Argentina: Alejandro Bunge and Raúl Prebisch." *The European Journal of the History of Economic Thought* 20, no. 2 (2013): 372–398.

4 Pan-American Intellectual Cooperation

Emergence, Institutionalization, and Fields of Action

Juliette Dumont

Through the problem of intellectual cooperation, this article contributes to the renewed historiographical interest in the Pan-American movement from a perspective that no longer considers Latin America as the passive recipient of US American Imperialism.[1] Intellectual cooperation within Pan-Americanism has been difficult to analyze. This is partly due to the elusive nature of the movement, for which it is difficult to elaborate a definition and partly to the ambiguity and ambivalence that characterized the proponents and agents of Pan-Americanism in the United States, which was the principal, if not unique driving force behind the movement. Finally, it is virtually impossible to distinguish identifiably Pan-American dynamics from those that should more rightly be attributed to the fields of either US–Latin American relations, or regional relations in Latin America. Mark J. Petersen's description of Pan-Americanism at the turn of the twentieth century as "a wide collection of movements that made the concept simultaneously more difficult to define and all the more fascinating,"[2] encapsulates the stimulating and arduous challenge posed by any investigation of intellectual cooperation. Moreover, the area of intellectual cooperation was conducive to idealistic rhetoric, the whole point being to encourage collaboration and better understanding between interested parties; such rhetoric should neither be dismissed out of hand as simply serving to conceal US economic interests and Latin American strategies, nor should it be taken at face value.[3]

This issue addressed, it remains to work out how to account for the galaxy that is Pan-American intellectual cooperation. This article draws on two hypotheses, one formulated by Mark J. Petersen, the other by Mark T. Berger. Petersen, in light of a historiography that insists on the protean nature of Pan-Americanism, has proposed making a distinction between two separate dimensions at the heart of the movement. The first includes those aspects that have been traditionally associated with Pan-Americanism: questions of security and the defense of US economic interests. From this perspective, emphasis is placed on the hegemonic ambitions of the United States and on Pan-Americanism as a tool at their disposal. The second dimension concerns what Leo S. Rowe referred to as "the larger aspects of Pan-Americanism," of which Mark J. Petersen has drawn up a list: "issues

DOI: 10.4324/9781003252672-5

of internal development and practical and technical matters of common concern among the American republics such as sanitation, urban housing, prevention of epidemic diseases, protection of patents and trademarks, communications, aviation, women's rights, scientific and cultural exchange, et cetera."[4] Intellectual cooperation is an integral part of all aspects of this second dimension, within which "controversy was actively avoided … and non-governmental actors were heavily involved."[5]

Mark T. Berger defines the concept as "a changing set of ideas, institutions, practices, and movements linked explicitly and implicitly to assumptions about a range of common experiences and aspirations held by peoples and governments in the Americas."[6] He continues: "Pan American narratives emphasize the commonality of the hemispheric experience in contrast to other parts of the world. They often point to the necessity and even the naturalness of closer cooperation and integration to the region." This definition focuses our attention on the multiple and shifting realities encompassed by Pan-Americanism but also on its discursive element, as well as on the actors and practices driving the movement.

If, in many respects, both these dimensions were incorporated into the building of an informal US American empire, the US Americanization of Latin America and the interests of the United States, two further elements cannot be overlooked. First, Latin Americans seized upon, appropriated, and cultivated the concept. Second, Latin Americans were often aware of the ambivalent nature of Pan-Americanism. The Chilean writer Arturo Torres Rioseco, who taught in a number of US universities, wrote an article in the academic journal *Hispania* in 1931 entitled "Towards a better Pan-American understanding," in which he expressed a widely held concern about US expansion ("The United States is constantly increasing their involvement in Latin America, which is turning towards the North, sometimes with a show of admiration, sometimes with a show of concern and fear … From Argentina to Cuba and Mexico we are under North American influence"[7]) while subscribing to what Arthur P. Whitaker referred to as the "Western Hemisphere Idea" ("We are experimenting, in the North and the South, with a new interpretation of life, a new form of expression and a new way of finding happiness. The two halves of the New World have so much in common that it is almost impossible to imagine the existence of one without the other."[8])

The rhetoric of "commonality" and allusions to the special position and role of "America" or "the Americas"[9] was also employed by a large number of Latin Americans, especially in the wake of the First World War. In order to understand this stance, it is essential to bear in mind the importance of discussions about identity taking place on a national and regional level throughout the region from the 1920s onwards that attempted to redefine the relationship with "Madre Europa."[10] In this context, Pan-American intellectual cooperation, as well as its European manifestation as promoted by the International Committee on Intellectual Cooperation, offered a range of actions, a space for interaction, and legitimization for Latin American actors anxious to better define the identity of their nation and their region, and to strengthen the positions of both on the international stage. Pan-American intellectual cooperation was one of the elements in the "vast transnational experimental workshop"[11] that was Latin America in the interwar period and a platform from which Latin Americans could exert their influence in the new world order that emerged in the aftermath of the war. As Mark J. Petersen has asserted: "Pan-American cooperation was ... an opportunity for Latin American states to engage with a broader trend of multilateralism."[12]

To effectively analyze the period under consideration, from the end of the nineteenth century to the dawn of the Second World War, this article draws as much on North American historiography as it does on that of Latin America and Europe, thereby yielding a diversity of viewpoints that constitute a useful kaleidoscope through which to comprehend this multifaceted phenomenon. In keeping with my intention to avoid reducing Pan-Americanism, explored here in relation to intellectual cooperation, to merely one of its dimensions or to a simple confrontation between the power of the United States and the Latin American world (in itself diverse), I have chosen to employ a multi-scalar analysis that cross-references developments on the national, regional, continental and transnational levels. Only the local level is not considered here, for reasons of space. Finally, this study privileges an institutional approach in an attempt to provide an initial framework for the proliferation characterizing the ensemble of phenomena stimulated by intellectual cooperation that can be associated with Pan-Americanism.

In the first instance, I will consider Pan-Americanism in a broader context than that of its continental manifestation, taking into account events at both the lower regional level and beyond at the international level in order to understand the dynamics of intellectual cooperation that nourished and reinforced the movement. I will go on in the second section to present three modalities for the institutionalization of Pan-American intellectual cooperation, whose susceptibility to appropriation and reinterpretation in Latin America will be discussed in the final section. This article represents an initial attempt to identify the origins and development of intellectual cooperation within the framework of Pan-Americanism. It is therefore intended to serve as a point of departure for further investigation, and does not represent the culmination of the research process.

United States–Latin American Relations and the Construction of an Informal Empire

The Pan-American dynamics of intellectual cooperation are part of a wider framework that encompasses all exchange between the two halves of the American continent, going back to the time of Latin America Independence, as has been shown by Juan Manuel Espinosa in his work *Inter-American*

68   *Juliette Dumont*

Beginnings of US Cultural Diplomacy.[13] The Spanish–American–Cuban War and the wave of anti-Americanism it incited reduced the level of exchange. However, between these events and 1914 the expansion of higher education in the United States started to attract Latin American students, and certain Latin American countries, notably Brazil and Argentina, requested US expertise, predominantly in the guise of scientific missions. Generally, exchange took place within areas that were considered priorities for young Latin American states seeking to modernize.

At the same time, the peace movement of the first decade of the twentieth century, which was reflected in the United States by the foundation of the Carnegie Endowment for International Peace (1909), the American School Peace League (1907), and the World Peace Foundation (1910), had an impact on the development of cultural and academic exchange. These institutions, encouraged by the recommendations of the Pan-American Conferences, began to take an interest in Latin America. Their work contributed to another phenomenon: the emergence of an ever-increasing interest in Latin America from US academics and teachers, resulting in the professionalization of Latin American studies. The historian Mark T. Berger connects the institutionalization of Latin American Studies with Pan-Americanism, and with the development of a set of narratives that constructed the idea of an America "with a common history and destiny," "posing questions in terms that reflected US expansion"[14] and "natural" leadership of the region. This movement resulted in the publication, from 1918, of the *Hispanic Historical Review*, founded by an historian from the University of California, as well as the launch of the review *Inter-America* by the Carnegie Foundation in 1917.

The US educational community's growing interest in Latin America also manifested itself in secondary education where, for example, the teaching of Spanish became increasingly widespread: at secondary level, the number of students taking the language rose from 6,406 in 1913 to 252,000 in 1922.[15] As a result of this interest in Spanish, teachers were encouraged to research the cultural, social and political life of Latin America. All of it led to the creation in 1917 of, among other things, the review *Hispania*, published by the *National Association of Teachers of Spanish*. Considered as a whole, these practices were part of what Ricardo Salvatore has called "the discursive formation of informal empire," which he defines as "a collective enterprise laden with representations."[16] This fell very much within the framework of the "enterprise of knowledge" whose purpose was "drawing South America into the orbit of 'American' collective knowledge."[17] This process was inseparable from the evolution and the structure of Pan-American intellectual cooperation.

Scientists: The Founding Fathers of Latin American Intellectual Cooperation

Intellectual cooperation was not characterized solely by ongoing United States-Latin American relations, as described above. It was also fueled by dynamics specific to Latin America, which developed from the end of the nineteenth century.[18] Indeed, during the process of modernization initiated by Latin American elites at the turn of the twentieth century, those elites were confronted with similar problems, and a certain number of actors, among them scientists, took it upon themselves to advocate the possibility of facing these problems collectively and coherently. For scientists in particular, the challenge was threefold. First, they had to help their country gain entry to the circle of "civilized nations." They then had to prove they were legitimate contributors to and representatives of an international scientific system dominated by Europe and the United States and finally, thereby secure from their countries the recognition and funding required for their work.

Attention to health issues, as well as the collaborations formed between natural science museums[19] came together at medical and scientific congresses, organized within a framework that was partly South American, partly Pan-American. This section addresses the Latin American congresses, which principally assembled countries of the Southern Cone. These congresses were evidence of a willingness to circulate scientific information and to contribute to the establishment of personal ties between men of science on the subcontinent. They can be regarded as the first attempt to develop a scientific community at a regional level. The first Latin American Scientific Congress (1898) was organized by the *Sociedad Científica Argentina* and gathered delegations from thirteen countries. The objective was to offer a complete panorama of the scientific work being undertaken in the realms of law, mathematics, engineering, the natural sciences, physics, chemistry, anthropology, agronomy, medicine, and hygiene.

Doctors felt it was necessary to organize their own gatherings and the initiative for the first Latin American Medical Congress (1902) was taken by a group of Chilean doctors and members of the *Sociedad Médica de Chile* who held positions at the university Faculty of Medicine and in the public health sector. According to their general rules, the Latin American Medical Congresses had to meet five objectives: to contribute to the progress of medical science; to disseminate scientific knowledge that would allow Latin American nations to meet their own particular challenges (such as the fight against tropical diseases and urban sanitation); to promote the adoption of uniform measures within the framework of international health protection; to forge and maintain links of solidarity between medical institutions, associations and leading figures of Latin America by encouraging intellectual exchange; and finally, to have purely scientific goals, in other words, to avoid turning these events into political or ideological rallies.[20] All of these objectives corresponded with the definition of intellectual cooperation, and resulted in the creation of networks. Indeed, the congresses offered spaces for sociability that allowed participants to forge personal links thus paving the way for future contact on an institutional and extra-institutional level within the context of missions, exchanges, and research projects. In fact, exchanges between doctors and scientists, especially those in Argentina, Brazil, and Chile, continued beyond the congresses and into the 1940s. This permitted a dynamic particular to South America, even though that dynamic had largely been integrated into the sphere of Pan-Americanism with the creation of the Pan-American Health Organization in 1902 and when the *Latin American* scientific congresses became *Pan-American* in 1908.

International Dynamics: The Role of the International Organization of Intellectual Cooperation

From the 1920s onwards, the regional dynamics of intellectual cooperation were strengthened, on the one hand, by the omnipresence of discussions about national and regional identity,[21] resulting notably in the emergence of cultural revues that generated transnational networks.[22] On the other hand, they benefited from the broader dynamics of European intellectual cooperation driven by the International Organization of Intellectual Cooperation (IOIC) operating under the auspices of the League of Nations.[23] In fact, the Latin American countries became increasingly involved in this organization, which fostered the construction of networks in the region through national commissions for intellectual cooperation.[24] Many Latin American intellectuals and diplomats, such as Gabriela Mistral, Alfonso Reyes, or Elyseu Montarroyos, advocated for the participation of their country in the work of the IOIC because it provided the opportunity to feature on the "map of the world's intellectual life."[25] This would allow them to gain prestige on the international intellectual stage, and on the international stage generally, but also to counterbalance the growing influence of the United States.[26] The work of the IOIC and the networks it created were instrumental in initiating and reinforcing dynamics specific to Latin America.[27] The increasingly dangerous situation in 1930s Europe was certainly connected to this process, which cemented the idea that "America" should come to the rescue of the civilization under threat on the Old Continent. The advent of the Good Neighbor Policy, which emphasized the need to reinforce ties, particularly cultural and intellectual, between American nations, in turn strengthened the channels of intellectual cooperation within the inter-American system. This was reflected, for instance, in the stimulus provided by the Pan-American conferences in Montevideo (1933), Buenos Aires (1936), and Lima (1938) to create national commissions for international cooperation, along the lines of the IOIC, but with the express purpose of participating in the Pan-American movement.

Institutionalization(s) of Pan-American Intellectual Cooperation: The Pan-Americanization of the Scientific Congresses

In his overview of the Pan-American "galaxy," the Chilean jurist, Alejandro Álvarez, called attention to the existence of the Pan-American Scientific Congresses which "dealt with all subjects relating to the sciences but studied them from a specifically American point of view."[28] We return here to the idea, present in the Pan-American Scientific and Medical Congresses, that there were challenges specific to the Western Hemisphere that required reflection and solutions tailored to their circumstances. This was not the case solely in the sciences; for Alejandro Álvarez, geography and history (in particular the wars of independence) had created the basis for "continental solidarity," represented since the end of the nineteenth century by "a policy of constant rapprochement and cooperation in all areas of international activity." He concluded: "This is what is referred to as Pan Americanism. Nothing like it exists or has ever existed in Europe."[29] In the words of fellow Chilean jurist, Hernán Castro Ossandón, in a work devoted to American intellectual cooperation, the Pan-American Conferences represented "political Pan-Americanism" while the scientific congresses achieved "practical Pan-Americanism."[30] The distinction drawn by Ossandón is consistent with the one made by Leo S. Rowe when he spoke of "the larger aspects of Pan-Americanism," which allowed Mark Petersen to identify "two separate dimensions" within the movement. "Political" and "practical," Pan-Americanism as defined by Ossandón was as much a principle as a repertoire of actions. Writing almost twenty years apart, the emphasis placed by these two Latin American authors on the scientific congresses is indicative of their central importance to Pan-American intellectual cooperation. In all likelihood, this was because the original initiative was one led by Latin Americans for Latin Americans.

Two further encounters[31] were to follow the first Latin American Scientific Congress organized by the *Sociedad Científica Argentina* (Buenos Aires, 1898), and with the full support of the Chilean government, the organizing committee for the Fourth Congress (Santiago de Chile, 1908) decided that the United States should participate in future congresses; the designation "Latin American" was therefore discarded in favor of "Pan-American." This decision was the result of a plurality of factors. First, there was the progressive politicization of this kind of event, as science was also a matter of competition between nation states: public authorities became aware that hosting and funding scientific events benefited the country's image abroad.[32] By inviting the United States, Chile not only interacted with the US on an equal basis, but also "earned its place at the forefront of Pan-Americanism."[33] As for Latin American scientists, the desire to build a scientific community capable of competing with that of Europe,[34] to resolve public health problems specific to America,[35] and to gain recognition within their own countries, explains why they wanted these scientific meetings to have continental scope: Pan-American gatherings would provide a wider platform from which to exchange models and information, and to publicize their research. Finally, this Pan-Americanization of the scientific congresses was linked to various factors: the South American tour of US Secretary of State Elihu Root in 1906, whose discourse about Pan-American sameness was well received among the intellectuals and elites he encountered;[36] the emergence of the "enterprise of knowledge" described by Ricardo Salvatore and Mark T. Berger; and the creation, following a resolution of the Second International Conference of American States (Mexico, 1902), of the Pan-American Health Organization (PAHO). It was also the result of the convergence of Latin American dynamics[37] and US-led initiatives[38] whose goals were to set health standards to combat the cholera and yellow fever epidemics that were hindering trade relations, and to promote urban sanitation policies.

The second Pan-American Scientific Congress (Washington, 1915–16), whose aim was to "increase the knowledge of America, to disseminate and allow the culture of each nation within the Americas to become the inheritance of all the American republics,"[39] as documented by Samuel Guy Inman, can be regarded as the most significant gathering yet of intellectuals from both sides of the continent.[40] It tackled questions of commerce, education, international law and science. This congress corresponded with the period when Woodrow Wilson was trying to improve relations between the United States and Latin America, notably in the form of the Pan-American Pact, which was intended to demonstrate hemispheric solidarity in the face of a Europe that was being engulfed in the trenches. The actions and discourse of Leo S. Rowe during the congress were part of this same resolve. His repeated calls for the strengthening of inter-American intellectual cooperation evoked a peaceful American continent that needed to work toward the resolution of its own problems, and find its own solutions in order to do this. He thereby pursued a project that had been initiated as early as 1906–7 through visits to Argentina[41] and Chile, during which he had forged ties with intellectuals and statesmen from both countries. He had already begun by "inciting them to change their outlook from a vision of progress focused on the European example to a new paradigm embodied by the United States.[42] This kind of discourse met with a positive response insofar as it echoed the determination of a certain number of Latin American intellectuals, and scientists in particular, to "contribute to the progress of humanity"[43] and to redefine their ties with Europe, which they were beginning to suspect was not the only incarnation of civilization.

After Washington, three further congresses took place.[44] These scientific assemblies became increasingly consequential as new areas of interest were added to the discussions. Moreover, the resolutions made during these congresses were submitted to the Pan-American Union, which undertook to include them in the program for subsequent Pan-American conferences. The increasing strength and scope of intellectual cooperation within the framework of Pan-Americanism was a double-edged and profoundly ambivalent development. On the one hand, the Pan-American arena represented a threefold opportunity for Latin American scientists: greater visibility and dissemination of their work,[45] but also a certain prestige for their countries; the achievement of aims already defined in South American arenas thanks to the debates and work undertaken by the PAHO and the scientific congresses;[46] and finally, material possibilities offered by the increasing involvement of philanthropic institutions in the Pan-American movement, in particular the Rockefeller Foundation.[47] On the other hand, this process was also strengthening the "informal empire" of the US PAHO policy was determined almost exclusively by its director, William Wyman.[48] Several authors have demonstrated, moreover, to what extent the boundaries between philanthropic foundations and US diplomatic circles were porous.[49]

Intellectual Cooperation at the Pan-American Conferences: An Ever-Growing Presence

There is no overview, in English,[50] of the role played by intellectual cooperation during the Pan-American Conferences. Such an overview, as will be provided here, is essential to understanding the evolution and evaluating the importance of intellectual cooperation, and to identifying the subjects considered relevant to reinforcing links between the different nations of the hemisphere. Even before the Pan-American Union adopted specific structures for organizing intellectual cooperation, a certain number of initiatives were launched that fell within its scope. Thus, according to Hernán Castro Ossandón:

The First International Pan American Conference, organized in Washington (1889–90), can be taken as the starting point for contemporary development of the Intellectual Cooperation Movement in America; because it was then that it was officially noted, for the first time, that it was necessary and important to cultivate intellectual relations in order to strengthen continental solidarity, and that the first collective initiative was taken directly for this purpose.[51]

Castro Ossandón's observations were based on the resolution formulated during this conference which called for the foundation of an American Library in Washington. It wasn't until the Second Pan-American Conference (Mexico, 1902) that the Columbus Library was formally established.

The Third Pan-American Conference (Rio de Janeiro, 1906) was a step forward in that intellectual cooperation would now fall within the prerogatives of what was then still known as the International Bureau of the American Republics: a recommendation stipulated that the Bureau address issues relating to education, in particular student exchanges. This momentum was consolidated in Buenos Aires in 1910, during the Fourth Conference, where many of the delegates were from intellectual or educational backgrounds. Moreover, when the Bureau was reorganized and renamed the Pan-American Union, intellectual relations were clearly identified as falling within its scope of action. Finally, a resolution was adopted which aimed to encourage American universities to set up exchanges between teachers and students. The need to increase academic exchange was subsequently reasserted at the Fourth Pan-American Conference (Buenos Aires, 1910) and at the Second Pan-American Scientific Congress in 1915–16, during which a resolution was formulated that required:

the teaching of the Spanish language be made general in the schools of the United States, and of the English language in Latin American schools, and that both be taught from the point of view of American customs, history, literature, and social institutions.[52]

The Fifth Pan-American Conference (Santiago, 1923) addressed another aspect of academic cooperation by adopting a resolution that encouraged the harmonization of university curriculums.

If the atmosphere at the conference in Havana (1928) was tense, especially when it came to political or legal issues, it nevertheless led to a certain amount of progress in matters of intellectual cooperation. Nine subjects relating to intellectual cooperation were included in the agenda. This conference thus precipitated the foundation of the Pan-American Institute of Geography and History and the resolution for the proposed creation of an Inter-American Institute of Intellectual Cooperation. The Inter-American Congress of Rectors, Deans, and Educators in General that took place in Havana in 1930 continued the work begun in 1928. It was the occasion for a veritable panegyric on inter-American cooperation, delivered by Ricardo Dolz, senator and dean of the Faculty of Law at the University of Havana, in which he gave an overview of inter-American intellectual cooperation.[53] His inventory is as much a list of the initiatives that took place either within the framework of exchange at a Latin American level, or which belonged to the sphere of bilateral relations between Latin American countries, as it is a list of those initiatives relating to Pan-American dynamics. Moreover, Dolz's speech highlighted another aspect pertinent to any analysis of these dynamics: the great variety of actors involved (he mentioned "scientific organizations, sections of cooperation, associations, colleges, federations, confederations, museums, offices, etc."), which is something Castro Ossandón also highlighted as a feature of intellectual cooperation on the continent.[54] This kind of discourse reflected the fact that both the rhetoric and the practices of Pan-American intellectual cooperation were sustained by as much as they nourished "the vast transnational experimental workshop" that was Latin America in the interwar period.

The Inter-American Conference for the Maintenance of Peace held in Buenos Aires in 1936 could well be considered the high point of the movement as well as the moment of transition into a new era. In fact, the conference marked the very beginnings of Roosevelt's "Good Neighbor Policy," coming at a time when the US State Department was envisaging playing a role in the realm of cultural relations, with the aim of countering German and Italian propaganda. A Special Commission was set up to examine issues of cooperation and to discuss the two main sources of problems: intellectual exchange and moral disarmament. This conference issued the highest number of recommendations (7), resolutions (9) and conventions (5) relating to intellectual cooperation in the history of the Pan-American Conferences, and in a great many different areas (the arts, performance, mutual exchange of publications, radio broadcasting, literature, education and academic exchange). The most important of these was the "Convention for the Promotion of Inter-American Cultural Relations," which was unanimously approved. Besides reinforcing academic exchange, this convention recommended the establishment of a service dedicated to the exchange of publications between the libraries of contracting states and contained resolutions on the peaceful orientation of the public education system, the diffusion of films of an educational nature, and art exhibitions. It was also recommended that national commissions for intellectual cooperation be established in countries where they did not already exist, similar to those associated with the IICI. These commissions would equally maintain links with the PAU, demonstrating the extent to which the dynamics of Pan-American intellectual cooperation interconnected with those of their international counterpart.

The Seventh and Eighth Pan-American Conferences (Montevideo, 1933; Lima, 1938) might seem less ambitious in comparison; nonetheless it should be noted that both conferences raised questions regarding the conservation of historic sites and artefacts, associated in 1938 with the conservation of natural areas. This recommendation of 1938 was the reformulation, within the Pan-American framework, of the processes of construction and redefinition of national identity that had begun in the 1920s and became, in the 1930s, the focus of public policies designed to define national heritage, but also to promote the growing tourist industry. Finally, it is worth mentioning that following the conference in Lima, the musical world began to be included in Pan-American intellectual cooperation. As for educational issues, they remained present and, along with scientific cooperation,[55] can be considered as both the leitmotif and catalyst for the expansion of Pan-American intellectual cooperation.

The Foundation and Development of the Division of Intellectual Cooperation

In 1917, the PAU created a small education department, a development that had its origins in a resolution taken at the Second Pan-American Scientific Congress (1915–16). The aims and activities of the department were outlined in a 1938 memorandum:

> gathering material on education, publishing a series of pamphlets on educational theory and practice, assisting Latin American educators interested in the educational movement of the United States, helping American students and teachers to learn something about the educational systems of Latin America, and guiding Latin American students in the United States. As a means of cooperating with college and university administrators in evaluating the credentials of prospective students from Latin America, special reports were issued on Latin American universities, secondary and normal schools.[56]

The activities of the department, as created in 1917, were clearly a prolongation and an expansion of the exchanges between the United States and Latin America described above. On the one hand, it recognized the attraction the United States held for Latin American students and its possible value as a role model in terms of pedagogy; on the other, it marked participation in the "enterprise of knowledge" identified by Mark T. Berger and Ricardo Salvatore. Indeed, it is within this context that a partnership was created between the PAU and more than fifty US higher education institutions,[57] as well as with a number of philanthropic organizations, such as the Carnegie, Rockefeller and Guggenheim Foundations, in order to set up a scholarship program for Latin American students wishing to study in the United States. The Guggenheim Foundation was approached directly by the Directorate General of the Pan-American Union in 1926 and the services of the PAU were used by the Foundation to conduct surveys in Mexico and South America that resulted in the establishment of fellowships for Mexico, Argentina, Chile and Cuba.[58] Links between the US academic community and the philanthropic foundations on the one hand, both of which overlapped substantially with the diplomatic community, and with the PAU on the other, were thus part of a general movement that seemed to leave little room for Latin American initiatives; one in which Pan-Americanism was defined solely in terms of exchange between the United States and the "rest" of America south of the Rio Grande. From this perspective, Pan-Americanism seemed to be a system with a core (US) and a periphery (Latin America).

The department subsequently evolved: in 1924, it became more autonomous from the Directorate General and in 1929 changed its name to become the Division for Intellectual Cooperation (DIC). In the October 1929 issue of the *Bulletin of the Pan-American Union*, it was announced that a Technical Advisory Committee, composed of "eminent figures from diverse intellectual backgrounds," all of whom were from the United States, had participated in the formulation of a work program for the Division.[59] It would henceforth have a much broader remit as it "not only carries on its original work in the field of education, but also follows as closely as possible the different phases of the cultural movement in the Americas."[60] In order to better understand the extent of its reach, Concha Romero James, then head of the DIC, referred to the documents preserved in the Division's archives, whose classification system reveals which subjects were addressed: "Archaeology, Art and Artists, Bibliography, Congresses, Education, Exchange of Teachers and Students, Letters, Practice of Professions, Societies, Treaties on Intellectual Cooperation."[61] The DIC, besides centralizing a certain amount of information, "makes a special effort to keep in personal contact with a large number of individuals in every conceivable field of intellectual endeavour."[62] These archives and the constitution of a register of key resource persons allowed the DIC to act as an information center for the entire continent: teachers, students, scientists, and intellectuals could all address the Division in order to obtain information about another country or region of the continent. Many examples of such demands were given by Concha Romero James in her 1938 report and the majority came from the United States. The Division thus seemed to exist in order to facilitate exchange between the United States and Latin America, but rarely between Latin American countries, which raises questions about the meaning and scope of Pan-Americanism: was it just a two-way encounter between the United States on one side and Latin America on the other? It seems that while the Latin Americans were eager to exchange with the United States, they were also keen to do so with the rest of the Americas, as illustrated by the categorization made by Concha Romero James of the various requests received by the department from the subcontinent:

The Bureau received countless numbers of requests from teachers, civil servants, administrators and students, who were planning to spend some time in the United States or study in one of the other American countries; authors needing information on the most varied of themes or who wanted to send their books to interested persons specializing in the same areas; school-age children eager to correspond with their foreign classmates in the United States and other sister Republics; artists wishing to exhibit their works in this country, men of science who wanted to exchange publications, identify our botanical and zoological species, even organize expeditions.[63]

Thus the "reinforcement of spiritual relations between the nations of the American continent,"[64] presented as the main goal of Pan-American intellectual cooperation, cannot be reduced to the relations between the United States on the one hand and Latin America on the other.

This ambiguity was particularly noticeable with regard to education, which was the subject of a series of publications issued by the DIC[65] consisting of, "pamphlets on the theory and methodology of education as a means of contributing to the exchange of ideas and experience within such an important sphere."[66] In 1939, 108 documents were published in Latin American educational reviews, written by authors from across the continent. These documents were issued every two months, in Spanish and in Portuguese.[67] Moreover, there was a publication entitled *Lectura para maestros*, distributed in Spanish and Portuguese, that "contains information on the educational movement in the Americas"[68] intended to "raise awareness of the reality of education in America" and to "create ties between the participants in this reality."[69] In addition to this, *Educational Trends in Latin America*, an English-language review "intended for the use of persons in the United States interested in comparative education," was published each semester. The number and nature of these publications demonstrated a major interest in educational innovations and experiences across the hemisphere. The combined mobilization of the PAU, US American universities and US philanthropic foundations to promote academic exchange, as well as the work of the Institute of International Education[70] might suggest that the US educational model would have a strong presence in the pages of these reviews. If we look at the table of contents of *Lectura para maestros*[71] however we see that the articles focus predominantly on Latin American subjects (with information supplied by the country in question) rather than subjects relating to the United States. The DIC thus also served as an intermediary between Latin American educators and teachers, adding momentum, in its own modest fashion, to the dynamic under way between Latin American countries.

Moreover, when in 1931 Eloise Brainerd, then head of the DIC, gave her assessment of intellectual cooperation in America, she highlighted the "continuous current of educators between the various Spanish-American nations."[72] She also noted a tendency to familiarize students in secondary and higher education with neighboring countries: "Courses relating to the other American Republics are given in secondary schools in all Latin American countries and in universities or teachers colleges in Argentina, Chile, Cuba, Ecuador, Mexico and Peru."[73] This Latin American dynamic developed in two stages. Initially, during the first two decades of the twentieth century, congresses were established by students[74] and by teachers.[75] Thereafter, in the 1930s and 1940s, countries such as Argentina, Brazil, and Chile in particular, seized upon academic exchange as a tool of cultural diplomacy.[76] At the same time several bilateral agreements were established between these countries regarding educational issues (the revision of textbooks[77] and teacher and student exchanges,[78] for example) and more generally regarding an intellectual rapprochement.[79] These agreements served as models for the recommendations of the Inter-American Conferences of Buenos Aires (1936) and Lima (1938).

Samuel Guy Inman, in a brief summary of the accomplishments of the Pan-American Union in matters of intellectual cooperation, deplored the fact that the intellectual cooperation department, which he considered "the most active section of the whole system,"[80] had only limited and underpaid staff.[81] Is it the case then that the DIC had a somewhat marginal and insignificant role in the sphere of Pan-American Intellectual cooperation? Rather it offered a point of intersection, a crossroads between the two dynamics identified above—the United States as the center and the driving force of Pan-Americanism, led principally by US universities and charitable foundations and the emerging Latin American multipolar vision of Pan-Americanism. If the DIC was in many respects a component of the informal empire of the United States, it also served as both a sounding board and a means of boosting the vitality of Latin American exchange. Thus Pan-Americanism, considered from the perspective of intellectual cooperation and its institutionalization, appears to have constituted an encounter between these two dynamics.

Latin American Appropriations of Pan-Americanism: When Internationalism Met Nationalism

I will present two examples of how the Latin Americans seized upon Pan-Americanism, and in particular the intellectual cooperation with which it was bound up, to defend and promote their own agenda. The Latin American dynamic identified above was fueled by national considerations, whether of national identity, foreign policy, or both.

In 1926, when Brazil withdrew in protest from the League of Nations, a Brazilian doctor, Xavier de Oliveira, published a series of articles in the *Jornal do Brasil*, calling for the creation of an organization whose purpose would be to reinforce American intellectual cooperation. In 1927, his initiative having been well received in certain Latin American countries, de Oliveira, who had links to both diplomatic and political circles in Brazil, pursued his editorial campaign. The intended outcome of the initiative was to put an end to the isolation of Brazil from the rest of America, and even to make Brazil the driving force behind continental dynamics. This position was the result of two different processes. First there was Brazil's detachment from Europe, evidenced by their withdrawal from the League of Nations. In another parallel process, stimulated by foreign policy developments since the beginning of the twentieth century, Brazil answered the "American calling" advocated by de Oliveira; this meant affecting a rapprochement with the United States according to the terms of an "unwritten alliance,"[82] rather than adhering to a Latin American bloc designed to resist the power of the United States.[83] The rapprochement was made manifest in the rhetoric adopted in favor of Pan-Americanism and the Monroe Doctrine, as understood and implemented in the United States.[84] It was in evidence when Xavier de Oliveira presented the project of the Inter-American Institute of Intellectual Cooperation (IAIIC)[85] as the culmination of a "doctrine accepted today by the entire of America"[86] and as "the result of the great work of the PAU."[87] This was an incredible rhetorical display, given the criticisms levelled by numerous intellectuals and politicians against the Monroe Doctrine and Pan-Americanism,[88] seen as the instruments of US imperialism. These criticisms did not go unheard in Brazil.

This rhetoric should not blind us to Brazil's ambitions to assume leadership of the subcontinent and to be considered the equal of the United States south of the Rio Grande. By placing the project under the aegis of the PAU, Xavier de Oliveira was able to present his country as the forerunner of American intellectual cooperation, the "vanguard of Pan-Americanism." The benefits to be reaped by Brazil through the foundation of this organization would therefore be twofold: on the one hand, the country pictured itself as the driving force behind Pan-Americanism, a position that up until that point had been monopolized by the United States; on the other hand, whereas it had once been thought of as the interloper in the "great family" of Latin America, it would now become the beating heart of its intellectual prestige. By consulting Latin American diplomats on the project and publicizing their positive reactions, de Oliveira offered a counterpart to his assertions regarding the Monroe Doctrine: he presented a Brazil attentive to the opinions of its neighbors, that wished to support and strengthen regional dynamics; a Brazil that was a friend and ally to the United States, but also thoroughly Latin American. For this purpose, the language of commonality (and the consequent differentiation from Europe) was constantly employed by Xavier de Oliveira and associated with Pan-Americanism, which was in this case used to serve the diplomatic agenda of Brazil.

Nationalism and Pan-Americanism United: The Case of Chile

As the result of pressure from certain Latin American delegates, an Inter-American Institute of Musicology (IAIM) was created, under the direction of Francisco Curt Lange, at the Eighth Pan-American Conference (Lima, 1938). Lange had been the editor of the *Boletín Latino-Americano de Música* since 1934, which had facilitated the emergence of a transnational network of Latin American music experts. The IAIM was short-lived as it was supplanted in July 1940 by the creation of the PAU Music Division (MD) "a wartime agency ... mainly sponsored by the US State Department and managed by US musicologists."[89] The Music Division was funded from the outset by the recently established Office of the Coordinator of Inter-American Affairs, which included a Music Committee, as well as by the Carnegie Foundation. The creation of the Music Division was part of the movement to assert US cultural diplomacy (the Cultural Affairs Division of the State Department dates from 1938) and within this framework, the emergence of US musical diplomacy,[90] led by a "clustering of organizations and agencies."[91] It would be natural to assume that this framework left Latin American actors little room for maneuver. Corinne Pernet has shown however that this development contributed to the assertion of Latin American national identities, notably in Chile.[92]

In order to understand this process, it is important to note that the Music Division's interest in folk and popular music was part of a wider movement taking place toward the end of the 1920s. Specialists in folklore and popular culture, from North and South America, engaged in collecting and promoting this type of cultural production, perceived as one of the authentic bedrocks of national identity. The movement was the stimulus for constant interaction between the national, regional, and continental spheres due to the emerging "transnational professional community"[93] eager to exchange knowledge and practices. Corinne Pernet has shown that "the US initiatives and resources resulted in increased networking activities among folklore scholars and helped to bring about the institutionalization of popular arts and folklore studies at museums and universities across Americas."[94]

This was particularly true in Popular Front Chile (1937–41), where those specializing in this area saw in the Pan-American constellation an opportunity to secure both intellectual and material resources that could then be used to promote their work, and in turn strengthen "*chilenidad*," that is to say Chilean national identity. The establishment of the Institute of Music Extension at the University of Chile in 1940, and its subsequent reincarnation as the autonomous Institute of Musical Folklore in 1944, were thus the result of both North American and Pan-American connections established by Domingo Santa Cruz Wilson and Eugenio Pereira Salas,[95] both from the University of Chile, that allowed them to obtain equipment and expertise from the United States.[96] This is just one of the examples that has led Pernet to conclude that "progressive nationalism and Pan-Americanism worked together to shape Chilean folklore."[97]

Conclusion

There was considerable risk involved in an article devoted to Pan-Americanism of falling into the trap of interpreting the phenomenon as nothing more than an instrument of North American interests, and of analyzing its evolution solely in this light, such is the extent to which the history of the growing influence of the United States in Latin America, be it in political, economic or intellectual terms, has been confused with the history of the inter-American system. I have tried to make the voice of the subcontinent heard, and to illuminate the issue of hegemony as it has been redefined by certain researchers, including Ricardo D. Salvatore, who has insisted on the fact that hegemony "does not necessarily mean replication or acceptance of the same," but should rather be considered as "a selective adaptation of a set of principles, value norms, and ideas emanated from the imperial center."[98] Resistance, adaptation, rejection and reappropriation, are all part of the dynamics of Pan-Americanism, which represented far more than a confrontation between Bolívar and Monroe. Without denying the considerable influence of the United States, I have tried to restore the complexity of the situation, going beyond the partisan interpretations that dominated studies undertaken against the backdrop of the Cold War. This complexity, like the ambivalent nature of Pan-Americanism, is as much the result of the driving impulses of Latin America as those of the United States. As for the Latin Americans, on various occasions they seized upon Pan-Americanism as a political and ideological concept, but equally as a set of practices, a means of sociability and a promise of profitable exchange between the two parts of the continent and between themselves.

To describe and analyze what exactly was meant by Pan-Americanism within the framework of intellectual cooperation it is possible to use the theories formulated by Ludovic Tournès to understand the phenomenon of Americanization, which he has studied by looking at the role of US American philanthropic organizations in the field of higher education and research in France. He proposes adopting "a circulatory perspective which accounts in the same analysis for the different parties in the relationship and their interactions," so as "to break with the dichotomy of transmitter/receiver and dissemination/reception, to analyze the respective dynamics of the two parties considered at one and the same time as transmitters and receivers, even when there is an imbalance of power between them."[99] This approach allows us to consider Pan-Americanism as a "co-production," to see that Latin America was not simply reacting to the United States but was at the origin of dynamics that pre-existed the US American initiatives. The US was confronted by processes

82 Juliette Dumont

already under way and Pan-Americanism can now be analyzed as the emergence of a communal language, allowing all those concerned "to pursue related projects, even if they were not identical."[100]

Notes

1 At its most basic level, intellectual cooperation can be defined as any international cooperation initiative designed to promote the exchange and dissemination of knowledge in order to encourage better understanding between peoples.
2 Mark Petersen, "The 'Vanguard of Pan-Americanism': Chile and Inter-American Multilateralism in the Early Twentieth Century," *Cooperation and Hegemony in US–Latin American Relations: Revisiting the Western Hemisphere Idea*, ed. Juan Pablo Scarfi and Andrew Tillman (New York: Palgrave Macmillan, 2016), 112.
3 Ibid.
4 Ibid., 113.
5 Ibid.
6 Mark T. Berger, "A Greater America? Pan Americanism and the Professional Study of Latin America, 1890–1990," *Beyond the Ideal: Pan Americanism in Inter-American Affairs*, ed. David Sheinin (Westport: Greenwood Press, 2000), 55.
7 Arturo Torres Rioseco, "Hacia una mejor comprensión panamericana," *Hispania* 14, no. 3 (May 1931): 218.
8 Ibid., 220.
9 Both expressions are employed by the Latin American actors in the reference sources consulted for this article.
10 See, for example, Patricia Funes, *Salvar la nación: Intelectuales, cultura y política en los años veinte latinoamericanos* (Buenos Aires: Prometeo Libros, 2006).
11 An expression borrowed from Anne-Marie Thiesse, *La création des identités nationales: Europe XVIIIe–XIXe siècle* (Paris: Éditions du Seuil, 2001), 13.
12 Petersen, "Vanguard," 116.
13 Juan Manuel Espinosa, *Inter-American Beginnings of US Cultural Diplomacy, 1936–1948* (Washington, DC: Government Printing Office, 1977).
14 Berger, "A Greater America?" 47.
15 Espinosa, *Inter-American Beginnings*, 47.
16 Ricardo D. Salvatore, "The Enterprise of Knowledge: Representational Machines of Informal Empire," *Close Encounters of Empire: Writing the Cultural History of US–Latin American Relations*, ed. Gilbert M. Joseph, Catherine C. Legrand, and Ricardo D. Salvatore (Durham, NC: Duke University Press, 1998), 71.
17 Ibid., 75–6. See also Ricardo D. Salvatore, *Disciplinary Conquest: US Scholars in South America 1900–1945* (Durham, NC: Duke University Press, 2016).
18 On the dense traffic of ideas, especially those of an intellectual nature, which characterized South America in particular, see Ori Preuss, *Transnational South America: Experiences, Ideas and Identities 1860s–1900s* (New York: Routledge, 2016).
19 On the role of natural science museums in the emergence of exchange between scientists from South America, see, among others, Maria Margaret Lopes, "Cooperação científica na América Latina no final do século XIX: os intercâmbios dos museus de ciências naturais," *Interciencia* 25, no. 5 (2000): 228–33.
20 Marta de Almeida, "Circuito aberto: idéias e intercâmbios médico-científicos na América Latina nos primórdios do século XX," *História, Ciências, Saúde—Manguinhos* 13, no. 3 (2006): 742.
21 This identity shift was mainly due to the weakening of Europe as a model of civilization in the wake of the First World War. See Olivier Compagnon, *L'adieu à l'Europe: L'Amérique latine et la Grande Guerre* (Paris: Fayard, 2013).

22 See Jussi Pakkasvirta, ¿Un continente, una nación? Intelectuales latinoamericanos, comunidad política y las revistas culturales en Costa Rica y en el Perú (1919–1930) (Tuusula: Academia Scientiarum Fennica, 1997); Alejandra Pita González, La Unión Latino Americana y el Boletín Renovación: Redes intelectuales y revistas culturales en la década de 1920 (México: El Colegio de México, Centro de Estudios Históricos, Universidad de Colima, 2009).
23 The IOIC emerged with the creation in Geneva of the International Commission of Intellectual Cooperation (1922) and was consolidated by the opening in Paris of the International Institute of Intellectual Cooperation (1926), which was designed as the "*organe exécutif*" of the Commission.
24 Each member state of the IOIC was supposed to create a national commission that would represent its country's intellectual landscape. The aim was both to build a more effective relationship with each country and to encourage the organization of intellectual activity to promote bilateral and multilateral relationships. Moreover, the function of the state delegate to the IOIC was established in 1925 in order to facilitate communication between the organization and each member state. In 1929, even if nineteen Latin American states had already nominated a delegate to the organization, only four had created a national commission. In 1939, nineteen states had a delegate (42.4 percent of the total and almost as many as Europe), thirteen of which had a commission (28.3 percent of the total).
25 The expression was used by Gabriela Mistral in a newspaper article published in *El Mercurio*, in which she called for the Latin American states to be involved in the work of the IOIC. AUN, AUN, A I 83, *El Mercurio*, July 13, 1927.
26 See Carl Doka, *Les relations culturelles sur le plan international* (Neufchâtel-Suisse: Éd. de La Baconnière, 1959), 11–12; Juliette Dumont, "De la coopération intellectuelle à la diplomatie culturelle. Les voies/x de l'Argentine, du Brésil et du Chili (1919–1946)," PhD in History, University of Sorbonne Nouvelle–Paris 3, 2013, 131–96.
27 The two American Conferences of National Commissions in Santiago de Chile (1939) and in Havana (1941), organized on the initiative of the Chilean and Cuban commissions, reflected the Latin American actors' reappropriation of the intellectual cooperation generated by the IOIC. See Juliette Dumont, *Diplomaties culturelles et fabrique des identités: Argentine, Brésil, Chili (1919–1946)* (Rennes: Presses Universitaires de Rennes, 2018), ch. 6.
28 Alejandro Álvarez, *La réforme du Pacte de la Société des Nations sur des bases continentales et régionales*, Report presented at the 5th Session of the International Juridical Union (June 1926), 15.
29 Ibid., 12–13.
30 Hernán Castro Ossandón, *Cooperación intelectual americana: Memoria de prueba para optar al grado de licenciado en la Facultad de Ciencias Jurídicas y Sociales de la Universidad de Chile* (Santiago de Chile: La Nación, 1944), 39.
31 Montevideo (1901) and Rio de Janeiro (1905).
32 For the Congress in Rio de Janeiro (1905), see Hugo Rogélio Suppo, "Ciência e relações internacionais: O congresso de 1905," *Revista da SBHC* 1 (2003): 6–20; and for the Santiago Congress, Oscar Calvo Isaza, "Conocimiento desinteresado y ciencia americana. El Congreso científico (1898–1916)," *Historia crítica* 45 (2011): 90–91.
33 Petersen, "Vanguard," 20.
34 Europe was regarded both as a model to be emulated and as a source of feelings of inferiority that needed to be resisted.
35 Among the presentations and subjects addressed during the congress, of particular note was the importance accorded to the fight against tropical diseases (mainly yellow fever, malaria, and ankylostomiasis).

84 *Juliette Dumont*

36 For an analysis of Elihu Root's tour, see Juan Pablo Scarfi and Andrew R. Tillman, "Cooperation and Hegemony in US–Latin American Relations: An Introduction," *The Hidden History of International Law in the Americas. Empire and Legal Network*, ed. Juan Pablo Scarfi and Andrew R. Tillman (New York: Oxford University Press, 2017), 19–30.
37 Cleide de Lima Chaves, "Power and Health in South America: International Sanitary Conferences, 1870–1889," *História, Ciências, Saúde—Manguinhos* 20, no. 2 (2013): 423; Marcos Cueto and Betty Rivera, "Entre la medicina, el comercio y la política: el cólera y el Congreso Sanitario Americano de Lima, 1888," *El rastro de la salud en el Perú*, ed. Marcos Cueto, Jorge Lossio, and Carol Pasco (Lima: IEP/UPCH, 2009), 111–50.
38 It is worth noting, for example, the role of Walter Wyman, appointed US Surgeon General in 1891, who made an important contribution to the Second Pan-American Medical Congress (Mexico, 1896) and the International Conference of American States in 1902. See Marcos Cueto, *El valor de la salud: Historia de la organización panamericana de la salud* (Washington, DC: Organización Panamericana de la Salud, 2004), 21–5, 38.
39 Samuel Guy Inman, "Backgrounds and Problems in Intellectual Exchange," *Inter American Intellectual Interchange* [no ed.] (Austin: Institute of Latin American Studies of the University of Texas, 1943), 7.
40 "This congress had 2238 attendees, representing 21 nations, 650 universities, 350 scientific and commercial bodies in the US and Latin America. This number surpassed all Latin American Congresses and it would not be exceeded in future congresses." Rodrigo Fernos, *Science Still Born: The Rise and Impact of the Pan American Scientific Congresses, 1898–1916* (iUniverse, 2003), 2.
41 Ricardo D. Salvatore, "The Making of a Hemispheric Intellectual-Statesman: Leo S. Rowe in Argentina (1906–1919)," *The Journal of Transnational American Studies* 2, no.1 (2010): 36.
42 Miguel Antonio Muñoz-Asenjo, "Las visitas de Leo Stanton Rowe a Chile y sus ideas en torno a la Cooperación Intelectual entre Sudamérica y Estados Unidos, 1907–1915," *Latin American Journal of International Affairs* 3, no. 1 (2011): 69.
43 This expression was first used by Leo S. Rowe at the Santiago Congress (1908).
44 Lima (1924), Mexico (1935), Washington (1940).
45 Thanks to the conferences and congresses, but also to the *Boletín de la Oficina Sanitaria Panamericana*.
46 For example, in 1924, eighteen countries approved the Pan American Sanitary Code, which committed its signatories to coordinate their efforts in the field of public health. Moreover, from 1922 the PAHO published the *Boletín de la Oficina Sanitaria panamericana*, in response to the express desire of scientists for the dissemination of information. Published on a monthly basis with a print run of 3,000 copies, it was one of the first periodical publications dedicated to international health (Marcos Cueto, *El valor de la salud*, 57).
47 The Rockefeller Foundation was particularly active in Latin America in the field of public health and epidemic control. See Marcos Cueto, "The Cycles of Eradication: The Rockefeller Foundation and Latin American Public Health, 1918–1940," *International Health Organizations and Movements 1918–1939*, ed. Paul Weindling (Cambridge: Cambridge University Press, 1995), 222–42; Steven Palmer, "Central American Encounters with Rockefeller Public Health, 1914–1921," *Close Encounters of Empire: Writing the Cultural History of US–Latin American Relations*, ed. Gilbert M. Joseph, Catherine LeGrand, and Ricardo D. Salvatore (Durham, NC: Duke University Press, 1998), 311–31.
48 Particularly as no funding had been provided for the four Latin American members to attend the meetings in Washington. and Theodore M. Brown, "100

Years of the Pan American Health Organization," *American Journal of Public Health* 92, no. 12 (2002): 1888–89.
49 See Frank N. Ninkovich, *The Diplomacy of Ideas: US Foreign Policy and Cultural Relations 1938–1950* (Cambridge: Cambridge University Press, 1981), chapter "Philanthropic Origins of Cultural Diplomacy"; Katharina Rietzler, "Before the Cultural Cold Wars: American philanthropy and cultural diplomacy in the interwar years," *Historical Research* 84, no. 223 (2011): 148–64. Juan Pablo Scarfi has highlighted the same phenomenon in the field of the law through an analysis of the links between the American Institute of International Law, the Carnegie Foundation and the State Department. See Scarfi, *The Hidden History*.
50 An overview I provided in French as part of my PhD thesis.
51 Ossandón, *Cooperación intelectual americana*, 11.
52 *Proceedings of the Second Pan-American Scientific Congress* (Washington, DC, 1915).
53 *Inter-American Congress of Rectors, Deans, and Educators in General (1928), Report of the Chairman of the Delegation of United States* (Washington, DC: United States Government Printing Office, 1931), 19–20.
54 Ossandón, *Cooperación intelectual americana*, 11.
55 In 1938, a recommendation was adopted for the coordination of the bodies of scientific and technical cooperation and a resolution for the coordination of scientific and technical research.
56 UNESCO Archives (UNA), A XI 11, memorandum attached to a letter addressed to Daniel Secrétan, September 27, 1939: "*Programa de cooperación intelectual de la Unión Panamericana*," by Concha Romero James.
57 Ossandón, *Cooperación intelectual americana*, 36.
58 Widener Library, "The Pan-American Union in the field of Inter-American Cultural Relations," a memorandum prepared by Concha Romero James, Head of the Division of Intellectual Cooperation (Washington, DC: n.p., 1938), 1.
59 Included among the members of this committee were: Stephen P. Duggan, director of the Institute of International Education; James Brown Scott, secretary of the Carnegie Endowment for International Peace and president of the American Society of International Law and J. David Thompson, secretary of the American National Committee for Intellectual Cooperation.
60 Widener Library, "The Pan-American Union in the field of Inter-American Cultural Relations," 2.
61 Ibid., 2.
62 Ibid., 3.
63 UNA, A III 63, *Primera conferencia Americana de comisiones nacionales de Cooperación intellectual, Actas e informes*, Imprenta Universitaria, Santiago, 1939, report by Concha Romero James, "Programa de cooperación intelectual de la Unión Panamericana," 113.
64 Francisco Walker Linares, *Cooperación intelectual* (Santiago de Chile: Publicaciones de la Comisión chilena de Cooperación Intelectual, 1943), 13.
65 There were also periodicals dedicated to the intellectual life of the continent, in Spanish (*Correo*), in Portuguese (*Correio*) and in English (*Panorama*).
66 AUN, A XI 11, "*Programa de cooperación intelectual de la Unión Panamericana* …"
67 AUN, A III 63, *Primera conferencia Americana*…, 115.
68 AUN, A XI 11, "*Programa de cooperación intelectual de la Unión Panamericana* …"
69 Widener Library, *Lectura para maestros*, no. 7 y 8, Oficina de Cooperación intelectual, Unión Panamericana, Washington, DC, June 1939.
70 Established in 1919 by Nicholas Murray Butler, Elihu Root and Stephen P. Duggan and maintained through private funding, the IIE opened a Latin

American Division in 1929 and, at the request of the Pan-American Union, organized a US tour for 22 Argentine academics. Between 1933 and 1935, the IIE also implemented a new wave of exchange programs. In 1934, with financial assistance from the Carnegie Foundation, 6 Chilean academics working on educational issues were hosted by various North American universities.
71 Eighteen issues were published between 1937 and 1945.
72 Eloise Brainerd, *Intellectual Cooperation between the Americas*, Education series, no. 15. Reprinted from the April 1931 issue of the *Bulletin of the Pan-American Union* (Washington, DC: The Pan-American Union, 1931), 3.
73 Ibid., 6.
74 There were three editions of *Congreso Internacional de Estudiantes Americanos* (Montevideo, 1908; Buenos Aires, 1910; Lima, 1912).
75 The First Congress of Latin American Teachers, which took place in Buenos Aires from 8 to 19 January 1928, brought together several delegations (from Mexico, Panama, Guatemala, Peru, Bolivia, Chile, Argentina, Uruguay, and Paraguay; also present was a representative from the Education Workers' International in Paris), and led to the foundation of the distinctly anti-imperialist *Internacional del Magisterio Americano*. Another Congress took place in Montevideo in 1930.
76 In 1940, the Division for Intellectual Cooperation of the Brazilian Ministry of Foreign Affairs devoted 30 percent of its budget to academic exchange; rising to 60 percent in 1946. At the end of the 1930s, half of the budget of the Chilean Commission of Intellectual Cooperation, attached to the University of Chile, was used to offer grants to Latin American students wishing to study in Chile.
77 Between Argentina and Brazil in 1933, and Argentina and Chile in 1938.
78 Between Argentina and Brazil in 1935, and Argentina and Uruguay in 1938.
79 Between Argentina and Chile in 1935.
80 Inman, "Backgrounds and Problems in Intellectual Exchange," 9.
81 In 1938, the Bureau's staff comprised two Mexicans, one Brazilian, two North Americans and one Chilean.
82 A term coined by E. Bradford Burns, *The Unwritten Alliance: Rio Branco and Brazilian–American Relations* (New York: Columbia University Press, 1966).
83 See Hugo Rogélio Suppo, "Ciência e relações internacionais"; Kátia Gerab Baggio, "A 'outra América': A América Latina na visão dos intelectuais brasileiros das primeiras décadas republicanas" (Doctoral diss., Universidade de São Paulo, 1998), 52–5.
84 See Juan Pablo Scarfi, "In the Name of the Americas: The Pan-American Redefinition of the Monroe Doctrine and the Emerging Language of American International Law in the Western Hemisphere, 1898–1933," *Diplomatic History* 40, no. 2 (2016): 89–218.
85 At the 1928 Pan-American Conference in Havana, a resolution was finally adopted calling for the establishment of the Institute, but this was never made a reality. See Juliette Dumont, "Latin America at the Crossroads: The Inter-American Institute of Intellectual Cooperation, the League of Nations and the Pan-American Union," *Beyond Geopolitics: New Histories of Latin America at the League of Nations*, ed. Alan McPherson and Yannick Wehrli (Albuquerque: University of New Mexico Press, 2015), 155–67.
86 Article "Os iniciadores do Intercambio universitario Argentino-Brasileiro" (August 24, 1926), reproduced in Xavier de Oliveira, *Intercambio Intellectual Americano. Contribuição brasileira á creação do "Instituto Inter-americano de cooperação intellectual"* (Rio de Janeiro: Imprensa nacional, 1930), 27.
87 This expression was used by Xavier de Oliveira in a circular letter sent in 1927 to American diplomats in Rio de Janeiro. Cited in the article "A palavra dos diplomatas americanos acreditados junto ao governo do Brasil" (n.p., 1927), 75.

88 See Juan Pablo Scarfi, "La emergencia de un imaginario latinoamericanista y antiestadounidense del orden hemisférico: de la Unión panamericana a la Unión Latinoamericana (1880–1913)," *Revista Complutense de Madrid* 39 (2013): 81–104.

89 Pablo Palomino, "Nationalist, Hemispheric, and Global: 'Latin American Music' and the Music Division of the Pan American Union, 1939–1947," *Nuevo Mundo Mundos Nuevos* (June 11, 2015) (doi:10.4000/nuevomundo.68062). Retrieved from http://journals.openedition.org/nuevomundo/68062

90 Jennifer Campbell, "Creating Something Out of Nothing: The Office of Inter-American Affairs Music Committee (1940–1941) and the Inception of a Policy for Musical Diplomacy," *Diplomatic History* 36, no. 1 (2012): 19–39.

91 Palomino, "Nationalist, Hemispheric and Global," 7.

92 Corinne Pernet, "The Popular Fronts and Folklore: Chilean Cultural Institutions, Nationalism and Pan Americanism, 1936–1938," *North Americanization of Latin America? Culture, Gender, and Nation in the Americas*, ed. Hans-Joachim König and Stephan Rinke (Stuttgart: Verlag, 2004), 253–77; Corinne Pernet, "'For the Genuine Culture of the Americas': Musical Folklore and the Cultural Politics of Pan Americanism," *De-centering America*, ed. Jessica Gienow-Hecht (New York: Berghahn Books, 2008), 132–68.

93 Pernet, "The Popular Fronts and Folklore," 136.

94 Ibid.

95 Domingo Santa Cruz Wilson and Eugenio Pereira Salas both spent a few months in the United States, at the invitation of the US Department of State. Eugenio Pereira Salas was also one of the founders and the first president of the Instituto Chileno Norteamericano de Cultura, created in 1938.

96 Pernet, "The Popular Fronts and Folklore," 266–8.

97 Ibid., 253–77.

98 Salvatore, "The Making of a Hemispheric Intellectual-Statesman," 11.

99 Ludovic Tournès, *Sciences de l'homme et politique. Les Fondations philanthropiques américaines en France au XIXe siècle* (Paris: Garnier, 2011), 11.

100 Ibid., 13–14.

Bibliography

Baggio, Kátia Gerab. "A 'outra América': A América Latina na visão dos intelectuais brasileiros das primeiras décadas republicanas." PhD diss., Universidade de São Paulo, 1998.

Berger, Mark T. "A Greater America? Pan Americanism and the Professional Study of Latin America, 1890–1990." In *Beyond the Ideal: Pan Americanism in Inter-American Affairs*, edited by David Sheinin, 45–56. Westport: Greenwood Press, 2000.

Burns, E. Bradford. *The Unwritten Alliance: Rio Branco and Brazilian-American Relations*. New York: Columbia University Press, 1966.

Calvo Isaza, Oscar. "Conocimiento desinteresado y ciencia americana: El Congreso científico (1898–1916)," *Historia crítica* 45 (2011): 86–113.

Campbell, Jennifer. "Creating Something Out of Nothing: The Office of Inter-American Affairs Music Committee (1940–1941) and the Inception of a Policy for Musical Diplomacy." *Diplomatic History* 36, no. 1 (2012): 19–39.

Compagnon, Olivier. *L'adieu à l'Europe: L'Amérique latine et la Grande Guerre*. Paris: Fayard, 2013.

Cueto, Marcos. "The cycles of eradication: the Rockefeller Foundation and Latin American public health, 1918–1940." In *International Health Organizations and*

Movements 1918–1939, edited by Paul Weindling, 222–242. Cambridge: Cambridge University Press, 1995.
Cueto, Marcos. *El valor de la salud: Historia de la organización panamericana de la salud*. Washington, DC: Organización Panamericana de la Salud, 2004.
Cueto, Marcos and Betty Rivera. "Entre la medicina, el comercio y la política: el cólera y el Congreso Sanitario Americano de Lima, 1888." In *El rastro de la salud en el Perú*, edited by Marcos Cueto, Jorge Lossio, and Carol Pasco, 111–150. Lima: IEP/UPCH, 2009.
de Almeida, Marta. "Circuito aberto: idéias e intercâmbios médico-científicos na América Latina nos primórdios do século XX." *História, Ciências, Saúde—Manguinhos* 13, no. 3 (2006): 733–757.
de Lima Chaves, Cleide. "Power and Health in South America: International Sanitary Conferences, 1870–1889," *História, Ciências, Saúde—Manguinhos* 20, no. 2 (2013): 411–434.
Doka, Carl. *Les relations culturelles sur le plan international*. Neufchâtel-Suisse: Éd. de La Baconnière, 1959.
Dumont, Juliette. "De la coopération intellectuelle à la diplomatie culturelle: Les voies/x de l'Argentine, du Brésil et du Chili (1919–1946)." PhD diss., University of Sorbonne Nouvelle–Paris 3, 2013.
Dumont, Juliette. *Diplomaties culturelles et fabrique des identités: Argentine, Brésil, Chili (1919–1946)*. Rennes: Presses Universitaires de Rennes, 2018.
Dumont, Juliette. "Latin America at the Crossroads: The Inter-American Institute of Intellectual Cooperation, the League of Nations and the Pan-American Union." *Beyond Geopolitics: New Histories of Latin America at the League of Nations*, edited by Alan McPherson and Yannick Wehrli, 155–167. Albuquerque: University of New Mexico Press, 2015.
Espinosa, Juan Manuel. *Inter-American Beginnings of US Cultural Diplomacy, 1936–1948*. Washington, DC: Government Printing Office, 1977.
Fee, Elizabeth and Theodore M. Brown, "100 years of the Pan American Health Organization," *American Journal of Public Health* 92, no. 12 (2002): 1888–1889.
Funes, Patricia. *Salvar la nación: Intelectuales, cultura y política en los años veinte latinoamericanos*. Buenos Aires: Prometeo Libros, 2006.
Fernos, Rodrigo. *Science Still Born: The Rise and Impact of the Pan American Scientific Congresses, 1898–1916*. iUniverse, 2003.
Lopes, Maria Margaret. "Cooperação científica na América Latina no final do século XIX: os intercâmbios dos museus de ciências naturais," *Interciencia* 25, no. 5 (2000): 228–233.
Muñoz-Asenjo, Miguel Antonio. "Las visitas de Leo Stanton Rowe a Chile y sus ideas en torno a la Cooperación Intelectual entre Sudamérica y Estados Unidos, 1907–1915." *Latin American Journal of International Affairs* 3, no. 1 (2011): 52–71.
Ninkovich, Frank. *The Diplomacy of Ideas: US Foreign Policy and Cultural Relations 1938–1950*. Cambridge: Cambridge University Press, 1981.
Pakkasvirta, Jussi. *¿Un continente, una nación? Intelectuales latinoamericanos, comunidad política y las revistas culturales en Costa Rica y en el Perú (1919–1930)*. Tuusula: Academia Scientiarum Fennica, 1997.
Palmer, Steven. "Central American Encounters with Rockefeller Public Health, 1914–1921." In *Close Encounters of Empire: Writing the Cultural History of US–Latin American Relations*, edited by Gilbert M. Joseph, Catherine LeGrand, and Ricardo D. Salvatore, 311–331. Durham, NC: Duke University Press, 1998.

Palomino, Pablo. "Nationalist, Hemispheric, and Global: 'Latin American Music' and the Music Division of the Pan American Union, 1939–1947." *Nuevo Mundo Mundos Nuevos*. (June 11, 2015) (doi:doi:10.4000/nuevomundo.68062). Retrieved from http://journals.openedition.org/nuevomundo/68062.

Pernet, Corinne. "'For the Genuine Culture of the Americas': Musical Folklore and the Cultural Politics of Pan Americanism," In *De-centering America*, edited by Jessica Gienow-Hecht, 132–168. New York: Berghahn Books, 2008.

Pernet, Corinne. "The Popular Fronts and Folklore: Chilean Cultural Institutions, Nationalism and Pan Americanism, 1936–1938." In *North Americanization of Latin America? Culture, Gender, and Nation in the Americas*, edited by Hans-Joachim König and Stephan Rinke, 253–277. Stuttgart: Verlag, 2004.

Petersen, Mark. "The 'Vanguard of Pan-Americanism': Chile and Inter-American Multilateralism in the Early Twentieth Century." In *Cooperation and Hegemony in US–Latin American Relations. Revisiting the Western Hemisphere Idea*, edited by Juan Pablo Scarfi and Andrew Tillman, 111–137. New York: Palgrave Macmillan, 2016.

Pita González, Alejandra. *La Unión Latino Americana y el Boletín Renovación: Redes intelectuales y revistas culturales en la década de 1920*. México: El Colegio de México, Centro de Estudios Históricos, Universidad de Colima, 2009.

Preuss, Ori. *Transnational South America: Experiences, Ideas and Identities 1860s–1900s*. New York: Routledge, 2016.

Rietzler, Katharina. "Before the Cultural Cold Wars: American Philanthropy and Cultural Diplomacy in the Inter-war Years." *Historical Research* 84, no. 223 (2011): 148–164.

Salvatore, Ricardo D. *Disciplinary Conquest: US Scholars in South America 1900–1945*. Durham, NC: Duke University Press, 2016.

Salvatore, Ricardo D. "The Enterprise of Knowledge: Representational Machines of Informal Empire." In *Close Encounters of Empire: Writing the Cultural History of US–Latin American Relations*, edited by Gilbert M. Joseph, Catherine C. Legrand, and Ricardo D. Salvatore, 69–105. Durham, NC: Duke University Press, 1998.

Salvatore, Ricardo D. "The Making of a Hemispheric Intellectual-Statesman: Leo S. Rowe in Argentina (1906–1919)." *The Journal of Transnational American Studies* 2, no. 1 (2010): 1–36.

Scarfi, Juan Pablo and Andrew R. Tillman, "Cooperation and Hegemony in US–Latin American Relations: An Introduction." In *The Hidden History of International Law in the Americas. Empire and Legal Network*, edited by Juan Pablo Scarfi and Andrew R. Tillman, 19–30. New York, Oxford University Press, 2017.

Scarfi, Juan Pablo. "In the Name of the Americas: The Pan-American Redefinition of the Monroe Doctrine and the Emerging Language of American International Law in the Western Hemisphere, 1898–1933." *Diplomatic History* 40, no. 2 (2016): 89–218.

Scarfi, Juan Pablo. "La emergencia de un imaginario latinoamericanista y antiestadounidense del orden hemisférico: de la Unión panamericana a la Unión Latinoamericana (1880–1913)." *Revista Complutense de Madrid* 39 (2013): 81–104.

Suppo, Hugo Rogélio. "Ciência e relações internacionais. O congresso de 1905." *Revista da SBHC* 1 (2003): 6–20.

Thiesse, Anne-Marie. *La création des identités nationales: Europe XVIIIe–XIXe siècle*. Paris: Éditions du Seuil, 2001.

Tournès, Ludovic. *Sciences de l'homme et politique: Les Fondations philanthropiques américaines en France au XIXe siècle*. Paris: Garnier, 2011.

5 Popular Pan-Americanism, North and South
International Relations and the Idea of "American Unity" in Argentina and the United States, 1939–45

Lisa Ubelaker

In September of 1941, community leaders in the town of Elkins, West Virginia decided to change the theme of their much-anticipated annual October Forest Festival. The statewide event, usually a homage to the fall foliage, would be refashioned as a demonstration of local support for Pan-Americanism. As in festivities past, thousands of West Virginians would descend on the town for three days of food, music, sports events, dancing, a parade and the ceremonial crowning of some thirty princesses and a queen. This year, however, the Fall Festival Queen would be tasked with the important work of "demonstrating how the hill people feel about their Latin American neighbors." A local paper extolled the communal effort: "the mountain people of West Virginia, who are right neighborly among themselves, aim to do their share toward spreading that traditional friendliness ... with a Pan-American jamboree."[1] On opening day, Latin American flags were flown high as the young women, donning pastel dresses, were crowned. A guest of honor, an emissary from the Panamanian embassy, celebrated the town's initiative and told participants that they were contributing to a larger effort of regional goodwill: "at least in this hemisphere, we love our neighbors as we love ourselves," he said, adding that "[as] humanity has gone mad in other continents, [Americans] have been charged with the enormous responsibility of saving the cultural humanity of mankind."[2] The festival's queen, her court, and the crowd of onlookers then attended a pageant titled "From the New World," which exhibited Latin American dances, presented by local dancers.

The "hill people" of Elkins put on a tremendous display, but they were far from alone in their demonstration of hemispheric solidarity. Local displays of support for the Good Neighbor Policy took place in small towns across the United States in 1941. Some events were quite elaborate. In April, the town of Greenfield, Iowa closed its schools for a massive day-long event celebrating local adoration for the peoples of the hemisphere. Some 1,800 locals participated; 8,000 outside attendees visited to see the procession. Men, women, and children sported Latin American costumes "improvised

DOI: 10.4324/9781003252672-6

by Greenfield sewing machines"; local businesses "displayed products from Latin-America, everything from tin and manganese ore to llama robes and brazil nuts in the husk";[3] after much practice, the high school band marched and played the national anthems of Latin American countries. Back in Elkins, long after the excitement of the annual pageant winded down, local papers continued to ignite Pan-Americanist Spirit. On Pearl Harbor Day, before news of the attack could be set to print, a headline in the West Virginia *Charleston Gazette* extolled local women and men to buy Argentine furs as Christmas gifts.[4] Women who wore furs, it explained, were bolstering economic ties with Latin America while also exhibiting their support for the Good Neighbor Policy.

In a brief period from 1939 to 1942, everyday forms of participating in Pan-Americanism flourished in towns and cities across the United States. While local town committees organized parades and hosted pageants, a slew of nationally circulating media and commercial outlets offered advice on how the US public might help the government build closer ties with Latin America from their homes, stores, and communities. Purchasing "Good Neighbor"-themed clothing, cooking Latin American recipes, hosting pageants, reading books, and learning Spanish were just some of the myriad ways a host of media outlets encouraged ordinary Americans to take international relations into their own hands.

Curiously, a parallel wave of Pan-Americanist energy was evident further south, in Argentina, although it took different forms and reflected different debates. Argentina would, at first glance, seem to be a rather unlikely place to cultivate strong Pan-Americanist sentiment: Argentina's representatives had long been outspoken voices against imperialist—and specifically US— interventions in the region, and residents typically emphasized their strong cultural and economic ties to Europe rather than the Americas. Moreover, from 1941 to 1945 Argentina stood out as the only nation to remain neutral and refuse to join forces with the Allied powers, rebuffing pressure from its neighbor states. Yet, despite (or perhaps because of) these factors, Pan-Americanism flourished as an idea in the public sphere.

What can be made of this abrupt surge in representing and imagining "the Americas"? For quite some time, treatments of twentieth-century Pan-Americanism have closely examined specific or isolated elite or intellectual projects, or emphasized the romanticism of the ideal and regarded its momentary popularity as a whimsical period of US interest in Latin America, with little bearing on the real economic and defense-driven foreign policy.[5] Other scholars have framed this particular wave of Pan-Americanist energy as an outcome of a top-down propaganda strategy set in motion by state offices like the United States' Office of the Coordinator of Inter-American Affairs (CIAA) for the purposes of advancing diplomatic and commercial goals in the region.[6] These approaches are valid and revelatory: the CIAA was, indeed, integral to the advance of many Pan-Americanist projects during the period, including some mentioned here. Too, Pan-Americanism appeared in various permutations since the late nineteenth century, and over the decades had been picked up and exalted by a number of groups who saw regionalism as a noble—or at least useful—political, economic, commercial and intellectual ideal.[7] Yet, most of these efforts recognized, either implicitly or explicitly, that true regionalism, a true unifying identity was a far-off ideal: although there were many Pan-Americanist initiatives, there seemed to be no genuine "Pan-America."

What made the late Good Neighbor Policy moment peculiar, and what previous examinations of Pan-Americanism have overlooked, was that during these years, Pan-Americanism momentarily became reinvented in everyday cultures and it transformed from something spoken about as a lofty ideal in elite circles to, momentarily, a participatory project that spread roots in local cultures, articulating tensions and ideas about how ordinary people fit into, or even impacted, large-scale global relations. During this brief period—and it was quite fleeting—regular persons spoke of daily actions—reading magazines and books, watching films, buying blouses, holding parades, listening to radio programs—as a form of personally engaging in, and actively constructing the regionalist idea.

Although the motivations and meanings of participating in Pan-Americanist trends were different in Argentina and in the United States, examining their forms and functions in each place illustrates how "American Unity" momentarily emerged as a way for regular persons to envision themselves as, in one way or another, taking part in the forging of international relations. The first section of this contribution details the emergence of the Good Neighbor-era trend and suggests that, during the still-isolationist period preceding US entry into the Second World War, the Christian rhetoric of the Good Neighbor Policy offered regular US Americans an invitation to demonstrate that the United States figured as a moral counter to Nazi power. Yet, as the following section shows, participants did not always agree on the moral bounds of Pan-Americanism. Its racial dimensions—and limitations—became a point of contention. The third section examines American Unity played out quite differently in Argentina. At first, evocations of regionalism became a way for a stifled press to express pro-Allied sentiment and circumvent state efforts to censor public opinion on the war. Over time, and particularly after the 1943 coup that generated a path to power for the populist Juan Domingo Perón, the idea of the United Americas also became a way to voice opposition to emerging nationalist state policies.

Pan-Americanism gradually disappeared from public discussion in the post-war era. Yet, the sentimentalism awakened in the final Pan-Americanist moment did not disappear. Rather its essential premise, that individuals could be participants and actors on the front lines of the construction of foreign policy, would become a key idea for a new era.

Popular Pan-Americanism in the United States

The popularity of Pan-Americanism in 1940 was unprecedented, but the concept of American regionalism was not new. To the contrary, Pan-Americanism had appeared intermittently as a part of US and Latin American political discourses since the independence era,[8] and by the end of the nineteenth century, it had gained favor among diplomats and businessmen who took up the term and refashioned it as a form of US-led commerce-driven international relations. A few decades later, it came into vogue again. Even as US military interventions in the region intensified during the 1910s, Pan-Americanism was inspiring renewed interest as a model for international relations, particularly among scholars and diplomats (including President Woodrow Wilson), who contrasted the Americas' relatively harmonious coexistence against European disunion.[9] Over the following two decades, Pan-Americanism became a flexible idea used in the organization of diplomatic forums, institutional meetings, professional networks, and social events that covered any number of subjects, including conflicts over US intervention, territorial disputes, scientific conventions and sports competitions.

This is to say, prior to the 1930s, privately led Pan American clubs were diverse in scope and origins, and were, in many cases, only tangentially connected to formal state projects like the PAU.[10] Beginning in the 1910s and even more so in the 1920s, an array professional organizations began to see Pan-Americanism and the field of cultural relations as an arena in which they could organize.[11] During this same period, in Latin America, and particularly in Argentina, private, non-state groups participated actively in Pan-Americanist forums. Although it was a widely felt that the connections between Argentina and Europe outweighed any real sense of "American unity," conferences on a variety of issues—legal, medical, professional—became important means of exchanging ideas.[12] Yet, most of these projects remained confined to a politically and socially active elite; as a result, Pan-Americanism remained a rather vague ideal onto which disparate groups could project their visions of collaboration.

The renewed escalation of conflicts in Europe in the 1930s changed the meaning of American Unity. By 1939, in a pre-Pearl Harbor United States, fears of Nazi incursion into South America stoked anxieties about the nation's regional ties. In 1940, a presidential executive order established the Office of the Coordinator of Inter-American Affairs (CIAA), which, with Nelson Rockefeller at the helm, was to shore up support for the United States and the Allied cause in Latin America. For Rockefeller, the goals of hemispheric defense and US economic hegemony were complementary; impending war made Latin American support critical, but also generated an opportunity for the United States to replace European countries as a primary trade partner in South America. The office capitalized on popular interest and the official policy of non-intervention to actively reframe US power as anti-imperialist, grounded in non-intervention and friendly commercial and cultural exchange. A myriad of cultural programs mobilized mass media in Latin America and the United States to insist that, going forward, US leadership would exemplify a benign and positive influence on the hemisphere, engaging in international relations through friendly trade and shared admiration, rather than military power.[13]

The CIAA brought the idea of hemispheric solidarity into the limelight of public media in the early 1940s. The agency provided government backing (in a variety of forms) for some of the period's most important Pan-Americanist consumer and intellectual projects. Along with the PAU, it also published material that encouraged regular US Americans to hold their own Pan-Americanist meetings and celebrations in small towns, and created and sponsored separate material, in radio, film, advertising and print media, for Latin American consumers. CIAA programs also flourished in the realm of mass media. A slew of new radio programs promised to help US listeners learn about their "neighbors to the south."[14] CIAA-sponsored films also attracted wide audiences. The films often followed a more longstanding tradition of depicting Pan-Americanism as a kind of benign romance between US male protagonists and Latin American women.[15] In *Down Argentina Way* (1940) and *Weekend in Havana* (1941) the interactions between US American male protagonists and the rising starlet Carmen Miranda captivated audiences.[16] In the Disney film *Los Tres Caballeros* (1944) Donald Duck articulated his fondness for Latin America by chasing women on a Brazilian beach before fixating on Carmen Miranda's sister in a strange, almost psychedelic encounter.[17] Some films produced music that crossed over into radio hits. The song, *Chica Chica Boom Chic*, featured in the film *That Night in Rio* (1941), became a national sensation. Although songs and movies like these were rather superficial, they offered an enticing message—in naming the foreign policy explicitly, they re-imagined diplomacy as a personal relationship.

Without a doubt, the CIAA propelled the language of Pan-Americanism—and, specifically, an imagery of international relations as a personal endeavor—into the public discourse at unforeseen levels. Yet, it did not work alone. Narrowly exploring the explosion of public culture that lauded the ideal of Pan-Americanism as a state-driven strategy ignores that the success of CIAA initiatives relied heavily on the popularity of the idea. Pan-Americanism resonated with audiences and generated enthusiastic participation. While stoking the trend, the CIAA could not have anticipated the degree to which US Americans would celebrate and see themselves as actively participating in the regionalist ideal.

Ms. Good Neighbor: Consumer Fashion and International Relations

In April 1940 the trade periodical *Women's Wear Daily* exuberantly told US clothing merchants that, inspired by a recent mass interest in Latin American relations, anything Latin American was ripe for selling.[18] Over the following two years, Latin American-styled clothing saw "superb" consumer responses. By 1941 the trend reached West Virginia—the *Charleston Gazette* lauded that Latin styles were arriving in local stores. It explained to local audiences that war in Europe may have brought a stop to traditional imports, but it had lit a new enthusiasm for a different kind of consumer encounter with Latin America. Latin American-inspired dresses and prints were novel, "exotic," and brought a contrast to Old World fashions.

The fact that designs and treatment in many instances are new to us simply adds to the enthusiasm with which we discover that the New World has artisans as skillful and materials as lovely as the Old World. Native Indian crafts that go back to the civilization of the Incas and the Aztecs for inspiration are available along with the sophisticated products of city industries.[19]

Women's Wear Daily concurred—by 1942 more and more local distributors were seeing success with Good Neighbor clothing. Saks Fifth Avenue decked out their storefronts with Latin American products and clothing and in Washington, Lansburgh & Bro. department store hosted a "salud a las Modas Pan Americanas"-themed promotion with Latin American-inspired clothing that had a "excellent response."[20] *Parents* magazine advertised Chesterfield coats sold with Disney Pan-American pins for children.[21] As with much of this era's Pan-Americanist fanfare, the clothing lines inspired by US–Latin American relations were presented in the US press as a kind of novel encounter between regular US Americans and their nearly mythical Latin American neighbors—an opportunity for US consumers (mostly women) to "discover" the products and styles of the South. Tailoring with Latin American "flair" offered a mix of exoticism and luxury, in which [overwhelmingly white] US consumers were to act as patrons and explorers, engaging in an act of "discovering" the New World.

However, the goods being sold were more than mere curiosities. Shoppers were expected to see each article as a unit of international trade, and to view the purchase as economic support for the Good Neighbor Policy. In 1941, Macy's Department Store in New York City, in coordination with the CIAA, developed an elaborate stage to present Latin America wares and fashion to US consumers. Billed and promoted as an opportunity to engage in diplomatic commerce, Macy's Latin American Fair was a two-month event that displayed Latin America food, home goods and "modernized" "Latin-inspired" clothing across various staged settings. The elaborate store displays included a replica of Mayan ruins (where jewelry was sold), a *Coffee Finca* modeled after a plantation hut, a Brazilian *Fiesta Square* which served as a tea room, *the Jungle* exhibiting exotic orchids, an *Indian Marketplace*, and a modern replica of a city street called *the Avenida 1942* where books and leather goods from Argentina were sold.[22] Concerts were held, and on a separate level, visitors could browse an exhibit of Latin American art.[23] *Vogue* hailed the event as a kind of simulated international travel experience in which US women could discover Latin America, purchase decorations for their home and clothing for themselves, and support the war effort. Over 850,000 visitors toured the event during its two-month exhibition.

Consumerism, in each of these cases, was entwined with a narrative of generating economic support, through the purchase of products and the exhibition of "friendship." Each shopper, in making their purchase and then displaying it publicly was thus helping to forge a sentimental and anti-imperial hemisphere. For those who could not tour the displays at major department stores, there were plenty of ways to engage in the trend. Major women's magazines encouraged that participation in "fashionable" international relations could also be crafted at home: the *Ladies' Home Journal* sold "Good Neighbor Patterns" that women could buy and sew at home—a portions of the proceeds went towards and Inter-American scholarship fund. The magazine also encouraged young girls to "continue the good neighbor policy" by knitting sweaters with Latin American wool.[24]

A racialized, gendered, and international power dynamic formed the groundwork of these exchanges. US consumers—depicted in nearly all of these texts as white US women—were encouraged to imagine themselves part of a second line of US defense. Empowered by their purchasing power and their benign "friendliness" they were engaging in international relations through local commerce, while also imbuing policy with sincerity. As they browsed goods staged in a controlled and pleasurable encounter, or used their dollars to purchase wool or furs, they ostensibly were helping male leadership steer Latin America away from trade with the Axis, while at the same time performatively "learning" about the Latin American other. *The Washington Post* reinforced the notion of feminine commercial aid, explaining: "[Uncle] Sam himself can be a good neighbor by lending money ... but when the neighbor's store is on the rocks, the women are the ones who must commence buying there to help him out."[25]

Pan-Americanism emerged as a way to imagine ordinary Americans, and in this case, women, as engaging in not just the performance, but also the production, of US power.

Homespun Relations

Although the Macy's fair in New York, the Forest Festival in West Virginia, and the parade in Greenfield, Iowa were different kinds of productions (the festivals and parades de-emphasized consumerism in favor of community performance), in all three, US participants donned "Latin" styles and engaged in an essentialized reproduction of Latin America. In the case of store-bought women's wear, the image of the young sexualized "señorita" made famous by film star Carmen Miranda could be worn at home, making it both a consumable good, and a form of more intimate performance of US international relations that mimicked the sexualized relations dramatized on screen.[26] Pageants also illustrated an essentialized reproduction of "Latin America" in which women bestowed with sashes and crowns were deemed representations of Pan-Americanist sentiments. A teacher in Waco, Texas described a local event there in which a queen, "Miss Pan America entered and was introduced by Miss Texas, then Ambassadors of the twenty-one Pan American countries were introduced, each carrying a flag we made":

> They sang America, the Beautiful around a throne, made of a box covered with bunting. The queen wore a white dress and crown and scepter made of cardboard covered with tinfoil ... each child was in Spanish costume ... one table displayed products from Latin America.[27]

The homespun décor of small-town initiatives contrasted against the flashy wares presented in *Vogue* magazine, or even at Macy's or Saks Fifth Avenue, but they also insisted that local acts of Pan-Americanist expression were relevant, and worth celebrating. In community papers, columnists coaxed readers to participate in the policy by studying Spanish, or organizing a Good Neighbor book club; others provided "Good Neighbor recipes" so homemakers might imitate Latin flavors at home.[28] Unlike the acts of consumption, which were billed as a more direct economic support to trade relations, these local practices—learning Spanish, joining a club, sewing flags or cooking a meal—articulated a sense that the nature of US role in the world ultimately depended on the attitudes, support, and collective efforts of regular people.

Activities like these were also actively encouraged by the Pan-American Union and the CIAA, which distributed pamphlets advising local groups to "further the cause of Inter-American unity" by issuing official proclamations on Pan-American Day, staging school assemblies, speech contests and creating local parades and beauty pageants.[29] Institutions Members of local community groups, in the United States and in Latin America, often registered with the Pan-American Union and signed up to receive bulletins or pamphlets with information on the Latin American Republics or on Pan American events. Materials were also available for purchase. The offices were prolific in providing ideas for local events, articles, and information. A personal archive kept by a former member of the Pan-American Student Forum provides evidence of the constant flow of the quantity and quality of resources that small local groups received from the organization. A pamphlet on "sources of Latin American Music" included a catalogue of Latin American folksongs with a list of phonograph records, band and orchestra arrangements, and simple sheet music available for purchase. A pamphlet on "What others have done for Pan-American Day Programs" included thirteen pages of ideas for small and large sized community events, titles for student addresses, and first-person accounts from local organizers.

Institutional programs like these encouraged a sense of mass participation, and made ideas and plans for performance easier to organize. Yet, without public enthusiasm and a sense of community support, they would never come to fruition. The practice of making Pan American displays caught on with gusto, particularly in US schools and women's groups. Typical events included parades featuring the twenty-one flags of the American republics, or pageants wherein judges crowned local women and girls "Miss Pan America," as in Lakewood California, or "Miss Unity," as in Albany, NY.[30] One "Pan American Friendship" pageant in San Antonio, Texas had local fourth and fifth graders each represent an agricultural product of the region as they sang about the benefits of cooperation; the pageant crowned one of the fifth graders "Miss Friendship";[31] a high school in Cambridge, Wisconsin chose to write and perform a three act play about Pan-Americanism at their graduation; the play coalesced in "a plea for the solidarity of the Americas" as the girls of the senior class presented the twenty-one flags of the American republics they had sewed by hand.[32] In Oklahoma, the chapters of the Pan American Student Forum held regular meetings and occasional statewide community events. At a Convention Dinner and Dance held on Pan-American Day 1939, members opened the ceremony and young women provided the night's entertainment: "Señorita Elisa Gusine from Uruguay gave a talk about 'La Cultura Uruguaya' and danced several numbers for the audience; local members Miss Margaret Murphy and Lucille Brown sang 'La Habanera.'"[33]

While many of the pageants and parades that took place around the United States bore the signs of small-town craftiness rather than mass consumerism or vogue couture, they also relied on US white participants "dressing up" as Latin Americans to demonstrate to one another their mutual endorsement of regional relations. Photographs suggest that participants did not only wear clothing they determined to be typical of Latin America, but also on occasion donned blackface and brownface, visually connecting the pageants and parades to an entrenched history of racist performances that upheld notions of white supremacy through costume. These types of homespun costumes were also suggestive of the fact that while these Good Neighbor performances lauded Americans' "common bonds," and "international friendship," US Pan-Americanist participation was quite often complementary, rather than a substantial challenge to prevailing racial, imperial, and gendered hierarchies.

The Limits of a Performed Alliance

The degree of interest in Pan-Americanism in the years approaching the Second World War raises the question: why, for this fleeting moment, did a US foreign policy develop such a powerful popular echo? At the center of these displays of Pan-Americanist solidarity was an argument about the moral nature of US power, one that succinctly connected sentimentalist feelings with capitalist commerce, wartime defense and Christian morality. An example could be taken from a typical script for a school Pan-Americanism play: "Pan American: A Pageant," distributed by the Pan-American Union and used in celebrations in many small US communities included a dramatic close that illustrated the message. Performers were instructed to "construct a cardboard mountain scene where a small image of Christ, such as is often found in ten-cent stores, be set up and the whole construction suitably illuminated, or if this seems too formidable, a large picture of Christ might be raised into view by the two nations while all look on with reverence, some kneeling and all sing the hymn."[34] The performance of hemispheric spirituality was followed by a staging of international commerce (described in the script as mutual "admiration and exchange of products") in which "northerners [walk about showing] toy cars and planes and southerners [do the same with] pottery, baskets, rugs, etc."[35] Here, US children performed friendly relations as a dramatization of trade under Christian symbolism, all while at the same time illustrating US technological superiority.

Publications echoed the emphasis on Christian connection. The *Pan American*, for example, noted that the policy itself was grounded in the "Christian doctrine that all of us should be good neighbors, doing unto others as we would be done by."[36] The Pan-American Student Forum, a group with followers across the Midwest, had at its motto, "of one blood He hath made all nations"[37] and the group's leadership described Pan-Americanism as "to live in a spirit of toleration, not only to believe in the reality of to live and let live, but also to sponsor and encourage more altruistic goals ... We can help outsiders most by helping those around us and showing the 'good neighbor' spirit."[38] In these diverse but coherent interpretations, Pan-Americanism was not merely a commercial or diplomatic project, but also a moral (and religious) model for US power—it was in this way built upon and expressed by the moral actions and displays of ordinary citizens.

As I have noted elsewhere, the emphases on Christian paternalism and "friendliness" also permitted both diplomats and ordinary Americans to contrast US dominance and Nazi ambition.[39] While Pan-Americanism was flourishing, media representations were also depicting German policy as an immoral, highly-scientific, and godless design for power.[40] The 1943 film *Why We Fight: a Prelude to War*, for example, described German Geopolitik strategy as a "military control of space" in which strategists are "in search of only two elements: labor and raw material."[41] Pan-Americanism stood to articulate Geopolitik's fundamental opposite: a pursuit of power, also driven by technological and commercial rationales, but grounded first in a humane sentimentalism; US policy was so moral that it could be modeled even by its women and children.[42] In such a context, learning Spanish, decorating one's house with Latin American rugs, or participating in a Pan-American Day Fair, was not only about expressing a sense of individual cosmopolitanism, it was also about participating in a specific ideation of moral superiority. Hemispheric peace, forged on the basis of sentimental engagement, was implicated in a story of the victory of good over evil, of the Good Neighbor over Nazi terror. It entwined the ordinary American in a hero's pursuit.

In this light, it bears noting that as many of these examples have already suggested, US Pan-Americanist sentiments were not anti-imperialist by any measure. US participants were inundated with a nearly cartoonish and sexualized idea of Latin America that was remodeled and refashioned to fit their tastes. Each activity depended on US consumers engaging in a discourse of a shared Americas while at the same time, in many cases, discovering their neighbors and performing their power over the continent, often in costume. These representations claimed a kind of anti-racism, anti-imperialist stance while nonetheless performing traditional hierarchies.

Activists for racial equality pointed out this paradox. Some found the momentary popularity of Pan-Americanism to be an opportunity to elevate their criticisms of the imperial and racist structures of US power.[43] Latino periodicals in Texas and California, for example, often included personal accounts that highlighted the contradiction between the evident spirit of "Good Neighboring" and the lived realities of discrimination were numerous.[44] In particular, Mexican American civil rights groups like the League of United Latin American Citizens (LULAC), mobilized to use the Good Neighbor Policy's positive rhetoric and the popularity of Pan-Americanism to fight discrimination, mobilizing to rally politicians on both sides of the border to protest the treatment of Latinos in the United States. Yet, in many instances, efforts to engage with white Pan-Americanists fell flat. Alonso Perales of LULAC wrote to many Pan-American organizations in the 1930s imploring their participation in civil rights. In the Pan-American Student Forum newsletter he urged students that genuine Pan-Americanism would mean "making every effort to eliminate racial prejudice in order that we may strengthen the ties of friendship between the two great races of the Western Hemisphere."[45] In 1939, he wrote the women running the Pan-American Round Tables of Texas to support efforts to address discrimination in the state. When the women denied their support, he wrote again, describing the injustices incurred by racial segregation in Texas public schools, parks, and public spaces, and to convey his disappointment. He vowed to "cease to participate" in any Pan-American organization that did not "strike at the very heart of the problem."[46] The Assistant Director of the Round Tables refuted Perales, responding that segregation in public parks was an "issue of sanitation"—a common pro-segregationist argument.[47]

Perales was not alone in seeing Good Neighbor fanaticism as both an opportunity to demand greater equality, as well as a rather empty performance of pleasant rhetoric. As early as 1936 *the Chicago Defender,* one of the most important Black newspapers of its time, warned readers to "beware the wolf in sheep's clothing" when it came to the Good Neighbor Policy, noting that the new language of kindness and equality was only rhetoric until the oppressed peoples of the United States saw an end to discrimination.[48] In 1941, Urban League founder George Haynes pointed out that racial discrimination in the United States contradicted the tenor of the Good Neighbor Policy: "the people of our neighboring nations to the South have mixed Negro and Indian ancestry ... and our treatment here of not only the Negro and Indians, but of the Jews, Chinese and Japanese has perceptibly weakened our influence in world affairs."[49]

Other interracial Pan-Americanist organizations did push for Good Neighbor advocates to take action on racial discrimination. In Chicago, a Pan-American group led by Ernst Schwarz and the YMCA spoke out against

Mexican American discrimination. As pressure mounted from both the US public and Latin American diplomats, Sumner Welles publicly condemned the treatment of Mexican-Americans in Texas. In a *Washington Post* op-ed, he concluded that racism and discrimination "create lasting resentments which no eloquent speeches by Government officials, nor governmental policies, however wise, can ever hope to remove."[50] In Texas in 1943, a Good Neighbor Commission was eventually established to attempt to address discrimination in the community. Pauline Kibbe, executive secretary of the Commission confronted Pan-American organizations on the need to address discrimination outright.[51] Read alongside the Pan-American activism of local, predominantly white communities, these confrontations underline the extent to which this era of popular Pan-Americanism largely upheld the racial and gendered status quo. The language of exotification, difference, and cultural appropriation so apparent in Pan-Americanist consumer culture, parades and performances reinforced white US power even while professing a new morality.

Pan-Americanism in Argentina

In 1942, S. Seeber, from Entre Rios, Argentina felt inspired to write to her favorite US magazine, *The Ladies' Home Journal*. In a letter published in February, she told readers that she had never felt much affinity with the United States and had long felt that Argentine women had much more in common with Europeans than with US Americans. Recently, however, there had been unprecedented talk of Pan-Americanism. While regionalist sentiment had not changed her mind about essential differences, it did compel her to write the magazine, with the hopes that US women might learn about their Argentine counterparts.[52] As Seeber's letter suggests, the sudden ubiquity of Pan-Americanist thought was not only evident in the United States; in many parts of Latin America, including in Argentina, it was also remarkable, intense, and fleeting. There, too, the sudden vogue of Pan-Americanism bore the marks of the CIAA's campaign. However, as in the United States, it also extended far beyond the realm of propaganda. There were pageants and parades on Pan-American Day, and rallies held by local organizing groups that celebrated the Good Neighbor Policy; the language of American Unity infiltrated the discourses of local activism, local print cultures, and the reflections of ordinary persons, like those of Seeber.

Yet, grounded in a different context, Pan-Americanism in Argentina acquired a vastly different meaning. Not an affirmation of US moral authority or Latin American exoticism, the idea of American Unity appeared, first, as a method for local media outlets and anti-fascist organizers to demonstrate implicit support for the Allied forces during a period of state censorship, effectively a form of bypassing executive restrictions on the press and organizers. Second, as the war progressed, the idea was repackaged in popular culture with an argument suggesting that new generations of Americans, north and south, shared a common middle-class culture, even if they were, in other aspects, culturally different. This essential idea persisted—and became more important—over the following decades, even while popular US-produced media of the Cold War era shed its references to regional identity.

As already noted, the notion of Pan-Americanism was not new to Argentine political discussions of the 1940s. Professionals and scholars participated in formal inter-American congresses and exchanges, activists had organized around the notion of American solidarity, and women from Buenos Aires had been key leaders in Pan-American feminist alliances in the 1920s. Moreover, Pan-Americanism had emerged in many instances as concept that excluded or remained critical of the United States—a method of regional organizing that was intended to emphasize bonds between Latin American countries and counter imperialist interventions.

What first changed in the 1940s, then, was a rapid proliferation of voices extolling the US Good Neighbor Policy and gradually coming to use "American Unity" as part of a local expression. In Argentina, the terms Pan-Americanism and American Unity were deployed interchangeably. The proliferation of these concepts was accompanied by a crescendo of media and public events promoted by Rockefeller's CIAA, though local organizers and outlets soon joined this chorus, vociferously supporting the notion that Americanism (inclusive of the United States) was a plausible, if not desirable, product of the war, and imbuing the American Unity idea with local meaning.

Discussions of the war in *El Hogar*, a widely read arts and home magazine, sheds light on this change. In 1939, editor Alberto Casal Castel observed that in Buenos Aires, a city largely composed of European immigrants, the European war was distant yet personal: "Only the Argentines allow ourselves, perhaps because of our geographic position or because of our racial composition, to look at foreign questions as internal dilemmas."[53] He asked readers to consider a map of the world and to imagine pins marking German victories. He told readers to consider each pin "as a nail in the heart of our map."[54] The relationship of Argentina to European conflict, here, was direct, in spite of, not because of, its location in the Americas. Pan-Americanism—whatever form it might have existed in the past—seemed quite outside the purview of sentiments about the war.

Yet, almost exactly a year later, it was a bond with the Americas, rather than a connection with Europe, that the editors saw infiltrating public discourse. The magazine noted that the idea of the Americas had taken over local discussion, becoming fashionable, particularly in the press. In March, writer Pedro Songreguer criticized the ubiquity of the idea of American Unity in Buenos Aires, critiquing in particular its fanatics among the those contributing to public discourse:

> The issue of "American culture." ... It is certainly fashionable these days. From the orators to the journalists, who talk about with it fervent

enthusiasm, inspired, at times, by a sincere love for the "esteemed destiny" of the New World, to the erudite writers, bored collectors of ideas, who never have an original thought for themselves, there is no one who does not consider it necessary to pronounce their opinion on this complicated and passionate topic.[55]

El Hogar appeared reticent to join the Pan-Americanist bandwagon, but the resistance was short lived. The magazine devoted an entire issue to "Liberty in America" in April. Collaboration with the CIAA was evident. The issue featured an article comparing the American cowboy to the Argentine gaucho, as well as essays by Nelson Rockefeller, Eleanor Roosevelt and Argentine journalist and CIAA-collaborator Alejandro Sux, who also hosted a radio news show that targeted Argentine audiences.[56]

El Hogar was far from alone in taking up Pan-American discourse. As Casal Castel had noted, by 1939, the language of American Unity had spread far beyond formal diplomatic meetings and into public culture—over the following five years it would appear in mass media that circulated among a vast array of political and social sectors and become the thematic focus of political rallies and local pageants. Yet, if so many seemed to agree that Argentines felt closer to Europe than to any notion of Pan-Americanism, what explained the sudden bombardment of Americanist vocabulary in the press. Was this just the power of US wartime propaganda at work? Although the heavy hand of the CIAA is certainly apparent in many of these examples, to assume that the sudden emergence of Pan-Americanist discourse is merely a question of external influence or imposition ignores the ways and the extent that local media, activists, and media consumers were using this language as a tool for political and popular expression at a time when the official state position was one of neutrality. Local adoptions of Pan-Americanism suggest that by 1940, regardless of CIAA influence, "American Unity" emerged as a way for individuals and collectives to question the government's position of neutrality without mentioning the war explicitly—a tool that became particularly useful as the state attempted to prevent activists and the press from meddling in international affairs.

Another Word for Anti-fascism

Of course, the breadth and scope of CIAA influence on local media can make it difficult to disentangle which outlets permitted the agency to use its publication to reach local audiences, and which took up Pan-Americanist discourse independently. Regardless, however, as Pan-Americanist discourse reached a fever pitch it compelled broader debate over the idea in places to which the CIAA would have struggled to gain access. Even the deeply anti-imperialist socialist magazine *Claridad* took up the mantle of American unity. It included a translated piece by US journalist John Gunther that closed with the exclamatory remarks, "The Good Neighbor Policy has truly been a triumph. That truth is a simple and indisputable fact."[57] Antonio Zamora, the magazine editor, endorsed "the new North American way of thinking—a new conscience and attitude towards the other American nations." Placing less of a focus on anti-imperialism and a stronger focus on solidarity, *Claridad* made a US-inclusive Americanism part of its public renouncement of fascism, as well as its growing concern about Argentine government policies relating to neutrality.

El Hogar was not alone in welcoming discussion of the Pan American ideal. From 1939 to 1941, a slew of public media outlets grappled with the term. The literary magazine *Sur* held two separate roundtables on the subject in 1940 and 1941. The historian Lewis Hanke and local CIAA-collaborator Maria Rosa Oliver directed one such discussion, engaging with a number of thinkers who had written on the concept of regional identity. They noted the sudden popularity and ubiquity of the idea of the "Americas," though several participants sustained that most Argentines would continue to identify with Europe rather than with the United States.[58] Nevertheless, none denied that a wave of interest in Americanism was palpable, particularly in light of European war: despite the idea of ties with Europe running deep, there had emerged a clear utility to the Pan American idea.

Rightist nationalist press outlets zeroed in on the sudden enthusiasm for Pan-Americanism. They rallied their followers by critiquing the trend as an adoption of US propaganda. The pro-Nazi magazine, *El Pampero* mocked Pan-Americanism as imperialist doctrine and *El Fortín*, a conservative and anti-Semitic nationalist paper took note of *Sur*'s recent discussion of Americanism and told readers that Pan-Americanism was a Yankee-Jewish imperialist plot.[59]

Meanwhile, nationally circulating newspapers took up the language of American Unity, promoting the trend as an anti-fascist rallying cry. When the Argentine government offered a tepid official response to the attack on Pearl Harbor, *El Mundo* invoked the idea of Pan-Americanism to critique the response. The article, "Practical Pan-Americanism" lamented that "the consolatory phrase of calling America the continent of peace is no longer true. The insatiable monster is coming to our shores."[60] *La Prensa* echoed the sentiment, criticizing the government's inaction and professing that it was unaligned with the will of the people, who were of and "with America."[61]

Pro-Allied activists adopted the language of Pan-Americanism in their demonstrations. In late November of 1941, the group Acción Argentina planned an anti-fascist rally at the Luna Park arena in Buenos Aires; the government shut it down as anathema to Argentine foreign policy. The executive power justified the shutdown in the press, noting that it was the responsibility of the government to determine if civilian actions conflicted with official state neutrality.[62] Activists regrouped. "American Unity" emerged as a veil for their organizing. Several groups, including the Anti-Nazi Journalists, the Radical Feminist Committee, the Socialist Party, the Worker's Socialist party, and the Austria Committee organized an event in honor of Roosevelt and his Good Neighbor Policy, again, at Luna Park. The Good Neighbor Policy, these grassroots organizers proclaimed, offered a model of friendly relations and respect for sovereignty. *El Mundo* reported that the federal police attempted to stop another meeting of anti-Nazi journalists gathering on similar grounds, but then allowed the meeting to continue on the condition that they made no mention of international affairs.[63] In a second press release, the state reasserted that citizens would not be permitted to organize meetings that aimed to influence Argentina's foreign relations.[64]

Government censorship became more explicit. On December 16, 1941, citing "the safeguarding of neutrality and the defense of the continent," the Ministry of the Interior began monitoring the press for editorial opinion on the war. It was not long before both foreign and local publications sold at kiosks came under scrutiny.[65] Anti-Nazi press and anti-fascist organizers reacted, with some publications further exalting the image of American unity as a counter-construction to censorship. *Claridad* printed blank pages in its editorial section, which it titled "America faces the destiny of the world."[66] The idea of America became a tool for political expression. Examples permeated other, more mass-oriented outlets. *Radiolandia*, a weekly magazine dedicated to the national mass media (film and radio, in particular) was at times obstinate in their dedication to national productions and refused to comment on US imported media. However, in 1943, an editorial questioned a new regulation that required radio presenters to take an exam in national history, its message wrapped around the icon of a United Americas and the slogan, "With Unity Liberty." Here, as elsewhere, the symbols of the Americas were not just contrasted against European War, but also pitted against nationalist regulation.[67]

Americanism and a Modern Connection

As *Radiolandia*'s proclamation suggests, on the radio, the language of Pan-Americanism found an even broader audience, but also experienced increased regulation. Radio was an important outlet for US propaganda and in Argentina, Rockefeller's CIAA sought to foment Americanism among audiences by launching overt and covert programming on Radio Splendid and Radio Belgrano. A number of Pan-Americanist radio programs appeared and disappeared over the 1942–5 period—musical shows sang typical songs from countries across the continent, news programs provided war updates, and radio theater dramatized inter-American relations.[68]

In 1943, the new military government extended the regulations set out in 1942, doubling down on some aspects of neutrality, and engineering new rules that promoted nationalist programs and took aim at foreign media. By 1944, all foreign-produced programming was required to be pre-recorded and reviewed, voices with foreign accents were permitted limited airtime and national folklore music and orchestras were granted special priorities.

106 *Lisa Ubelaker*

By this time, most programs produced by the CIAA were discarded—those that were being sent by NBC for reproduction on the local station Radio Splendid were cut immediately; CBS Daily News, which CBS recorded and sent for rebroadcasting by Radio Belgrano, underwent major editing.[69] Some of the most popular and locally produced CIAA programs remained on the air by modifying their content and their methods of production; new locally-produced shows tailored the more standard message of American defense to fit local context. Musical, theater and educational programing that did not explicitly address European war but strictly promoted "American Unity" could sometimes escape censors and find sizeable audiences.

In this context, references to American Unity began to appear with greater frequency, and as in other media, the concept seemed to serve as a veiled response to new censorship. By 1944, *Sintonía* another widely read magazines for radio fans, advocated for the programming and inundated their content with "American" radio references. *Sintonía* informed readers as late as 1944 that entertainment and news shows produced by the Inter-American Broadcasting Association were bringing the Americas closer together. A typical piece emphasized that "continental unity" was all the more necessary in an age when "the oppressed peoples of the Old World" looked to the Western Hemisphere as a light of "liberty and peace."[70]

By 1944, vast portions of the local press had taken up the idiom of "American Unity," and, in short measure, Argentine cities began to host their own Pan-Americanist pageants and parades.[71] However, the most notable trend in Americanist sentiment could be found in the kinds of mass media that generated a notable popular audience; there, the construction of US-Argentine connection became a more elaborately developed idea. CIAA documents are useful for tracing the trend. The Coordinating Committee for Argentina received 1,643,000 letters from listeners when they offered to send free booklets about "Pan American heroes" to any written request; they sent out another 41,000 bound radio scripts to Argentines who wrote their offices.[72] These numbers offer some indication of interest in Pan American themes, but it was not until 1944, when Radio Belgrano began broadcasting *Del Brazo con los Varela* that a program that heightened "American Unity" truly resonated with local popular culture. The theater show dramatized the experiences of Alfredo Varela, the son of a middle-class Argentine family who went to the United States to study. Each episode recounted Alfredo's daily life in the United States, framed by letters he exchanged with his family in Buenos Aires. *Del Brazo con los Varela* was an instant hit, occupying a key timeslot in Radio Belgrano's programming and thanks to feedback tools used by the CIAA, we know that many listeners were actively following along as Alfredo journeyed through the United States. Not long into the show's first season, the coordinating office received over 135,000 requests from local listeners who requested postcards and booklets describing Alfredo's travels and experiences.[73]

Unlike the United States, where Pan-Americanist programming imagined Latin America as an exotic place to be "discovered," on *Del Brazo con los Varela*, personal inter-American relations were grounded in the mundane: each episode dramatized how both the US and the Argentine middle classes, while different, professed similar modern, connected lifestyles. Simple family dramas emphasized cultural similarities, personified cultural exchanges, exaggerated the ease of travel and communication with the United States, and heightened the reputation of the United States as the site of scientific innovation. In Argentina, the Varela family was depicted as typically urban and close-knit. A promotional article featured in *Radiolandia* included photos of the clan in their best Sunday clothes, walking arm and arm, feeding the ducks together at a park, and seated at home. The people and places Alfredo encountered in the United States were not that different from what his family had access to back home.

Del Brazo con los Varela conjured an idea of continental cultural cohesion built by an international, modern, educated and "ordinary" families. Articles about the show coaxed listeners that through the Varelas' experiences, they would "get to know the problems that affected households across the continent, and form closer ties" with similar families:

> They are a symbol of a sincere and pure aspiration for continental peace and harmony; a demonstration of the role that destiny holds for us as a race, as a people, as inhabitants of these hard-working peaceful lands ... Their name is Varela, a common and everyday name, because for them, there is no such thing as exclusion. All of us could be, or are, in some way, the Varela, who walk together, arm in arm.[74]

Here, international bonds were intimate, personal, and forged independent of a state or other institutions.

Del Brazo con los Varela was not alone in conjuring this image. One of the most popularized US media ventures ever to take root in Argentina, launched at the same time. *Selecciones del Reader's Digest* offered a similar narrative of unity for modern professional families. An offshoot of the US *Reader's Digest*, the Spanish-language magazine was designed and edited to advance inter-American relations; early issues made a point of exalting the Pan-American idea, telling audiences that the region's peoples, "in sharing the same hemisphere, also shared many problems and interests, as well as a similar character and political philosophy."[75] Advertisements and articles described modern media as providing a bond between disparate peoples: Ana de Martínez Guerrero, a leader of the Pan-American women's movement in Argentina, for example told *Selecciones* readers in 1941 that even if they could not board a plane to travel to see the Americas themselves they could have a modern relationship with the peoples of the region by reading.[76] Like the promotional material for *"Del Brazo con los Varela,"* testimonials about *Selecciones* encouraged local readers to use media to imagine themselves "connected" to a broader community of consumers, as never before.

Unlike *Selecciones*, *Del Brazo con los Varela* had a relatively short run, despite its popularity. In late 1944, at the end of its second season, state censors cracked down on transnational programming. After several episodes of *Del Brazo con los Varela* were severely edited for content, the controlling office explained to the network that the show would be permitted on the air but only if the writers complied with an important change in the plot line—Alfredo had to return home. Under new nationalist policies, *Del Brazo con los Varela* could continue to depict "an ordinary Buenos Aires family," but it could no longer illustrate the affinity of that family with the United States, at least not through travel.[77] The request is compelling, not only because it illustrates the specificity of nationalist radio regulation, but also because it serves to highlight what made media like *Del Brazo con los Varela* and *Selecciones del Reader's Digest* stand out. The plotlines of American Unity, as it appeared in these locally-popular programs and in the local press, suggested that regular Argentines could participate in the construction of international relations through cultural connection—and that, perhaps, these relations could form independently of the politics of the state.

Conclusion

By 1947, attitudes about American Unity had changed. Pan-Americanism receded from public view, largely retaining relevance only among the sparse elite groups and social clubs that had rallied around the concept in the years preceding the war. In the United States, the most poignant legacy of Pan-Americanism was, perhaps, not its efforts to construct a regional identity, but a clear articulation of the possibility for ordinary men and women to participate in and critically engage with US international relations by buying into, defining, and contesting it.[78] In Argentina, the idea of American Unity was initially a compelling symbol for anti-fascist and anti-Peronist activists. However, the political utility of this idea evaporated when the recently arrived US Ambassador in Argentina, Spruille Braden, organized a political intervention in the country's 1945 election, circulating a confidential "Blue Book" that cited Perón's connections to fascist Europe and Argentina's pro-Nazi factions, but generated Argentine accusations of US intervention in Argentine federal election. The Blue Book was leaked and Perón's campaign was quick to use the event to remind voters that each vote cast would be for one of "Braden or Perón," thereby setting up a powerful dichotomy between national sovereignty (via Peronism) and US imperialism. The evidence of intervention obliterated the moral power of a US-led Pan-American ideal.

Yet, Perón was wise to not do away with the metaphor of regional solidarity entirely. Perón's own *Blue and White Book*, circulated in response to the *Blue Book*, was laced with references to the idea of regional solidarity. The text discredited Braden's campaign as revealing the Good Neighbor policy to be a shallow endeavor while reaffirming Argentina's ties with its the sister republics.[79] Over the following years, new Peronist mass media made reference to Argentina's role in the Americas, reconjuring a previous version of Pan-Americanism that exalted Argentina's role and excluded the United States.[80] Still, the notion of American Unity never returned on a pre-1945 scale.

As in the United States, the idea of that international relations could be an intimate affair did live on in public discourse. In the late 1940s and 1950s *Selecciones* retained its nearly unrivaled popularity in Argentina, eliding censorship by making no reference to Peronism. In the 1950s it was joined by new examples of transnational culture that abandoned the language of Pan-America but retained a discourse that centered US media as a means for Latin Americans to "connect" to a global community. Although most mentions of the "Americas" had evaporated, the notion that knowledge and shared culture could generate personal international ties was still a potent political concept—and one all the more relevant in a Cold War era.

The wave of Pan-Americanist discourse in US and Argentine public cultures was fleeting but intense. Although these phenomena would not have existed without the United States government and the CIAA, the popularity and utility of these ideas as local interpretations of Pan-Americanism extended far beyond the reach of these initial propaganda projects. In the United States, Pan-Americanism became a cultural craze, a consumable good, and a means of expressing moral internationalism during the pre-Second World War era. Foreign policy momentarily became popular culture. The idea of the Good Neighbor became celebrated as a way for US Americans to imagine themselves as participants in the construction of moral empire. In Argentina, the utility of this idea was quite different. Rather than a true consumer craze, Pan-Americanism inundated media representations as a method for the press, anti-fascist groups and ordinary persons to express their criticisms of government neutrality, and then to construct and debate a sense of international connection in concert with emerging nationalist government policies. The Pan-Americanist energies that emerged in the United States and Argentina differed in form and function, a testament to the flexibility of Pan-American ideals.

Notes

1 "Charleston Girl Coronated Queen Silvia XII," *The Charleston Gazette*, October 3, 1941, 20; "Neely to Crown Local Girl at Forest Festival Today," *The Charleston Gazette*, October 2, 1941, 11.
2 "Neely Crowns Queen Silvia," *The Charleston Gazette*, October 3, 1941, 20.
3 "Mexican official delighted with Greenfield fete," *Waterloo Daily Courier*, April 14, 1941, 2.
4 "Be patriotic, buy furs and aid in Uncle Sam's Defense Program," *The Charleston Gazette*, December 7, 1941, 2.
5 Stephen M. Park, *The Pan American Imagination: Contested Visions of the Hemisphere in Twentieth Century Literature* (Charlottesville: University of Virginia Press, 2014); Ricardo D. Salvatore, "The Enterprise of Knowledge: Representational machines of Informal Empire," *Close Encounters of Empire. Writing*

the *Cultural History of US–Latin American Relations*, ed. Gilbert M. Joseph, Catherine C. Legrand, and Ricardo D. Salvatore (Durham: Duke University Press, 1998), 69–107.
6 Frank Ninkovich, *The Diplomacy of Ideas: US Foreign Policy and Cultural Relations, 1938–1950* (Cambridge: Cambridge University Press, 1981); Darlene Sadler, *Americans All: Good Neighbor Cultural Diplomacy in World War II* (Austin: University of Texas Press, 2012).
7 David Sheinin, ed., *Beyond the Ideal: Pan Americanism in Inter-American Affairs* (Westport, CT: Greenwood Press, 2000).
8 As Caitlin Fitz's work on the revolutionary period has shown, ordinary persons in the United States had previously entered into moments of fascination, and romanticized sympathy, with the peoples of Latin America. Caitlin Fitz, *Our Sister Republics: The United States in an Age of American Revolutions* (New York: Liveright Publishing Corporation, 2016).
9 This sentiment can be captured in any number of publications during the period. For an example see, George H. Blakeslee, "True Pan-Americanism: A Policy of Coöperation with the Other American Republics," *The Journal of Race Development* 7, no. 3 (January 1917): 342–60. Also see, Mark T. Gilderhus, *Pan American Visions: Woodrow Wilson and the Western Hemisphere (1913–1921)* (Tucson: University of Arizona Press, 1986).
10 For example, William Wachs, "Student Pan American Activity," *Hispania* 23, no. 1 (February 1940): 59–64; "Good Neighbor Forum Explains Latin America," *Chicago Tribune*, August 4, 1940, 3; Fernanda Perrone, "Inventory to the Papers of Frances R. Grant," (New Jersey: Rutgers University, 2000). www2.scc.rutgers.edu/ead/manuscripts/grantf.html;*Pan American Society: Historical Note and Secretary's Report for the Year 1941* (New York: Pan American Society, 1941), 1; Committee on Cultural Relations, Inc., "Two Conferences on International Relations, Summer of 1940," (New York: Committee on Cultural Relations, Inc., 1940).
11 See for a few examples, Meagan Threlkeld, *Pan American Women: US Internationalists and Revolutionary Mexico* (Philadelphia: University of Pennsylvania Press, 2014); Dina Berger, "Raising Pan Americans: Early Women Activists of Hemispheric Cooperation, 1916–1944," *Journal of Women's History* 27, no. 1 (2015): 38–61.
12 See for example, Juan Pablo Scarfi, "La emergencia de un imaginario latinoamericanista y antiestadounidense del orden hemisférico: de la Unión Panamericana a la Unión Latinoamericana (1880–1913)," *Revista Complutense de Historia de América* 39 (2013): 81–104.
13 See Gisela Cramer and Ursula Prutsch, eds., *Americas Unidas! Nelson Rockefeller's Office of Inter-American Affairs (1940–1946)* (Madrid: Iberoamericana Vervuert, 2012); Sadler, *Americans All*; Justin Hart, *Empire of Ideas: The Origins of Public Diplomacy and the Transformation of US Foreign Policy* (Oxford: Oxford University Press, 2012).
14 Ben Grauer, "Latin Influence on the Air," *Pan American* (February 1941): 34.
15 This theme has been explored in Carmen Miranda's rise to fame has been examined by a number of scholars, including Cynthia Enloe; see her *Bananas, Beaches and Bases: Making Feminist Sense of International Politics* (Berkeley: University of California Press, 2000).
16 *Down Argentine Way*, directed by Irving Cummings, Hollywood, California: Twentieth Century Fox, 1940; *That Night in Rio*, directed by Irving Cummings, Hollywood, California: Twentieth Century Fox, 1941; *Weekend in Havana*, directed by Walter Lang, Hollywood, California: Twentieth Century Fox, 1941; *Springtime in the Rockies*, directed by Irving Cummings, Hollywood, California: Twentieth Century Fox, 1942; *The Three Caballeros*, Walt Disney Productions, Burbank, California: Walt Disney Productions, 1944.

17 Julianne Burton-Carvajal, "Surprise Package: Looking Southward with Disney," *Disney Discourse: Producing the Magic Kingdom*, ed. Eric Loren Smooden (New York: Routledge, 1994), 131–47.
18 "The South American Way Points to Success," *Women's Wear Daily*, April 18, 1940, 18; "South American Idea Takes Hold in Prints and Colors—Better Cottons Selling," *Women's Wear Daily*, February 2, 1942, 8.
19 "Good Neighbor Policy." *The Charleston Gazette*, December 25, 1941, 5.
20 "Consumer Response to Pan American Styles Termed Excellent," *Women's Wear Daily*, May 7, 1941, 28.
21 "Saludos! ... Chesterfield Coats and Tailored Suits," *Parents' Magazine*, 18, no. 3, March 1943, 82.
22 "Latin Americans honored at fair," *New York Times*, January 17, 1942, 30; "Macy's unfurls a magic carpet to Latin America," *New York Times*, January 17, 1942, 10.
23 I have written about the fair and its connection to earlier Pan-Americanist production in the United States in Lisa Ubelaker Andrade, "Bazar Panamericano: culturas de consumo y participación en el poder estadounidense (1939–1942)," *Avances de Cesor* 12, no. 13 (2015): 181–203. On the art exhibit at the fair, see, Lisa Crossman, "Macy's Latin American Fair: A Temple Built on the Anxieties of Inter/Americanism," *Material Culture Review* 79 (Spring 2014), https://journals.lib.unb.ca/index.php/MCR/article/view/24329/28171
24 Wilhela Cushman, "Good Neighbor Patterns." *Ladies' Home Journal*, February 1942, 59.
25 Clarke Beach, "US Counts on Women to Aid Pan-Americanism," *The Washington Post*, May 18, 1941, B8.
26 As Kristin Hoganson and William Leach have highlighted, US women had a long history of envisioning fashion as an arena for global engagement. Kristin L. Hoganson, *Consumers Imperium: The Global Production of American Domesticity, 1865–1920* (Chapel Hill: University of North Carolina Press, 2007). Even as far back as the Revolutionary War, American women waged their power as consumers to participate in emergent national politics. For more on consumer politics during the Revolution see, T. H. Breen, *The Marketplace of Revolution: How Consumer Politics Shaped American Independence* (New York: Oxford University Press, 2004).
27 *What Others Have Done for Pan-American Day Programs*. (Washington, DC: Pan-American Union: 1940). Courtesy of Andrew Konove, from the personal collection of Paulina Markenson.
28 "Dishes from the Other Americas," *Good Housekeeping* 114, no. 5 (May 1942): 140–41.
29 Office of the Coordinator of Inter-American Affairs, *Some Specific Suggestions for Inter-American Programs* (Washington DC: OCIAA, 1942); Office of the Coordinator of Inter-American Affairs, *The National Extempore-Discussion Contest of Inter-American Affairs* (New York City: National Public Discussions Committee, Inc., 1942); Pan-American Union, *Pan-American Day Handbook: A Guide for Use in Organizing Special Programs for Observance or Celebration of "the Day of the Americas"* (Washington, DC, 1942); Silvia Brull, *Latin America Bound, a Play* (Washington, DC: Pan-American Union, 1942). Margaret S. Crowther, *The Promise of the Americas, a Pageant* (Washington, DC: Pan-American Union, 1943); Dorothy Kathryn Egbert *A Pan American Friendship Party* (Washington, DC: Pan-American Union, 1940); Glenna C. Fogt, *Let Us Be Friends, a Play* (Washington, DC: Pan-American Union, 1942).
30 "Lakewood Pan-American Day Festival," *Independent Press Telegram*, April 21, 1940, 11 Z5; "Pan-American Day in the Americas," *Boletín Pan Americano* (May 1943): 42.

31 "Friendship Play at Briscoe School," *The San Antonio Light*, December 12, 1940, 6C.
32 "Pan American Pageant at Cambridge Commencement," *Madison Capital Times*, May 8, 1941, 8.
33 "Oklahoma Fourth State Convention Dinner and Dance," (Oklahoma: Pan American Student Forum, 1939). Courtesy of Andrew Konove. From the personal collection of Paulina Markenson.
34 Grace H. Swift. *Pan America: A Pageant for High Schools* (Washington, DC: Pan-American Union, April 14, 1940), 3.
35 Ibid.
36 "Good Neighbors," *Pan American* (December 1941), back cover.
37 Pan American Student Forum, *Year Book, 1937–1938* (Pan American Student Forum, 1938), ch. 19. Courtesy of Andrew Konove, from the personal collection of Paulina Markenson.
38 W. H. Butler, "Notes," *The American Student*, December 1937, 1.
39 Gearóid O'Tuathail, *Critical Geopolitics* (Minneapolis: University of Minnesota Press, 1996).
40 Ibid.
41 *Why We Fight: A Prelude to War*, directed by Frank Capra (Hollywood: Twentieth Century Fox, 1943).
42 For example, the film "Why We Fight," closed on a vision of the globe divided into two hemispheres as the narrator resolved: "two worlds stand against each other, one must die, one must live." Two hemispheres appeared—the Americas bathed in light, and Europe and Asia in darkness.
43 Thomas A. Guglielmo has examined the transnational effort by Mexican-American activists to engage in the discourse of the Good Neighbor Policy in more detail. Thomas A. Guglielmo, "Fighting for Caucasian Rights: Mexicans, Mexican Americans, and the Transnational Struggle for Civil Rights in World War II Texas," *The Journal of American History* 92, no. 4 (March 2006), 1212–37; Neil Foley, *The White Scourge: Mexicans, Blacks, and Poor Whites in Texas Cotton Culture* (Berkeley: University of California Press, 1997).
44 See "El caso trágico de Sleepy Lagoon," *Pueblos Hispanos*, August 14, 1943, 9; Alonso S. Perales, "Informe Núm 4. Acerca del Estado de las Gestiones Encaminadas a Terminar con la Discriminación," *La Prensa*, February 4, 1945, 5; "La voz del público: discriminación racial," *La Prensa*, November 15, 1942, 7.
45 Alonso S. Perales, *The American Student* (December 1937), 1.
46 Alonso S. Perales to Florence Griswold, November 25, 1939. Pan American Roundtables of Texas Archives. Original Archived Documents, 1939 September to December 14. Miscellaneous Correspondence and State Board Meeting September 26 1939. Pan American Roundtables of Texas Archives. Retrieved from www.partt.org/archives1940/19390905_FTGdoc.html.
47 W. W. Dee to Alonso Perales, April 8, 1940. Pan American Roundtables of Texas Archives. Original Archived Documents, 1939 September to December 14. Miscellaneous Correspondence and State Board Meeting September 26, 1939. Pan American Roundtables of Texas Archives. Retrieved from www.partt.org/archives1940/19390905_FTGdoc.html.
48 Similar articles reappeared throughout the Second World War. Examples include: "Race Issue Jeopardizes Good Neighbor Policy," *Chicago Defender*, April 11, 1942, 2; "Good Neighbor Periled By Prejudice," *Chicago Defender*, March 1, 1941, 5; "US Racism Undermines Good Neighbor Policy," *Chicago Defender*, April 13, 1943; For more on Black organizing and Pan Americanism see, Millery Polyné, *From Douglass to Duvalier: US African Americans, Haiti and Pan Americanism, 1870–1964* (Gainesville: University Press of Florida, 2010).
49 George Haynes, "Good Neighbors," *Chicago Defender*, March 1, 1941, 5.

Popular Pan-Americanism, North and South   113

50 Sumner Welles, "Mexican Nationals," *The Washington Post*, February 16, 1944, 10.
51 Pauline R. Kibbe to Jacob I. Rodriguez, September 1, 1944. Houston Metropolitan Research Center at the Houston Public Library, the Portal to Texas History. Retrieved from https://texashistory.unt.edu/ark:/67531/metapth249883/
52 S. Seeber, "Our Readers Write Us: South American Way," *Ladies' Home Journal* 59, no. 2 (February 1942), 4.
53 Alberto Casal Castel, "Afilares en el Corazón de las Mapas," *El Hogar*, May 17, 1940, 3
54 Ibid.
55 Pedro Songreguer, "El error más grave," *El Hogar*, March 21, 1941, 2.
56 Alejandro Sux, "La cordialidad de Roosevelt: impresión de diez minutos de charla...," *El Hogar*, July 4, 1941, 8.
57 John Gunther, "El drama de América," *Claridad*, December 1941, 167–9.
58 Discussants included Carlos Cossio, Germán Arciniegas, and Pedro Henríquez Ureña. "Debates sobre temas sociológicos," *Sur*, November 1941, 1.
59 *El Pampero*, January 3, 1941, 2; "Judaísmo y propaganda yanqui." *El Fortín*, April 1–14, 1941, 3.
60 "Panamericanismo Práctico," *El Mundo*, December 10, 1941, 6.
61 "La Argentina y la agresión contra América," *La Prensa*, December 11, 1941, 11.
62 "Acción Argentina Contesta," *El Mundo*, December 2, 1941, 30; "Dáse a Conocer el Mensaje de Acción Argentina que Debió Leerse en el Acto Prohibido," *El Mundo*, December 2, 1941, 6; "Postergan el Homenaje Preparado en Honor del Presidente F. D. Roosevelt," *El Mundo*, December 20, 1941, 4.
63 "Diferente Interpretación Acerca del Uso de Derechos Fundamentales," *El Mundo*, December 2, 1941, 3.
64 "Decretáse el Estado de Sitio en Toda la Nación," *El Mundo*, December 17, 1941, 8.
65 Ibid.
66 "América Frente el Destino del Mundo," *Claridad*, December, 1941, 1–3.
67 "Una acertada resolución de radiocomunicación," *Radiolandia*, June 3, 1943, 1.
68 Gisela Cramer, "How to Do Things with Waves: United States Radio and Latin America in the Times of the Good Neighbor," *Media, Sound, and Culture in Latin America and the Caribbean*, eds. Alejandra Bronfman and Andrew Grant Wood (Pittsburgh: University of Pittsburgh Press, 2012), 37–54.
69 Don Francisco, to Sumner Welles, Under Secretary of State, Dec. 17, 1941. General Records. Central Files. Information. Radio. Country Files. Record Group 229. United States National Archives College Park, Maryland.
70 "La Unión de América," *Sintonía*, January 1944, 4.
71 "Clara afirmación de solidaridad americana," *El Orden*, July 27, 1944, 1. Retrieved from www.santafe.gov.ar/hemerotecadigital/diario/4531/
72 G. F. Granger, to Sumner Welles, Under Secretary of State. Argentine Radio Report. Nov. 20, 1944. General Records. Central Files. Information. Radio Country Files. Argentina. Record Group 229. United States National Archives College Park, Maryland.
73 G. F. Granger, to Sumner Welles, Under Secretary of State. Argentine Radio Report. Nov. 20, 1944. General Records. Central Files. Information. Radio Country Files. Argentina. Record Group 229. United States National Archives College Park, Maryland.
74 "Los Varela, símbolo de concordia y paz," *Radiolandia*, April, 1943, 17.
75 *Selecciones del Reader's Digest*, August 1941, back cover.
76 Ana de Martínez Guerrero, *Selecciones del Reader's Digest*, July 1943, back cover.
77 G. F. Granger to Nelson Rockefeller, Coordinator of Inter-American Affairs, Jan. 3, 1944. Memo No 2260. General Records. Central Files. Information. Radio Country Files. Argentina. Record Group 229 National Archives, College Park, Maryland.

114 Lisa Ubelaker

78 As scholars like Christina Klein have demonstrated, a broader notion of forming an emotional bond with the world became a central component of US culture during the Cold War. See Christina Klein, *Cold War Orientalism: Asia in the Middlebrow Imagination, 1945–1961* (Los Angeles: University of California Press, 2003).
79 Juan D. Perón, *Libro Azul y Blanco* (Buenos Aires: Azul y Blanco, 1946), 3.
80 The Peronist magazine *Continente* serves as one example. Published from 1947 until 1955, it billed itself as Argentine and Pan-American and included texts and articles on Argentine culture and arts in English, Portuguese, and Spanish. The arts magazine *Sexto Continente* similarly revised the idea of Pan-Americanism, heralding itself a cultural magazine grounded in the Peronist perspective but that replaced US hegemony with Argentine leadership in regional transnational ties.

Bibliography

Berger, Dina. "Raising Pan Americans: Early Women Activists of Hemispheric Cooperation, 1916–1944." *Journal of Women's History* 27, no. 1 (2015): 38–61.
Breen, T. H. *The Marketplace of Revolution: How Consumer Politics Shaped American Independence*. New York: Oxford University Press, 2004.
Burton-Carvajal, Juliane. "Surprise Package: Looking Southward with Disney," In *Disney Discourse: Producing the Magic Kingdom*, edited by Eric Loren Smooden, 131–147. New York: Routledge, 1994.
Cramer, Gisela. "How to Do Things with Waves: United States Radio and Latin America in the Times of the Good Neighbor," In *Media, Sound, and Culture in Latin America and the Caribbean*, edited by Alejandra Bronfman and Andrew Grant Wood, 37–54. Pittsburgh: University of Pittsburgh Press, 2012.
Cramer, Gisela and Ursula Prutsch, eds. *Americas Unidas! Nelson Rockefeller's Office of Inter-American Affairs (1940–1946)*. Madrid: Iberoamericana Vervuert, 2012.
Crossman, Lisa. "Macy's Latin American Fair: A Temple Built on the Anxieties of Inter/Americanism." *Material Culture Review* 79 (Spring 2014). Retrieved from https://journals.lib.unb.ca/index.php/MCR/article/view/24329/28171.
Enloe, Cynthia H. *Bananas, Beaches and Bases: Making Feminist Sense of International Politics*. Berkeley: University of California Press, 2000.
Fitz, Caitlin. *Our Sister Republics: The United States in an Age of American Revolutions*. New York: Liveright Publishing Corporation, 2016.
Foley, Neil. *The White Scourge: Mexicans, Blacks, and Poor Whites in Texas Cotton Culture*. Berkeley: University of California Press, 1997.
Gilderhus, Mark T. *Pan American Visions: Woodrow Wilson and the Western Hemisphere, (1913–1921)*. Tucson: University of Arizona Press, 1986.
Guglielmo, Thomas A. "Fighting for Caucasian Rights: Mexicans, Mexican Americans, and the Transnational Struggle for Civil Rights in World War II Texas." *The Journal of American History* 92, no. 4 (March 2006), 1212–1237.
Hart, Justin. *Empire of Ideas: The Origins of Public Diplomacy and the Transformation of US Foreign Policy*. Oxford: Oxford University Press, 2012.
Hoganson, Kristin L. *Consumers' Imperium: The Global Production of American Domesticity, 1865–1920*. Chapel Hill: University of North Carolina Press, 2007.
Klein, Christina. *Cold War Orientalism: Asia in the middlebrow imagination, 1945–1961*. Los Angeles: University of California Press, 2003.

Ninkovich, Frank. *The Diplomacy of Ideas: US Foreign Policy and Cultural Relations, 1938–1950*. Cambridge: Cambridge University Press, 1981.

O'Tuathail, Gearóid. *Critical Geopolitics*. Minneapolis: University of Minnesota Press, 1996.

Park, Stephen M. *The Pan American Imagination: Contested Visions of the Hemisphere in Twentieth Century Literature*. Charlottesville: University of Virginia Press, 2014.

Polyné, Millery. *From Douglass to Duvalier: US African Americans, Haiti and Pan Americanism, 1870–1964*. Gainesville: University Press of Florida, 2010.

Sadler, Darlene. *Americans All: Good Neighbor Cultural Diplomacy in World War II*. Austin: University of Texas Press, 2012.

Salvatore, Ricardo D. "The Enterprise of Knowledge: Representational machines of Informal Empire." In *Close Encounters of Empire. Writing the Cultural History of US–Latin American Relations*, edited by Gilbert M. Joseph, Catherine C. Legrand and Ricardo D. Salvatore, 69–107. Durham: Duke University Press, 1998.

Scarfi, Juan Pablo. "La emergencia de un imaginario latinoamericanista y antiestadounidense del orden hemisférico: de la Unión Panamericana a la Unión Latinoamericana (1880–1913)." *Revista Complutense de Historia de América* 39 (2013): 81–104.

Sheinin, David, ed. *Beyond the Ideal: Pan Americanism in Inter-American Affairs*. Westport, CT: Greenwood Press, 2000.

Threlkeld, Meagan. *Pan American Women: US Internationalists and Revolutionary Mexico*. Philadelphia: University of Pennsylvania Press, 2014.

Ubelaker Andrade, Lisa. "Bazar Panamericano: culturas de consumo y participación en el poder estadounidense (1939–1942)." *Avances de Cesor* 12, no. 13 (2015): 181–203.

6 The Colombo–Lanusse Doctrine

Cold War Anti-interventionism and the End of Pan-Americanism

David M. K. Sheinin

From the late nineteenth century to the 1930s, many diplomats and political leaders framed Pan-Americanism as the promotion of peace and harmonious interchange in the Americas.[1] The historian Juan Pablo Scarfi has argued that after 1932 the Good Neighbor Policy, the voiding of the Platt Amendment, and US adherence to the principle of non-intervention "paved the way for the construction of a more solid system and body of multilateral inter-American cooperation." This included "the transition from Pan-Americanism to inter-American multilateralism" as a shift in the language of Western Hemisphere international law and inter-American relations.[2] Others have held that after the Second World War, with efforts to weaponize the movement by transforming it into a military alliance-focused entity, Pan-Americanism died a slow death. The historian Thomas M. Leonard tied what he called the 1930s non-interventionist US Good Neighbor Policy toward Latin America to a "new cooperative Pan Americanism." The latter was maintained by a "combination of domestic needs, trade necessities, and wartime strategic concerns rather than by a cooperative ideal." In this US-centric analysis, with Cold War conflict and the US-led 1954 invasion of Guatemala, the new Pan-Americanism "came to an end."[3] The historian W. Michael Weis traced the end of Pan-Americanism to Brazil's 1960s decision to abandon its "historic role of mediator between the United States and Spanish America," and the United States decision to "use the Alliance for Progress as an instrument of the cold war instead of economic development."[4]

Did Pan-Americanism end? One might argue that the movement continues apace in the work of the Pan-American Health Organization, the Inter-American Commission on Human Rights, the Pan-American Games and dozens of other bureaucracies, non-government organizations, and political projects that reflect both longstanding Pan-American ideals and organizations structured under the umbrella of the Pan-American Union/Organization of American States to promote social and political change.[5] In addition, a rich scholarly literature underscores the varied and lasting cultural, social, and political components of Pan-Americanism.[6] That said, the Scarfi, Weis, and Leonard analyses address fundamental and defining features in the diplomatic, political, and economic structuring of a Pan-American movement after 1889.

DOI: 10.4324/9781003252672-7

Drawing on those analyses, this chapter focuses on a mid-1960s endpoint for diplomatic renderings of Pan-Americanism around the question of peace and intervention: the Colombo–Lanusse Doctrine (after Ricardo Colombo, the Argentine ambassador to the Organization of American States (OAS) and Lieutenant General Alejandro Agustín Lanusse, commander of the Argentine Army and a future *de facto* president of Argentina).

Colombo–Lanusse was a juridical, military, and diplomatic justification in Latin American diplomatic and military circles for an Argentine initiative to transform the longstanding Pan-American disdain for foreign military interventions into a hemispheric rebuff of international communism. Along with Brazil and the United States, in attempting to militarize anti-communism under the umbrella of the OAS, Argentina came as close as any nation to finishing what the 1948 Inter-American Treaty for Reciprocal Assistance (TIAR) had begun in promoting and institutionalizing a US-led military alliance under the umbrella of Pan-Americanism. In addition, by defining communist-inspired "subversion" as the preeminent threat to hemispheric security, the Colombo–Lanusse Doctrine linked Pan-Americanism to anti-communism and laid the foundation for right-wing inter-American cooperation in the 1970s and 1980s, most notably through Operation Condor. I write "came as close" because through the collapse of Pan-Americanism, no trans-hemispheric military alliance was ever forged as demonstrated poignantly in the mixed response of the American republics to the Malvinas War.[7]

At times before 1850, anti-interventionist sentiment was aligned with the spirit and failed promise of the Monroe Doctrine. After 1870, it was typically directed against the imperial powers as an affront to Pan-American ideals. It was outlined as a matter of international law in the Calvo and Drago doctrines. Argentina and other nations advanced it vehemently at Pan-American conferences (1923, 1928, and 1933) while José Enrique Rodó, José Martí, and other leading intellectuals decried military intervention even as they aspired to a new kind of lyrical modernity in Latin America that they imagined in contrast to the ugly, workaday capitalism in the United States.[8]

Despite the fervent sense among some that a binary divided Latin American anti-interventionist sentiment from United States military interventions, there were contradictory grey zones in how Argentines and others approached foreign incursions. The Colombo–Lanusse Doctrine reflected a long history in Argentina of multiple motives for and meanings of anti-intervention. Anti-intervention sometimes papered over a range of deeper political, diplomatic, and cultural interests. In 1847, the Argentine minister in Washington Carlos de Alvear defended the US invasion of Mexico at the same time as he bemoaned US military violence.[9] In the late 1880s, the Argentine diplomat Vicente Quesada railed against US imperialism in the Caribbean but in 1905, the Argentine minister in Washington, Epifanio Portela, called the Roosevelt Corollary to the Monroe Doctrine a civilizing force.[10] In 1912, in the face of widespread African-Cuban insurrections, the Argentine chargé d'affaires in

Havana, Jorge Reyes, spoke to the damaging force of US imperialism in Cuba but justified a US military intervention as the reasonable protection of US business interests and the restoration of stability in the face of what Reyes called "negradas," a racist description of violent insurrection.[11] At the Sixth Pan-American Conference in Havana (1928), Argentina's famous anti-interventionist diplomatic stand contradicted Argentine foreign ministry instructions to its delegation. Mission chief Hónorio Pueyrredón's rhetoric hostile to the United States likely had more to do with his domestic political aspirations than with a passionate defense of national sovereignty in the Americas.[12]

With the Great Depression, the accompanying Good Neighbor Policy in the United States, and the impact of anti-intervention militancy in the Caribbean basin, the urgency of Pan-American anti-intervention diplomacy dulled.[13] *What became of the link between Pan-Americanism and anti-intervention diplomacy during the Cold War?* The formation of the Organization of American States (OAS) as a postscript to the core diplomatic currents of Pan-Americanism consigned anti-intervention to a diplomatic back burner in the Americas for four reasons. First, important as they were in the early twentieth century, from the 1954 US intervention in Guatemala through the Cuban Revolution and the Bay of Pigs invasion, the 1965 Dominican intervention, and the overthrow of Chilean president Salvador Allende in 1973, the stakes of military intervention became higher during the Cold War. Now, many of the heartiest opponents of US military intervention conceded an urgent global context, in the shadow of unprecedented Cold War dangers, foremost of which was nuclear warfare. In Argentina and elsewhere, home-grown, escalating anti-communism in government did not follow and was sometimes at odds with US anti-communist foreign policies. However, Latin American diplomats and political leaders often shared with US leaders a disdain for the revolutionary left and were reluctant to pile on in a joint Pan-American rebuke of the United States of the sort that had emerged at the Fifth (1923) and Sixth (1928) Pan-American Conferences. Implicitly and explicitly, OAS diplomacy often cast military intervention as an antagonist of an international communist menace.[14]

Second, by the 1960s, for reasons that included a tacit anti-communism and the professionalization of diplomatic corps (and their distancing from an earlier link to intellectuals in other fields) many Latin American diplomats had set aside idealistic notions of a link between anti-interventionism and the *arielismo* of Rodó and others. At the same time, while a broader swath of Latin Americans across class and racial lines now vociferously criticized US military intervention in a context of US involvement in the promotion of brutal military rule, increasing numbers of governments took a military turn, either in dictatorship or in weak democracies bearing the weight of a constant threat of military intervention. The 1973 coup d'état in Chile resonated particularly harshly across the hemisphere for all of the above reasons but in part because it marked the collapse of what many viewed as a last bastion of long-term democratic rule in the Americas, in the past a pillar of anti-interventionist sentiment.

Third, in the 1950s and the 1960s, OAS bodies, like their United Nations equivalents, began to link democratization to economic and social development, in the context of violence, hunger, and poverty. Military and non-military governments sympathetic to US modernization theory and economic models often promoted these linkages. In the diplomacy of economic and social development in authoritarian governments, US military intervention became a less pressing problem than a putative communist menace anxious to take advantage of Latin American poverty. Fourth, with the democratization of the idea of human rights, Amnesty International and a range of other transnational and national organizations often sympathetic to Cuban and other revolutionary projects took over the anti-intervention mantle as Pan-American anti-intervention faded.[15]

In 1965, the Argentine ambassador to the OAS Ricardo Colombo gave a speech at the Inter-American Defense College that marked a last gasp of Pan-American anti-intervention. It drew, as such Pan-American arguments often had, on precedent in diplomacy and the law. Like many Latin American diplomats of the time across the political center-right and center-left, Colombo was a Cold War warrior. He sketched a conceptual and international legal line from Bolivar through Calvo and Drago to his arguments on what defined intervention. In addition, Colombo emphasized that left-wing insurgencies—like the Montoneros in Argentina and the Tupamaros in Uruguay—were in fact, foreign interventions. In so doing, he tried to make Cold War Pan-Americanism relevant to the strategic positions of military regimes and set the stage for officials from military dictatorships stepping into positions of authority at the OAS. But Colombo also presaged the marginalization of the OAS in other international contexts and the quick triumph of the Inter-American Human Rights Commission after its founding in 1959 as an inheritor of Pan-American ideals, distinct from the OAS institutionally and philosophically. In 1968, Lieutenant General Alejandro Agustín Lanusse, Commander of the Argentine Army, added to Colombo's arguments with an even sterner attack on subversion in Latin America at the behest of international communism. At the same time, though, he added a new emphasis, *desarrollista* economics and the idea that the communist incursion was drawing on profound social and economic inequalities in the hemisphere.[16]

Colombo–Lanusse was a faithful reflection of Argentine government 1950s domestic policies, foreign policies, and global strategy—and the lasting anti-communist sentiment of many Argentines.[17] While Peronist politics domestically and internationally occupied a range of ideological drivers, their most consistently clear position on global strategy incorporated a fierce anti-communism that was also evident domestically in the persecution of Communist Party members and in other ways.[18] Colombo–Lanusse also reflects continuities, not only in the invocation of Drago and Calvo in the defense of anti-intervention, but also in Argentine diplomacy through democratic and dictatorial regimes and within the OAS itself.

An Inter-American Defense Board Without Teeth

The Colombo–Lanusse Doctrine came in response to the longstanding failed promise of a combined inter-American military force. The formation of the Inter-American Defense Board (IADB) had been a compromise without teeth. US military and political leaders had wanted the IADB as a step toward a formal military alliance. Latin American diplomats and political leaders while sympathetic to that plan in a Second World War context became skeptical immediately following the war. The IADB languished as largely irrelevant to military strategic planning in the Americas until the early 1960s when Brazilian and other Latin American military officers saw it as a possible wedge toward creating a transcontinental anti-communist military force. First proposed in 1942 by Resolution XXXIX of the Third Meeting of Consultation of Latin American Ministers of Foreign Affairs, delegates approved the creation of a committee of military and naval technical experts named by each of the governments in the Americas to study and recommend measures for continental defense. The notion of "technical" experts was meant to emphasize the apolitical nature of the future military force. This vague, supposedly non-political function was reinforced by Resolution IV of the Inter-American Conference on War and Peace (1945) that proposed a committee to foster improved military cooperation and better defense of the Western Hemisphere. Resolution XXXIV of the Ninth International Conference of American States (1948) established the IADB with no clear mandate, while article 44 of the OAS Charter stated that a Defense Advisory Committee (DAC) would assess the OAS on military collaboration and collective security. Delegates to the Fourth Meeting of Consultation of Latin American Ministers of Foreign Affairs (1951) shaped the beginnings of a clear role for the IADB when they passed Resolution III charging the IADB with preparing and maintaining plans for a common hemispheric defense against international communist aggression. However, in 1954, during the US-sponsored overthrow of the Jacobo Arbenz presidency in Guatemala, the IADB played no role.[19]

In May 1963, at the Conference of American Air Chiefs, General Curtis E. LeMay, Chief of Staff of the US Air Force, proposed transforming the IADB into a military assessment unit for the OAS. But LeMay wanted the United States to remain in the background and have Argentina or another Latin American country suggest the plan.[20] Argentine political authorities were unready to commit to the change. In April 1964, in a last gasp of Argentine Pan-Americanism, Constantino Ramos, cabinet chief to the minister of foreign relations, argued against changes to the IADB. He told the minister of defense in the administration of President Arturo Illia, Leopoldo Suárez, that OAS solidarity and a pacifist inter-American tradition had influenced Latin American resistance to the IADB as a military body in the late 1940s. That had led to the creation of the DAC, meant in part—according to Ramos—to keep the IADB outside the OAS bureaucratic structure. The

DAC, not the IADB, would advise the OAS on collective security, presumably outside the overwhelming influence of the US military. Ramos pointed out correctly that both the IADB and the DAC had been poorly structured and had been given ambiguous mandates in a reflection of Latin American suspicions that the United States would dominate any multilateral military force. Despite numerous applications of TIAR, on no occasion had the DAC ever been called on to advise, not even with the discovery of Russian nuclear launch sites in Cuba in October 1962. For Ramos, this was a clear signal that Latin American governments were disinterested in a standing body responsible for collective military security. He warned in addition of US military influence in the hemisphere and that Argentine military interests would be better served by a continuation of the status quo.[21]

In October 1962, the IADB asserted itself. It proposed that governments instruct their OAS representatives to allow the IADB to take over the DAC's failed mandate and to assume a military advisory capacity provisionally in regard to the US assertion that the Soviet Union was installing medium range missiles in Cuba. The urgency of the moment had had no impact within the OAS. The suggestion was sent to a working group that reported back in April 1963—long after the Cuban Missile Crisis—that the IADB proposal be referred to each hemispheric government for study. In 1964, Panama asked the OAS to intervene in response to US aggression in that country. The OAS council dispatched a team that helped the two countries reopen diplomatic ties, with no IADB participation. The IADB remained functionally marginal to diplomatic and military flare-ups in the hemisphere.[22]

In September 1964, Enrique Benjamín Vieyra, the Argentine chargé d'Affaires at the OAS, represented a shift rightward in the Argentine diplomatic corps and a waning of the influence of Ramos and those who thought as he did about hemispheric defense and US influence. Vieyra wrote to Foreign Minister Miguel Angel Zavala Ortiz that the IADB had been conceived to address what he called classic warfare. It had to be updated to deal with guerrilla warfare, secret international weapons transfers, and other forms of modern military aggression. In the case of Cuban military activity in Venezuela, he continued, the definition of aggression need not be confined to an armed attack. The concept of "aggression" was in flux as a result of new forms of communist penetration of the hemisphere. The IADB must be reconstituted to consider such change. Vieyra walked a questionable fine line that had blurred less than a year later when Colombo spoke. Without wishing to politicize the IADB, Vieyra argued, the body would have to adopt a strategy to confront the ideology of "communist penetration."[23]

Not surprisingly, military leaders were generally at the forefront of the move to weaponize the IADB, though some expressed a *desarrollista* link between the fight against communism, persistent poverty, and the need for economic development across the region. In January 1966, at a meeting of the IADB council of delegates, with the support of Brigadier General Ary

Presser Bello (Brazil), Brigadier Major Adolfo Teodoro Álvarez (Argentina) called on the IADB to find a way to integrate improvements to the economic, political, and social situation in the hemisphere with the problem of military defense. In reference to what he and others saw as IADB ineptitude, Vice Admiral Carlos Monge Gordillo (Peru) announced that it was time the IADB ceased being "some sort of illegitimate child" while Lieutenant Coronel Guillermo Castro (Costa Rica) argued that it was necessary for the IADB to prepare in the event it had to repel a foreign invasion, especially in light of the war being waged by free countries against international communism.[24]

After the 1964 coup d'état, Brazil began to push hard for a militarization of the inter-American system. In Rio de Janeiro, at the Second Extraordinary Inter-American Conference in early 1965, Brazilian de facto president Humberto Castello Branco called for a reconsideration of the organization and its approach to global strategy. New mechanisms for the peaceful resolution of controversies were required to deal with subtle forms of aggression in military and political infiltration and subversion. There could be no pretense of collective security without collective action against these threats. While OAS secretary general José Mora did not counter Castello Branco, he argued for a milder, more ambiguous set of reform measures to avoid divisions among Latin American governments and to keep the peace in the Caribbean region. A career diplomat and long-time OAS and Pan-American Union official, Mora was cautious about militarizing the OAS. Delegates referenced cooperation under the umbrella of the Alliance for Progress, and underlined the need for social and economic reform in the hemisphere. In the end, there was no majority in favor of Castello Branco's proposals.[25]

The Doctrine

On April 6, 1965, Colombo gave a speech at the Inter-American Defense College that combined anti-communist strategic planning, the case for a robust inter-American military force to confront communist subversion, and a Pan-American justification for the latter. Present were the director of the college, General Roland Del Mar (United States), the vice director, General Juan E. Aguirre (Paraguay), the chief of studies, General Manuel Iricibar (Argentina) as well as the heads of the armed forces of all member states of the OAS. Colombo focused on non-intervention making his speech the last major defense of that principle in a Pan American context. He began by citing independence era generals José de San Martín (Argentina) and Francisco de Paula Santander (Colombia) as the architects of non-intervention. Warning his audience implicitly against leftist insurgency in the present day, Colombo noted that Santander had attacked foreign interventions as "subversive" assaults on the sovereign rights of peoples in the new Latin American republics. Carlos Calvo's 1868 criticism of the French-British intervention in the Río de la Plata and the French incursion into Mexico could be read as harbingers of more recent Soviet-inspired interventions as an assault in the context of civil war, insurrection, or violent local uprisings.[26]

Colombo drew extensively on Ann Van Wynen Thomas and A. J. Thomas, Jr.'s *Non-Intervention: The Law and Its Import in the Americas*[27] to make three key arguments, all grounded also in Calvo's writings. Intervention was not restricted to a military landing. It could be a subtle, subversive set of dangerous political maneuvers in a Latin American country by a small political group at the behest of international communism. In addition, Colombo was taken with the book's argument that the assent of a quarry state to an intervention or an intervention for self-defense meant that neither could be considered an "intervention." Colombo was anticipating the formation of an inter-American military force that might cross national borders in the suppression of communist subversion.[28]

He dismissed arguments that intervention could only occur between two states at peace when what he described as powerful nations (meaning the Soviet Union) "render of intervention a perfect and permanent facet of political warfare." Economic pressure, diplomatic acts, political threats, and "subversive activities" could be considered under the modern juridical definition of intervention. Moreover, these forms of intervention should be viewed—as Calvo had argued—as a prelude to armed intervention. He drew in addition on the 1959 findings of the Inter-American Judicial Committee that intervention might include political, social, economic, or cultural acts of influence against a state; coercive economic or political acts; and permitting the trafficking of arms destined to an armed struggle. The last case likely referenced the 1954 supply of arms from Czechoslovakia to the Guatemalan government as well as the alleged 1963 Cuban government arms drop to the Fuerzas Armadas de Liberación Nacional (FALN) revolutionary group in Venezuela. The term "permitting" allowed for the authorship of such an action by a third party, specifically the Soviet Union. Colombo also identified as intervention the willingness of a state to allow a group to train militarily toward rebellion or sedition in another American state. This anticipated early 1970s Tupamaro insurgency unit training camps in Chile.[29]

Three months later, Colombo expressed still greater urgency in a confidential memorandum to Argentine foreign minister Miguel Angel Zavala Ortiz. Over that short time span, US forces had invaded the Dominican Republic during that country's civil war. They had subsequently withdrawn and an OAS "peacekeeping" force had replaced them. Recent developments in the Dominican Republic, Colombo argued, had tested the inter-American system with respect to a "new style of warfare" and had reinforced the need for strengthening the IADB into a rapid deployment military instrument of collective security. Now, Colombo introduced a new point of argument that would be taken up three years later by Lieutenant General Alejandro Agustín Lanusse, Commander of the Argentine Army. There would be more turmoil of the sort seen in the Dominican Republic, the result of growing "social-economic" disparities and political instability, which limited economic development in the Americas. In addition, arguing to his Argentine superiors with less than a year left in the shaky democratic presidency of Arturo Illia—overthrown by a military coup d'état in June 1966—Colombo maintained that the subversive action of communists had led to the need for unexpected investments in many countries to prepare for "repressive" operations. The threat of communism, then, prompted military repression and was part of Colombo's justification for his recommended changes to the IADB. While Colombo understood that most Latin American governments had thus far failed to endorse a militarization of the IADB, he pressed the issue of a shared inter-American ideology and politics. Latin Americans would have to develop "doctrinal unity" and "educational unity" in laying the foundations for a joint military defense force. *This was Colombo's absurd and fatal flaw.* There would be no "doctrinal unity" across the Americas on the question of communist subversion.[30]

Once the Inter-American Peace Force (IAPF), staffed largely by US troops, had been sent to the Dominican Republic in keeping with resolutions from the Tenth Meeting of Consultation of Ministers of Foreign Affairs (1965), intense opposition began to mount within the OAS toward military collective action, and any effort to create a standing inter-American military force. Hostility reached a head at the Eleventh Meeting of Consultation of Ministers of Foreign Affairs (Second Meeting, February 15–26, 1967) in Buenos Aires. The Argentine government, now under military rule, proposed again the creation of a Consultative Committee on Defense. The vote was six in favor (Argentina, Nicaragua, El Salvador, Honduras, Brazil, and Paraguay) versus eleven against (Venezuela, Ecuador, Dominican Republic, Costa Rica, Uruguay, Haiti, Mexico, Chile, Guatemala, Peru, and Colombia), with three abstentions (United States, Panama, and Bolivia). Those countries most firmly opposed were Chile, Uruguay, Ecuador, and Mexico. Venezuela and Colombia led what the Brazilian journalist Mario Busch called a "violent" opposition to the Argentine proposal. Some believed the Venezuelan government found itself unable to position itself otherwise. The Cuban-allied FALN had kidnapped Julio Iribarren Borges, brother of Venezuelan foreign minister Ignacio Iribarren Borges. The Venezuelan Foreign Ministry was locked into diplomatic stasis fearing the eventual outcome, the torture and killing of Julio Iribarren Borges.[31]

The Brazilian foreign minister attempted to salvage the plan. In October 1966, Juraci Magalhaes travelled to Chile, Bolivia, Argentina, and Uruguay to make his case for a collective security military force and picked up on Colombo's argument that such a force would not constitute a violation of the OAS Charter principle of non-intervention as the multilateral force would have as its sole objective blocking any intervention sponsored by Moscow or Beijing.[32] He also hoped to woo political leaders not yet having closed the door on the project as long as there was a parallel prospect of US economic assistance to participant countries. Magalhaes hoped to convince the Chilean government that the force would not be a proxy for US military intervention in the region but that the *a priori* promise of US economic assistance by treaty, insisted upon by Chile, was an impossible goal. The Brazilian and Argentine governments worried meanwhile that the debate over the force might generate a rift between democratic governments and the military regimes in Argentina and Brazil.[33]

As the likelihood of an OAS-sanctioned inter-American defense force waned, the Argentine and Brazilian militaries continued to plan secretly for that objective, as did military officers in other countries. A January 1966 memorandum from the Argentine military delegation to the IADB pointed out that a hurdle to overcome for the Argentine plan was that there was no specific reference to "armed aggression" in TIAR and in the OAS Charter.[34] That language might have to be built into a revision of those documents to allow for a multilateral military force to counter such aggression. The commander in chief of the Argentine Army was sharper still. In August 1966, Pascual A. Pistarini wrote to Argentine Foreign Minister Nicanor Costa Méndez of a more tough-minded approach. TIAR was ineffective in that it could easily be sidestepped as an instrument of collective defense if the treaty conflicted with the interests of individual member governments. Unlike Colombo, he was the first Argentine official to recognize that the project to create an inter-American defense force was impractical in that there could likely be no consensus among OAS member governments on what might constitute armed aggression or intervention. TIAR did not contemplate the sort of aggression carried out by international communism. To move forward, Pistarini urged that the foreign ministry and the armed forces develop a new policy. The OAS could not be strengthened by a military component until all member states came to understand that "communism is the fundamental enemy that threatens peace on the continent and that poverty and economic weakness are the motives for its expansion." On the connection between the advance of poverty and the surge of communism in the Americas, Pistarini cited a speech US defense secretary Robert McNamara gave in Montreal on May 18, 1966 to that effect. Like TIAR, the OAS Charter required an urgent updating to address the "real enemy," communism and the need to adopt "all possible provisions" to nullify that threat.[35]

Even if other states could be convinced of the perils of Soviet aggression, Pistarini insisted that to strengthen the OAS as an instrument in the war on communism, Argentine authorities would have to keep in mind the preeminence of Argentine national interests in the creation of a multinational military force. The Argentine military should never cede its liberty of independent action. Moreover, Pistarini argued that in the process of reforming the OAS, Argentina should "achieve a position of pre-eminence in Latin America" that would be reflected in leadership positions for Argentina in the OAS and the IADB, as well as the development in Argentina of courses for military officers from across the Americas on the fight against international communism. At the same time, Pistarini defended Alliance for Progress projects as an economic bulwark against communism.[36]

In October 1966, the Argentine ambassador to Brazil, Mario Amadeo met informally with the director of the Latin America section of the Brazilian Foreign Ministry, Pimentel Brandao who insisted that with communism in a moment of stasis in the Americas—that is, with no Dominican Crisis or Cuban Revolution on the immediate horizon—now was the time to act decisively in bringing a new multinational defense force to fruition. In keeping with some of Pistarini's ideas, the Brazilian military projected that each country would maintain a military unit within its own armed forces, on its own territory, ready to act immediately and effectively on behalf of the planned multinational defense force against any subversive action that might threaten the security of the continent. Even as the idea of an inter-American defense force was failing as an OAS political project because political leaders in the Americas understood that they could not agree on what might represent a threat to hemispheric security, Brazilian, Argentine, and other military officers acted on the assumption that the threat posed by international communism was self-evident. Consultation mechanisms for multilateral military action, Brandao continued, would have to be extremely fast. He imagined that participating countries would be connected to the OAS council by a telephone hotline, like the one linking the White House and the Kremlin. The system would ensure that the United States had no reason to intervene unilaterally as it had in the Dominican Republic because other countries had refused to act.[37]

By June 1967, the military government in Argentina had reoriented its efforts toward an exclusively military solution to the problem of a common defense against communism that would by-pass civil society decision-making. The Argentine ambassador in Guatemala, Gabriel Gálvez, reported to foreign minister Nicanor Costa Méndez on private talks he had had with representatives to the Central American Defense Council. The Costa Rican delegate, Lieutenant Colonel Renato Delcore, insisted that the Central American militaries were with Argentina on its proposal to modify the function of the IADB. But the Guatemalan foreign minister, Arenales Catalán, confirmed a view shared in Latin American military circles. The Argentines had rushed their plan unnecessarily in February 1967 without a strong understanding of possible political opposition in several countries. Central American military officers with whom Gálvez spoke confirmed a sense that the problem should be removed from the hands of diplomats and civil government officials. They urged Gálvez to suggest to Argentine military government authorities that the problem be raised in 1968 at the next meeting of hemispheric commanders in chief. For military officers, the IADB remained dysfunctional in its present form. Any exchange of ideas on a hemispheric defense update would have to take place at the commanders in chief meetings. Delcore argued that at the Eleventh Meeting of Consultation in Buenos Aires, many foreign ministers (presumably those opposed to the Argentine motion) were at odds with military thinking in their respective countries on this question and the unanticipated Argentine proposal allowed some to launch into "international demagoguery." Arenales told Gálvez that the Argentine motion was doomed to failure both for the need for the unanimity of delegates for its approval (never possible with opposition from Mexico and Chile) and for the lack of diplomatic preparation on the part of Argentina. While Arenales had no objections to the Argentine proposal, he could neither abstain nor vote in favor because of the political impact in Guatemala of the "demagogic diatribes of the [Latin American] foreign ministers that attacked the Argentine project."[38]

In October 1967, Rear-Admiral Jorge Alberto Boffi, head of the Joint Chiefs of Staff of the Argentine Armed Forces, found it necessary to instruct the Argentine military delegation to the IADB on their role, the first such formal directive since 1957. Recognizing now that there was unlikely to be a standing multilateral military force, Boffi wanted to make clear to the delegation that their responsibility was not to the OAS or to its member governments. Moreover, the delegation was answerable to the Argentine Joint Chiefs of Staff, not to the Argentine government, and under some circumstances, the Argentine military delegation might have functions apart from the IADB. As a dependency of the Argentine Joint Chiefs of Staff, Boffi went on, the delegation might be charged with secret intelligence and logistics activities. The Argentine military, then, while still advocating a greater role for the IADB, had resigned itself to the unlikelihood of that outcome. The goal of breaking communist subversion and incursions remained unchanged. Now, the Argentine forces would undertake inter-American operations on their own and in conjunction with like-minded military commands in the Americas. Boffi indicated that in future, the military delegation chief to the IADB would be high ranking as an Army Division General, a Navy Vice-Admiral, or an Air Force Brigadier Major in two-year rotations.[39]

A December 1967 secret internal IADB memorandum was out of step with Boffi's new instructions to his subordinates. The IADB remained committed to the lost idea of a political solution in the necessity for the American Republics to develop their military capacities in reference to TIAR, and in a combined effort to confront international communism. The IADB would maintain an advisory role to governments toward this end. However, for the first time, the IADB recognized what would be a central theme of Alejandro Lanusse's call for action six months later—the Soviet goal of implanting communism in developing countries by taking advantage of disaffection primed by poverty. "To achieve their subversive ends and to hide their real intentions," communist governments and their agents exploited the weakest members of society and their aspirations.[40]

In September 1968, in a speech to Latin American armed forces commanders, Alejandro Agustín Lanusse amplified Colombo's juridical, Pan-American justification for a non-interventionist military force. Lanusse's language was more blunt than Colombo's and without the historical references. The threat was subversion sponsored by international communism. But in a reflection of the *desarrollista* economic influences on his brief, future tenure as *de facto* president (1971–3), Lanusse contemplated subversion as a threat to the "complex problems that block or delay development in our countries." It was the growing disparity between rich and poor around the globe that had brought about political unrest on which international communism had fed "in its global imperial advance that had covered almost half the world in a few short years." In an echo of the all-but-defunct Alliance for Progress, he argued that economic "development is the key force in the fight against subversion, leaving military security in a complementary role."[41]

Unlike Colombo, Lanusse did not frame his argument in a context of international law and non-intervention. But he said something similar in outlining the fundamentals of a proposed inter-American military system. The common enemy was international communism. Under Soviet tutelage, Cuba had become the jumping-off point for a "mechanism of aggression" in three stages. Cuban revolutionaries fomented insurrection, organized revolutionary vanguards, and primed the formation of liberation armies throughout the Americas. Lanusse altered the Pan-American origins narrative by arguing for a military integration of the region into "'la Gran América' for which our ancestors fought and dreamed. The independence era epics in the Americas ('las epopeyas libertadoras') structured a common destiny that our generation is just now beginning to better understand." Debate over intervention and the niceties of Pan-Americanism were done. A functioning inter-American military alliance was needed, complemented by economic integration in a stronger Latin American Free Trade Association (LAFTA), culminating in a common market that would *exclude* the United States. Lanusse's never-realized plan also anticipated Operation Condor by calling for a transnational network of military intelligence and the elaboration of a common anti-communist doctrine in the Americas.[42]

Lanusse's shift in emphasis toward economic and social development in the fight against communism was too little too late as a mechanism to promote an inter-American defense force. The momentum for that force was lost. At the Thirteenth Meeting of Consultation of Ministers of Foreign Affairs (1969), when the OAS intervened to resolve the burgeoning military conflict between El Salvador and Honduras, the president of the IADB, US General James D. Alger, offered meeting organizers the collaboration of the IADB in planning and logistics for a defense force in Central America equivalent to the IAPF. The response was sharp and quick. Several delegations retorted that the IADB would have no role to play in this case. The Argentine military government, meantime, held to its public stand in favor of an inter-American military force while its military leaders understood that there was no longer the possibility of such an outcome. Alger was bothered by his antagonists in the OAS and made his views known to a handful of sympathetic OAS ambassadors. At the same time, the military government of *de facto* Argentine president Juan Carlos Onganía pressed for closer cooperation between the Argentine mission to the OAS and the Argentine military delegation to the IADB. For the first time, each was instructed to make certain that they held identical public policy positions on "almost all occasions."[43]

The Legacy of Colombo–Lanusse

Alejandro Lanusse's September 1968 warnings on the links between poverty, social unrest, and political subversion may have struck him as prophetic in the months and years that followed. In May 1969, seven months after Lanusse gave his speech to Latin American armed forces commanders, students and workers in Córdoba launched a series of violent uprisings that became the most significant challenge to authoritarian rule in twentieth-century Argentina. For Lanusse, the *Córdobazo* marked the start of left-wing armed revolution in Argentina and the dramatic failure of military rule under *de facto* president Juan Carlos Onganía. Lanusse attributed the collapse of government authority and the rise of the insurgent left to Onganía's inability to grasp a core principle of military governance in Argentina. Until then, most Argentines had accepted military rule as an unpleasant but constitutionally enshrined government mechanism to stave off political or economic chaos until democratic rule might return in short order. Lanusse blamed Onganía for failing on two related fronts. First, he lost track of the imperative to bring democracy back expeditiously. And second, his government paid no heed to the legitimate concerns of working- and middle-class Argentines whose dismay unleashed the *Córdobazo*.[44]

Lanusse identified his own subsequent military presidency (1971–3) as politically center-left and in keeping with equivalent left-leaning military governments in Peru and Bolivia at the time. He did what Onganía had not done in ushering the country back to democratic rule in 1973. Furthermore, he became a critic of the ferocity of Argentine military rule after March 1976. Even so, in his role as commander of the Argentine army under Onganía, Lanusse had played a central role in a political process that had not only undermined the prospect for democratic rule in Argentina for a decade and a half but had marginalized his own notions of military governance concerned with social and economic hardship, and keen on restoring democracy. In Argentina, the Colombo–Lanusse Doctrine represented the entrenchment of military power over civil society after 1955 in a way that had no precedent in military-civil society interactions. But in addition, the strategic imperatives on anti-communism that Colombo and Lanusse helped advance not only contributed to the destruction of a non-military Pan-American cooperative diplomatic ethos in the Americas. In Argentina, Brazil and elsewhere, they set in place a firm division between the military and the government *even when the former governed*.[45]

Increasingly, military officers made strategic and military decisions by way of their respective commands, not through the appropriate government ministries and agencies. By the time plans for a militarized Pan-American IADB fell apart for good after the Dominican intervention, Latin American militaries had already begun to lay the groundwork for an alternative network of military and intelligence cooperation that would bypass any remnant of diplomatic Pan-Americanism, the OAS and their own civil societies.

This was manifest in dozens of operations in the 1970s and 1980s that included the 1976 assassination of Orlando Letelier in Washingotn by the Chilean military, the secret mission of Argentine troops to Central America in the early 1980s, and the kidnappings and assassinations carried out by Operation Condor. Ironically, despite the anti-communism that informed the Colombo–Lanusse Doctrine and radically shifting Latin American military strategy in the 1960s and early 1970s, Latin American dictatorships often maintained strong trade and diplomatic ties with communist regimes—China in the case of 1970s Chile and the Soviet Union in the case of late 1970s Argentina.[46]

Notes

1 Daniel Antokoletz, *Manual teórico y práctico de la Liga de Naciones* (Buenos Aires: Talleres Gráficos Editorial Jurídica, 1926), 25–26. Many, including the Argentine jurist and diplomat Estanislao S. Zeballos, had a more cynical view of the movement and the oversized role of the United States in it. In 1917, Zeballos argued that, "the whole Pan-American policy [throughout the Americas] ... has always been commercial." Mark T. Gilderhus, *Pan American Visions: Woodrow Wilson in the Western Hemisphere, 1913–1921* (Tucson: University of Arizona Press, 1986), 99. See also, David Sheinin, "Rethinking Pan Americanism: An Introduction," *Beyond the Ideal: Pan Americanism in Inter-American Affairs*, ed. David Sheinin (Westport: Praeger, 2000), 1–8.
2 Juan Pablo Scarfi, *The Hidden History of International Law in the Americas: Empire and Legal Networks* (New York: Oxford University Press, 2017), 147.
3 Thomas M. Leonard, "The New Pan Americanism in US-Central American Relations, 1933–1954," *Beyond the Ideal: Pan Americanism in Inter-American Affairs*, ed. David Sheinin (Westport: Praeger, 2000), 95; Lisa Ubelaker, "Bazar panamericano: Cultura de consume y participación popular en poder estadounidense (1939–1942)," *Avances del Cesor* 12, no. 13 (2015): 181–203.
4 W. Michael Weis, "The Twilight of Pan-Americanism: The Alliance for Progress, Neo-Colonialism, and Non-Alignment in Brazil, 1961–1964," *The International History Review* 23, no. 2 (2001): 343–4; Jeffrey F. Taffet, *Foreign Aid as Foreign Policy: The Alliance for Progress in Latin America* (New York: Routledge, 2007), 63–65.
5 Mark Petersen and Carsten-Andreas Schulz, "Setting the Regional Agenda: A Critique of Posthegemonic Regionalism," *Latin American Politics and Society* 60, no. 1 (2018): 115–16.
6 See Rodrigo Booth, "Turismo, panamericanismo e ingeniería civil. La construcción del camino escénico entre Viña del Mar y Concón (1917–1931)," *Historia* 47, no. 2 (2014): 277–311; Perla Zusman, "Panamericanismo e imperialismo no formal: Argentina y las exposiciones universales estadounidenses de Búfalo (1901) y San Francisco (1915)," *Scripta Nova: Revista electronica de geografía y ciencias sociales* 16, no. 418 (2012). Retrieved from www.ub.edu/geocrit/sn/sn-418/sn-418-64.htm;

Maria José Canelo, "Producing Good Neighbors: Carmen Miranda's Body as Spectacular Pan-Americanism," *Revue française détudes américaines*, 2, no. 139 (2014): 60–76; Richard Cándida Smith, *Improvised Continent: Pan-Americanism and Cultural Exchange* (Philadelphia: University of Pennsylvania Press, 2017); Antonio Sotomayor, "Colonial Olympism: Puerto Rico and Jamaica's Olympic Movement in Pan-American Sport, 1930 to the 1950s," *The International Journal of the History of Sport* 33, no. 1–2 (2016): 84–104.

7 Stella Paresa Krepp, "Between the Cold War and the Global South: Argentina and Third World Solidarity in the Falklands/Malvinas Crisis," *Estudios Históricos* 30, no. 60 (2017): 141–60; Henry Torres-Vásquez, "La Operación Condor y el terrorismo de estado," *Revista Eleuthera* 20 (2018): 114–34; Francesca Lessa, "Operation Condor on Trial: Justice for Transnational Human Rights Crimes in South America," *Journal of Latin American Studies* 51, no. 2 (2019): 409–39; J. Patrice McSherry, "Operation Condor and Transnational State Violence Against Exiles," *Journal of Global South Studies* 36, no. 2 (2019): 368–98; Julieta Carla Rostica, "La Confederación Anticomunista Latinoamericana: Las conexiones civiles y militares entre Guatemala y Argentina (1972–1980)," *Desafíos* 30, no. 1 (2018): 309–47.

8 Jack Child, "The 1889–1890 Washington Conference Through Cuban Eyes: José Martí and the First International American Conference," *Inter-American Review of Bibliography* 20, no. 2 (1989): 443–56; José Martí, *Argentina y la primera conferencia panamericana* (Buenos Aires: Ediciones Transiciones, 1955), 45–53; Enrique Gil, *Evolución del panamericanismo* (Buenos Aires: Casa Editora Jesús Méndez, 1933), 150–62; Scarfi, *Hidden History*, 4–7; Ignacio E. Vitacca Morales, "Herencia y alteridad en el panamericanismo hispánico del siglo XX: José Enrique Rodó y Manuel Baldomero Ugarte," *Fronteras contemporáneas: identidades, pueblos, mujeres y poder: Actas del V Encuentro de Jóvenes Investigadores en Historia Contemporánea*, vol. 2, ed. Cristian Ferrer González and Joel Sans Molas (Barcelona: Departament d'Història Moderna i Contemporània de la Universitat Autònoma de Barcelona, 2017), 271–89; Carlos Pereyra, *El mito de Monroe* (Buenos Aires: Ediciones el buho, 1959), 180–84.

9 Thomas D. Davis, *Carlos de Alvear, hombre de la revolución* (Buenos Aires: Emecé, 1964), 165–99.

10 No. 78, Quesada to Norberto Quirno Costa, Argentine foreign minister, March 23, 1888, File 9/888, Box 1, First Pan American Conference, Political Division (POL), Ministry of Foreign Relations Archive (AMREC), Buenos Aires; no. 60, Quesada to Quirno Costa, April 16, 1889, File 9/888, Box 1, First Pan American Conference, POL, AMREC; Eduardo A. Zimmermann, "Ernesto Quesada, la época de Rosas y el reformismo institucional del cambio de siglo," *La historiografía argentina en el siglo XX*, vol. 1, ed. Fernando J. Devoto (Buenos Aires: Centro Editor de América Latina, 1993), 28; Vicente G. Quesada, "Las teorias del Doctor Alberdi," *Nueva Revista de Buenos Aires* 1 (1881): 352–84; no. 93, Portela to Foreign Ministry, November 21, 1905, File 9/888, Box 1, First Pan American Conference, POL, AMREC; Antonio Bermejo, Lorenzo Anadon, and Martín García Mérou, *Informe que la delegación de la República Argentina presenta a la Segunda Conferencia Pan-Americana* (Mexico City: Tipográfia de la Oficina Impresora de Estampillas, Palacio Nacional, 1902).

11 Reyes to Ernesto Bosch, Argentine minister of Foreign Affairs, File 8, March 12, 1912, File 5, Box 4, United States, POL, AMREC; Bosch to Rómulo S. Naón, Argentine ambassador, Washington, July 13, 1912, File 5, Box 4, United States, POL, AMREC; Aline Helg, "Race in Argentina and Cuba, 1880–1930," *The in Latin America, 1870–1940*, ed. Richard Graham (Austin: University of Texas Press, 1990), 37–69; Eduardo A. Zimmermann, "Racial Ideas and Social Reform: Argentina, 1890–1916," *Hispanic American Historical Review* 72 (1992): 23–46; Louis A. Pérez, Jr., "Politics, Peasants and People of Color: The 1912 Race War in Cuba Reconsidered," *Hispanic American Historical Review* 56 (1986): 509–39.

12 Alberto A. Conil Paz, *La Argentina y los Estados Unidos en la Sexta Conferencia Panamericana (La Habana—1928)* (Buenos Aires: Editorial Huemul, 1965), 25–33; David M. K. Sheinin, *Argentina and the United States at the Sixth Pan American Conference (Havana 1928)* (London: Institute for Latin American Studies, 1991), 18–25; Scarfi, *Hidden History*, 119–45; Fernando A, *Estrategia y*

132 David M. K. Sheinin

    poder militar: Bases para una teoría estratégica (Buenos Aires: Instituto de Publicaciones Navales, 1965), 122–3.
13 Alan McPherson, *The Invaded: How Latin Americans and Their Allies Fought and Ended US Occupations* (New York: Oxford University Press, 2014), 263.
14 E. Ramirez Novoa, *La farsa del panamericanismo y la unidad indoamericana* (Buenos Aires: Editorial Indoamérica, 1955), 145–96; Robert A. Potash, *The Army & Politics in Argentina, 1962–1973* (Stanford: Stanford University Press, 1996), 144–8.
15 Bernabé Malacalza, "The Politics of Aid from the Perspective of International Relations Theories," *Aid, Power and Politics*, ed. Iliana Olivié and Aitor Pérez (London: Routledge, 2019), 12–13; Stella Krepp, "Development before Democracy: Inter-American Relations in the long 1950s," *Forum for Inter-American Research* 11, no. 3 (2018): 94–109; Par Engstrom, "El sistema interamericano de derechos humanos y los relaciones Estados Unidos-América Latina," *Foro Internacional* 55, no. 2 (2015): 454–502; Tomás Moulian, *En la brecha: Derechos humanos, críticas y alternativas* (Santiago, Chile: LOM Ediciones, 2002), 73–5.
16 David M. K. Sheinin, "Making Friends with Perón: Developmentalism and State Capitalism in US-Argentine Relations, 1970–1975," *Federal History Journal* 5 (2013): 99–120.
17 "Public Opinion Survey," Field Work: Buenos Aires and Suburban Area, May 13–15, 1964, Instituto IPSA, S.A., Box 1, Entry 1018, Record Group (RG), 306, National Archives and Records Administration (NARA), College Park, MD; "Public Opinion Survey," Field Work: Buenos Aires, November 1961, Instituto IPSA, S.A., Box 3, Entry 1015, RG 306, NARA; "Survey of Television Households," Field Work: Buenos Aires—February 1963, Box 4, Entry 1015, RG 306, NARA; A-452. Robert M. McClintock, US ambassador to Argentina, "Summary of Recent Conversations with Peronist and Neo-Peronist Labor Leaders," May 7, 1961, Box 2437, Central Decimal File, RG 59, NARA.
18 On the origins and persistence of Cold War anti-communism in Argentina see, Cecil B. Lyon, Acting Assistant Secretary of State, "Various Matters Concerning Argentina," December 20, 1955, 735.00/12-2055 CS/E, Reel 1, LM 123, Central Decimal File, RG 59, NARA; 498, Hugh C. Reichard, US Labor Attaché, Buenos Aires, "Conversation with Dr. Raúl C. Migone," December 29, 1955, 735.00/12-2955, Reel 1, LM 123, Central Decimal File, RG 59, NARA; Humberto Sosa Molina, Minister of Defense, to Hipólito Paz, Minister of Foreign Relations, March 16, 1951, File "Estudio Técnico-Militar," Working Group, no. 1, File IV, AMREC; Senado de la Nación (Argentina), *Represión del comunismo: Proyecto de Ley, Informe y Antecedentes por el Senador Matías G. Sánchez Sorondo*, vol. 1 (Proyecto de Ley/Infomre) (Buenos Aires: Imprenta del Congreso Nacional, 1938); Senado de la Nación (Argentina), *Represión del comunismo: Proyecto de Ley, Informe y Antecedentes por el Senador Matías G. Sánchez Sorondo*, vol. 2 (Antecedentes) (Buenos Aires: Imprenta del Congreso Nacional, 1940); Jerónimo Remorino, *Política internacional argentina, 1951–1955*, vol. 1 (Buenos Aires: Standard, 1968), 299–315; Alberto Ciria, *Partidos y poder en la Argentina moderna* (Buenos Aires: Ediciones de la La Flor, 1975), 3rd edition, 187–92. Mario Rapoport, "Argentina," *Latin America Between the Second World War and the Cold War, 1944–1948*, ed. Leslie Bethell and Ian Roxborough (Cambridge: Cambridge University Press, 1992), 92–119.
19 Argentina, Ministry of Foreign Relations, Memorandum, "Junta Interamericana de Defensa," May 19, 1965, 122 OEA, POL, AMREC; Brig. Gen. Eugene L. Strickland, US Air Force, director, general staff, IADB, "Ubicación de la Junta Interamericana de Defensa dentro del Sistema Interamericano," January 17, 1966, 122, OEA, POL, AMREC; William C. Spracher, "The Inter-American Defense Board: A Study in 'Alliance Politics'," Master of Military Art and Science Thesis,

US Army Command and General Staff College, 83-4579, 1983, Fort Leavenworth, KS, 10–12.
20 Argentina, Secretariat of State, Air Force, to Leopoldo Suárez, Minister of Defense, Argentina, April 29, 1964, 122, OEA, POL, AMREC; Hernán Cortes, Subsecretary of Defense, to Miguel Angel Zavala Ortiz, Minister of Foreign Relations, April 30, 1964, 122, OEA, POL, AMREC; Constantino Ramos, Cabinet Chief to the Minister of Foreign Relations, May 6, 1964, 122, OEA, POL, AMREC.
21 Ramos to Leopoldo Suárez, April 30, 1964, 122, OEA, POL, AMREC.
22 Ramos to Leopoldo Suárez, April 30, 1964, 122, OEA, POL, AMREC; Tanya Harmer, "The 'Cuban Question' and the Cold War in Latin America, 1959–1964," *Journal of Cold War Studies* 21, no. 3 (2019): 114–51.
23 No. 597, Enrique Benjamín Vieyra, Argentine chargé d'affaires, OAS, to Zavala Ortíz, September 1, 1964, 122, OEA, POL, AMREC.
24 C-1003, Junta Interamericana de Defensa, Cosenjo de Delegados, Acta, Sesión 454, January 10, 1966, 122, OEA, POL, AMREC.
25 Argentina, Ministry of Foreign Relations, Department of International Organizations, "El Programa de la Segunda Conferencia Interamericana Extraordinaria," February 26, 1965, 122, OEA, POL, AMREC; "O.A.S. Chief to Ask Major Revisions," *New York Times*, October 20, 1964. Retrieved from www.nytimes.com/1964/10/20/archives/oas-chief-to-ask-major-revisions-mora-plan-includes-annual-foreign.html; C-1004, Vice-Admiral, US Navy, Bernard L. Austin, chair, IADB, "Informe Sobre la Segunda Conferencia Interamericana Extraordinaria, Río de Janeiro, 17–30 de noviembre de 1965," January 10, 1966, 122, OEA, POL, AMREC; José Briceño Ruiz, "Del panamericanismo al ALCA: la difícil senda de las propuestas de una comunidad de intereses en el continente Americano (II)," *Anuario Latinoamericano Ciencias Políticas y Relaciones Internacionales* 4 (2017): 145; A-6, William W. Lehfeldt, US consul, Córdoba, Argentina, "Political: University Student Attitudes, Córdoba," December 14, 1962, 835.432/12-1462, Box 2444, Central Decimal File, 1960–1963, RG 59, NARA.
26 "Conferencia sobre el principio de no intervención pronunciada en el Colegio Interamericano de Defensa del día 6 de abril de 1965 por S. E. el Señor Embajador argentino ante la organización de los Estados Americanos, Dr. Ricardo Colombo," April 6, 1965, 122, OEA, POL, AMREC.
27 Ann Van Wynen Thomas and A. J. Thomas, Jr., *Non-intervention: The Law and Its Import in the Americas* (Dallas: Southern Methodist University Press, 1956).
28 "Conferencia sobre el principio de no intervención."
29 Ibid.
30 No. 381, Colombo to Zavala Ortiz, "Relación de la Junta Interamericana de Defensa con la OEA," July 22, 1965, 122, OEA, POL, AMREC. As was frequently the case for Cold War Argentine foreign policy, the recovery of Malvinas entered into Colombo's rationale. He lamented the ambiguity of international legal definitions of "border" or "territorial" disputes or controversies including that over Malvinas. In reference both to the threat of international communism and to Argentina's claim to Malvinas, he asked rhetorically, "Can a controversy be defined based solely on the position of one of the parties to the conflict?" "Does an international dispute refer to questions of fact or questions of rights, or of both?" No. 73, Colombo to Zavala Ortiz, February 14, 1966, 122, OEA, POL, AMREC; Colombo, "Observaciones sobre el informe sobre la II Conferencia Interamericana Extraordinaria, Presentado por el Vicealmirante B. L. Austin, Presidente de la Junta Interamericana de Defensa," February 14, 1966, 122, OEA, POL, AMREC; David M. K. Sheinin, *Argentina and the United States: An Alliance Contained* (Athens: University of Georgia Press, 2006), 143–5.

134 David M. K. Sheinin

31 Raúl A. Quijano, Argentine ambassador, OAS, to Luis María de Pablo Pardo, Foreign Minister, September 16, 1970, 122, OEA, POL, AMREC; Mario Busch, "Argentina certa," *O Estado de Sao Paulo*, July 2, 1967, 7.
32 Chilean and Mexican authorities found (while senior Brazilian and Argentine military officers did not) that Articles 15 and 17 of the OAS Charter blocked the creation of a military force of the sort Magalhaes proposed. Article 15 entrenched the principle of non-intervention and Article 17 assured the inviolability of the territory of member states. Article 19 established that any new agreement for the maintenance of peace and security not violate articles 15 and 17.
33 No. 228, Guillermo de la Plaza, Director, Department of South American Affairs, POL, Memorandum, November 22, 1966, 122, OEA, POL, AMREC.
34 Argentine military delegation, IADB, "Memorandum," January 28, 1966, 122, OEA, POL, AMREC.
35 "La reunion de ejercitos," *La Prensa* (Buenos Aires), August 30, 1966, 10; "'Afirmar la realidad de América Libre y Unida,' Asi definió los fines de la reunion el Tte. Gral. Pistarini," *La Prensa*, August 30, 1966, 10; 169/66, Pistarini to Costa Méndez, August 25, 1966, 122, OEA, POL, AMREC.
36 Sheinin, *Argentina and the United States*, 131–2.
37 No. 625, Amadeo to Costa Méndez, November 1, 1966, 122, OEA, POL, AMREC.
38 No. 296, Gálvez to Costa Méndez, June 16, 1967, 122, OEA, POL, AMREC.
39 No. 569/67, Boffi to Nicanor Costa Méndez, October 10, 1967, 122, OEA, POL, AMREC; Boffi, "Instrucciones Generales para el Jefe de la Delegación Militar Argentina ante la Junta Interamericana de Defensa," October 10, 1967, 122, OEA, POL, AMREC.
40 No. T-0170, General Staff, IADB, "Bases para el planeamiento military de la defensa común," December 14, 1967, 122, OEA, POL, AMREC.
41 Lanusse, "Conferencia a cargo del comandante en jefe del Ejercito Argentino:Alejandro Agustín Lanusse, Teniente General, Comandante en Jefe del Ejército Argentino," September 24, 1968, 122, OEA, POL, AMREC; Argentine Army, General Staff, Fifth Command, "Puntos de Vista que sustentara la delegación del Ejército Argentino en la IXna CEA [Conferencia de Ejercitos Americanos]," 122, OEA, POL, AMREC.
42 Felipe Pereira Loureiro, Hamilton de Caravalho Gomes, Jr., and Rebeca Guerreiro Antunes Braga, "A preicentric Punta del Este: Cuba's failed attempt to join the Latin American Free Trade Area (LAFTA) and the limits of Brazil's independent foreign policy," *Revista Brasileira de Política Internacional* 61, no. 2 (2018) (doi: 10.1590/0034-7329201800203).
43 No. 846, Quijano to de Pablo Pardo, September 16, 1970, 122, OEA, POL, AMREC; María Cecilia Míguez, "Los debates sobre defensa entre Argentina y Brasil en la X Conferencia de Ejercitos Americanos," IX Jornadas de Sociología de la UNLP, December 2016, La Plata, Argentina. Retrieved from www.memoria.fahce.unlp.edu.ar/trab_eventos/ev.9004/ev.9004.pdf
44 Alejandro A. Lanusse, *Mi testimonio* (Buenos Aires: Lasserre, 1977), xv, 223–44; Guillermo Vázquez, "El Cordobazo: apuntes entre memorias e historiografias," *El pensamiento alternativo en la Argentina contemporánea*, vol. 3, ed. Hugo E. Biagini and Gerardo Oviedo (Buenos Aires: Biblos, 2016), 219–29; Juan B. Yofre, *Volver a matar: Los archivos ocultos de la "Cámara del terror" (1971–1973)* (Buenos Aires: Sudamericana, 2009), 18–20, 29–30.
45 Martín Vicente, "América Latina según el liberal-conservadurismo argentine: entre la modernización, el panamericanismo y la Doctrina de Seguridad Nacional (1959–1973)," *Circule por la derecha: Percepciones, redes y contactos entre las derechas sudamericanas, 1917–1973,* ed. Joao Fábio Bertonha and Ernesto Bohoslavsky (Los Polvorines: Universidad Nacional de General Sarmiento, 2016), 247–66; Alberto Benito Viola, *La guerra de guerrillas y la foto-interpretación* (Buenos Aires: Círculo Militar, 1968), 12–15; Enrique Rauch, *Un juicio al proceso politico argentino*

(Buenos Aires: Editorial Moharra, 1971), 116–29; José Levitán, *Estado de sitio: arma de la reacción* (Buenos Aires: Cardemar, 1972), 131–43.

46 "La URSS nos ofrece crédito barato," *Solidaridad: voz de la insurgencia obrera y popular* (Mexico City), 72, July 15, 1972, 35; Felipe Marini, "La lucha por la América Latina," *Revista del Círculo Militar*, 675 (1965): 113–17; Alan McPherson, *Ghosts of Sheridan Circle: How a Washington Assassination Brought Pinochet's Terror State to Justice* (Chapel Hill, NC: University of North Carolina Press, 2019).

Bibliography

Booth, Rodrigo. "Turismo, panamericanismo e ingeniería civil: La construcción del camino escénico entre Viña del Mar y Concón (1917–1931)." *Historia* 47, no. 2 (2014): 277–311.

Briceño Ruiz, José. "Del panamericanismo al ALCA: la difícil senda de las propuestas de una comunidad de intereses en el continente Americano (II)." *Anuario Latinoamericano Ciencias Políticas y Relaciones Internacionales* 4 (2017): 145–167.

Cándida Smith, Richard. *Improvised Continent: Pan-Americanism and Cultural Exchange*. Philadelphia: University of Pennsylvania Press, 2017.

Canelo, María José. "Producing Good Neighbors: Carmen Miranda's Body as Spectacular Pan-Americanism." *Revue française détudes américaines*, 2, no. 139 (2014): 60–76.

Child, Jack. "The 1889–1890 Washington Conference Through Cuban Eyes: José Martí and the First International American conference." *Inter-American Review of Bibliography* 20, no. 2 (1989): 443–456.

Ciria, Alberto. *Partidos y poder en la Argentina moderna*, 3rd edition. Buenos Aires: Ediciones de la La Flor, 1975.

Conil Paz, Alberto A. *La Argentina y los Estados Unidos en la Sexta Conferencia Panamericana (La Habana—1928)*. Buenos Aires: Editorial Huemul, 1965.

Davis, Thomas D. *Carlos de Alvear, hombre de la revolución*. Buenos Aires: Emecé, 1964.

Engstrom, Par. "El sistema interamericano de derechos humanos y los relaciones Estados Unidos-América Latina." *Foro Internacional*, 55, no. 2 (2015): 454–502.

Gilderhus, Mark T. *Pan American Visions: Woodrow Wilson in the Western Hemisphere, 1913–1921*. Tucson: University of Arizona Press, 1986.

Harmer, Tanya. "The "Cuban Question" and the Cold War in Latin America, 1959–1964." *Journal of Cold War Studies* 21, no. 3 (2019): 114–151.

Helg, Aline. "Race in Argentina and Cuba, 1880–1930," In *The Idea of Race in Latin America, 1870–1940*, edited by Richard Graham, 37–69. Austin: University of Texas Press, 1990.

Krepp, Stella Paresa. "Between the Cold War and the Global South: Argentina and Third World Solidarity in the Falklands/Malvinas Crisis." *Estudios Históricos*, 30, no. 60 (2017): 141–160.

Krepp, Stella. "Development before Democracy: Inter-American Relations in the long 1950s," *Forum for Inter-American Research*, 11, no. 3 (2018): 94–109.

Lanusse, Alejandro A. *Mi testimonio*. Buenos Aires: Lasserre, 1977.

Leonard, Thomas M. "The New Pan Americanism in US-Central American Relations, 1933–1954." In *Beyond the Ideal: Pan Americanism in Inter-American Affairs*, edited by David Sheinin, 95–114. Westport: Praeger, 2000.

Lessa, Francesca. "Operation Condor on Trial: Justice for Transnational Human Rights Crimes in South America." *Journal of Latin American Studies*, 51, no. 2 (2019): 409–439.

Leviтán, José. *Estado de sitio: arma de la reacción*. Buenos Aires: Cardemar, 1972.
Malacalza, Bernabé. "The Politics of Aid from the Perspective of International Relations Theories," In *Aid, Power and Politics*, edited by Iliana Olivié and Aitor Pérez, 11–33. London: Routledge, 2019.
Marini, Felipe. "La lucha por la América Latina." *Revista del Círculo Militar*, 675 (1965): 113–117.
McPherson, Alan. *Ghosts of Sheridan Circle: How a Washington Assassination Brought Pinochet's Terror State to Justice*. Chapel Hill, NC: University of North Carolina Press, 2019.
McPherson, Alan. *The Invaded: How Latin Americans and Their Allies Fought and Ended US Occupations*. New York: Oxford University Press, 2014.
McSherry, J. Patrice. "Operation Condor and Transnational State Violence Against Exiles." *Journal of Global South Studies*, 36, no. 2 (2019): 368–398. (doi: doi:10.1353/gss.2019.0042)
Míguez, María Cecilia. "Los debates sobre defensa entre Argentina y Brasil en la X Conferencia de Ejércitos Americanos." *IX Jornadas de Sociología de la UNLP*, December2016, La Plata, Argentina. Retrieved from www.memoria.fahce.unlp.edu.ar/trab_eventos/ev.9004/ev.9004.pdf.
Milia, Fernando A. *Estrategia y poder militar: Bases para una teoría estratégica*. Buenos Aires: Instituto de Publicaciones Navales, 1965.
Moulian, Tomás. *En la brecha: Derechos humanos, críticas y alternativas*. Santiago, Chile: LOM Ediciones, 2002.
Pereira Loureiro, Felipe, Hamilton de Caravalho Gomes, Jr., and Rebeca Guerreiro Antunes Braga. "A Preicentric Punta del Este: Cuba's Failed Attempt to Join the Latin American Free Trade Area (LAFTA) and the Limits of Brazil's Independent Foreign Policy." *Revista Brasileira de Política Internacional*, 61, no. 2 (2018). (doi: doi:10.1590/0034-7329201800203)
Pereyra, Pereyra. *El mito de Monroe*. Buenos Aires: Ediciones el buho, 1959.
Pérez, Jr., Louis A. "Politics, Peasants and People of Color: The 1912 Race War in Cuba Reconsidered." *Hispanic American Historical Review* 56 (1986): 509–539.
Petersen, Mark and Carsten-Andreas Schulz. "Setting the Regional Agenda: A Critique of Posthegemonic Regionalism," *Latin American Politics and Society*, 60, no. 1 (2018): 102–127.
Potash, Robert A. *The Army & Politics in Argentina, 1962–1973*. Stanford: Stanford University Press, 1996.
Ramirez Novoa, E. *La farsa del panamericanismo y la unidad indoamericana*. Buenos Aires: Editorial Indoamérica, 1955.
Rapoport, Mario. "Argentina." In *Latin America Between the Second World War and the Cold War, 1944–1948*, edited by Leslie Bethell and Ian Roxborough, 92–119. Cambridge: Cambridge University Press, 1992.
Rauch, Enrique. *Un juicio al proceso político argentino*. Buenos Aires: Editorial Moharra, 1971.
Rostica, Julieta Carla. "La Confederación Anticomunista Latinoamericana: Las conexiones civiles y militares entre Guatemala y Argentina (1972–1980)." *Desafíos*, 30, no. 1 (2018): 309–347.
Scarfi, Juan Pablo. *The Hidden History of International Law in the Americas: Empire and Legal Networks*. New York: Oxford University Press, 2017.
Sheinin, David M. K. *Argentina and the United States: An Alliance Contained*. Athens: University of Georgia Press, 2006.

Sheinin, David M. K. *Argentina and the United States at the Sixth Pan American Conference (Havana 1928)*. London: Institute for Latin American Studies, 1991.

Sheinin, David M. K. "Making Friends with Perón: Developmentalism and State Capitalism in US-Argentine Relations, 1970–1975." *Federal History Journal* 5 (2013): 99–120.

Sheinin, David. "Rethinking Pan Americanism: An Introduction." In *Beyond the Ideal: Pan Americanism in Inter-American Affairs*, edited by David Sheinin, 1–8. Westport: Praeger, 2000.

Sotomayor, Antonio. "Colonial Olympism: Puerto Rico and Jamaica's Olympic Movement in Pan-American Sport, 1930 to the 1950s." *The International Journal of the History of Sport*, 33, no. 1–2 (2016): 84–104.

Taffet, Jeffrey F. *Foreign Aid as Foreign Policy: The Alliance for Progress in Latin America*. New York: Routledge, 2007.

Torres-Vásquez, Henry. "La Operación Condor y el terrorismo de estado." *Revista Eleuthera*, 20 (2018): 114–134. (doi:doi:10.17151/eleu.2019.20.7)

Ubelaker Andrade, Lisa. "Bazar panamericano: Cultura de consume y participación popular en poder estadounidense (1939–1942)." *Avances del Cesor* 12, no. 13 (2015): 181–203.

Vázquez, Guillermo. "El Cordobazo: apuntes entre memorias e historiografías." In *El pensamiento alternativo en la Argentina contemporánea*, vol. 3, edited by Hugo E. Biagini and Gerardo Oviedo, 219–229. Buenos Aires: Biblos, 2016.

Vicente, Martín. "América Latina según el liberal-conservadurismo argentine: entre la modernización, el panamericanismo y la Doctrina de Seguridad Nacional (1959–1973)." In *Circule por la derecha: Percepciones, redes y contactos entre las derechas sudamericanas, 1917–1973*, edited by Joao Fábio Bertonha and Ernesto Bohoslavsky, 247–266. Los Polvorines: Universidad Nacional de General Sarmiento, 2016.

Viola, Alberto Benito. *La guerra de guerrillas y la foto-interpretación*. Buenos Aires: Circulo Militar, 1968.

Vitacca Morales, Ignacio E. "Herencia y alteridad en el panamericanismo hispánico del siglo XX: José Enrique Rodó y Manuel Baldomero Ugarte." In *Fronteras contemporáneas: identidades, pueblos, mujeres y poder: Actas del V Encuentro de Jóvenes Investigadores en Historia Contemporánea*, vol. 2, edited by Cristian Ferrer González and Joel Sans Molas, 271–289. Barcelona: Departament d"Història Moderna i Contemporània de la Universitat Autònoma de Barcelona, 2017.

Weis, W. Michael. "The Twilight of Pan-Americanism: The Alliance for Progress, Neo-Colonialism, and Non-Alignment in Brazil, 1961–1964." *The International History Review* 23, no. 2 (2001): 343–344.

Yofre, Juan B. *Volver a matar: Los archivos ocultos de la "Cámara del terror" (1971–1973)*. Buenos Aires: Sudamericana, 2009.

Zimmermann, Eduardo A. "Ernesto Quesada, la época de Rosas y el reformismo institucional del cambio de siglo," In *La historiografía argentina en el siglo XX*, vol. 1, edited by Fernando J. Devoto, 352–384. Buenos Aires: Centro Editor de América Latina, 1993.

Zimmermann, Eduardo A. "Racial Ideas and Social Reform: Argentina, 1890–1916." *Hispanic American Historical Review* 72 (1992): 23–46.

Zusman, Perla. "Panamericanismo e imperialismo no formal: Argentina y las exposiciones universales estadounidenses de Búfalo (1901) y San Francisco (1915)." *Scripta Nova: Revista electronica de geografía y ciencias sociales* 16, no. 418 (2012). Retrieved from www.ub.edu/geocrit/sn/sn-418/sn-418-64.htm.

7 Pan-American Human Rights

The Legacy of Pan-Americanism and the Intellectual Origins of the Inter-American Human Rights System

Juan Pablo Scarfi

Pan-Americanism has been long associated to an aspirational ideal towards hemispheric cooperation and harmony between the US and Latin America, which had limited effects on the concrete reality of inter-American affairs. Similarly, human rights have long been regarded as a normative ideal concerning the inviolability of the individual rights of the human person, a standard according to which both domestic and international communities around the world should adapt their behavior and performance in real politics. There is an important element that they both have in common since their inception in the Americas: they have been regarded as a guiding horizon to orient and accommodate the practice of global politics on the continent. The genealogies of Pan-Americanism and human rights in the Americas have tended to be framed in different periods within the historical evolution of US–Latin American relations and the so-called Inter-American System. While the former is often associated to the foundational period of the Inter-American System between 1890 and 1945, the evolution of the latter in the Americas is situated between the 1940s and 1970s. Yet they overlapped with one another. The purpose of this chapter is to trace and historicize these important overlaps and connections. The term "Pan-American human rights" seeks to capture the inter-connections between the legacy of Pan-Americanism and its intellectual influence on the emergence of early Inter-American human rights ideals and institutions that led eventually to the construction and consolidation of the so-called Inter-American Human Rights System. This chapter focuses on the Pan-American legal approach advanced by the Chilean jurist Alejandro Álvarez and the US jurist James Brown Scott through the American Institute of International Law (AIIL), founded by both of them in 1912, and the early ideals of human rights advocated primarily by the former.

The AIIL was a precedent of the Inter-American Human Rights System and the institutions associated with the Liberal International Order (LIO) of 1945. Therefore, the Pan-American and international legal ideas of its founding members, Scott and Álvarez, contributed to shaping the orientation of the inter-American legal institutions that were constructed in the aftermath of the Second World War and the LIO. While Scott was the

DOI: 10.4324/9781003252672-8

President of the AIIL, Álvarez remained as its Secretary General from its creation to 1927. Funded by the Carnegie Endowment for International Peace, the AIIL joined together all the national societies of international law of the Americas and it was designed under the model of the American Society of International Law, also founded by Scott and a group of jurists and diplomats associated to the so-called American Peace movement.[1]

This chapter traces the connections between the precedent of the AIIL and Pan-Americanism and the inter-American and global institutions created in the 1940s. It shows that the AIIL provided the institutional and ideological foundations for the inter-American institutions associated to the so-called Inter-American Human Rights System and the LIO. The Pan-American international law promoted by the AIIL offered the grounds for creating inter-American legal institutions, especially those devoted to promoting international human rights and peace. Therefore, the notion of Pan-American human rights seeks to grasp early notions of human rights in the Americas when they were envisioned in connection to the ideals of Pan-American solidarity and American international law before they were institutionalized. Yet these early notions of human rights, originally proposed for the Americas by Álvarez, were also at the core of the intellectual and doctrinal foundations of the so-called LIO.

The chapter also offers an intellectual genealogy of human rights, as they emerged from and were articulated within the Pan American legal tradition of the Americas and the AIIL and then projected globally towards Europe and the LIO. At the same time, it provides an alternative insight into the nature and scope of Pan-Americanism. Rather than presenting it as a continental isolated movement within the Americas, it focuses on its broader global effects and how the Pan American legal designs of the AIIL, and its early Pan American human rights ideals in particular, were projected as an exceptional model and framework for the reconstruction of the European international order and the international law of the future in the context of the First and Second World Wars.

A pioneering regional promoter of the idea of the individual rights of the human person in international law, Álvarez was the principal ideologue of Pan-American human rights, so will be argued in this chapter, for he was one of the most persistent Latin American advocates of Pan-Americanism and Pan-American legal solidarity, American international law and early notions of the rights of the human person. His advocacy was supported and institutionalized in cooperation with Scott through the AIIL. Álvarez believed that the continental tradition of American international law, as a unitary synthesis of the Latin American (continental) and US (Anglo-Saxon) legal traditions, offered the most advanced international legal framework for the reconstruction of international society following the two world wars. In this critical context for European civilization and diplomacy, Álvarez published two important works about the international law of the future (*Le droit international de l'avenir*) (1916) and the reconstruction of international law (*La reconstrucción del derecho de gentes*) (1944), putting forward ideas and projects for the codification of international law, international organization and the recognition of the international rights of the human person.[2] In a series of conferences delivered at the University of Buenos Aires, Álvarez affirmed categorically that international law was in crisis and thus it should be significantly redefined as a discipline in the aftermath of the Second World War.[3]

This chapter also argues that the Pan American movement and the legal tradition of the Americas were projected by AIIL and Álvarez in the context of the twenty years crisis as a global model and framework to be delivered to (European) international society for the construction of a new international order and the international law of the future. This critical context for European legal culture and diplomacy created the scope for envisioning alternative spatial conceptions of world order, decentering European hegemony in the name of new ideas of peace, continental solidarity, and human rights. As a legal thinker of the twenty years crisis, Álvarez inherited and envisioned his own conception of human rights and the promotion of peace from an American continental legal tradition, one that he himself conceived as a unified "Hegelian" synthesis between the US and Latin American traditions.[4] Paradoxically influenced by the French solidarist approach and writing in Paris, Álvarez was convinced that European conceptions of international law needed to be, if not discarded, at least significantly redefined in the aftermath of the First and Second World Wars.

In recent years, the literature on Pan-Americanism and US–Latin American relations has moved away from US-centric diplomatic approaches to Pan-Americanism and US–Latin American relations, emphasizing instead two-sided and mutual cultural and disciplinary influences and exchanges, and the great scope of action and agency that Latin America projected towards Pan-Americanism and inter-American affairs more broadly.[5] Similarly, recent scholarship on human rights has shown that the Latin American contributions to the consolidation of human rights ideals and declarations in the 1940s was foundational and informed the UN Declaration of 1948, and has touched upon the global effects of human rights as a regional movement in the 1970s and their cultural legacies in the 1990s.[6] Yet the precedents of Pan-Americanism and the role of the AIIL, especially the role of Álvarez, in these developments has been glossed over. This chapter contributes to a new revisionist literature on the history of human rights, which stresses their positive and dark effects on global politics and their lasting impact.[7] At the same time, it proposes a hemispheric and global approach to Pan-Americanism. For it explores its continental scope as a movement of the Americas, as well as its broader impact, through the AIIL, on European international society and the consolidation of the LIO.

The First World War, the Emergence of the AIIL, and the Pan-Americanization of International Law

Like US exceptionalism, the power of Pan-Americanism resided in its compelling force as an ideal to be promoted and the hopes and faith devoted to this ideal, rather than as a manifestation of a concrete state of affairs in the Western Hemisphere.[8] However, originally conceived as a US-led policy of economic, political, legal and cultural cooperation towards Latin America by 1880s and 1890s, Pan-Americanism has been always the "the friendly face of US dominance in the hemisphere."[9] The AIIL, founded by Scott and Álvarez, provided an institutional and legal basis for renovating the Pan-American movement by 1915 and promoting thus a Pan-American hemispheric approach to international law. In its early trajectory, the AIIL drew heavily on the international legal ideas of Álvarez in terms of its intellectual inspiration. For it was Álvarez the one who put forward the idea of American international law, but this idea developed and institutionalized thanks to Scott's institutional design and coordination in his role as Secretary General of the CEIP. The AIIL operated as a hemispheric legal network of hegemonic interaction with a common set of beliefs and practices. Its members shared a common adherence to the legitimacy of the Monroe Doctrine and Pan-Americanism as principles of continental solidarity; the acceptance of US hegemonic role in the development of international law in the Americas and its legal tradition as exemplary for the continent; the condemnation of violent interventions, territorial conquest and war; and the formal support for the principle of sovereign equality.[10] Although Scott and Álvarez shared these common beliefs and maintained a similar liberal internationalist vision, they adopted different approaches. Scott promoted a US-led, ethnocentric and elitist vision of Pan-Americanism and American international law within the AIIL, regarding US legal values and institutions as the model for the Americas. He believed that Pan-Americanism had to be based on an extension of US legal values, traditions and institutions to the Americas as a whole. By contrast, Álvarez sought to construct a more multilateral approach to Pan-Americanism. Álvarez was convinced that it was possible to forge a unitary Pan-American approach to international law based on a Hegelian synthesis between the US and Latin American legal traditions.[11] Yet for both of them US traditions were in principle the primary basis for constructing a continental legal tradition, since Álvarez regarded the US Monroe Doctrine as a foundational principle of American international law.[12]

The AIIL as a foundational legal network of the Inter-American System played a central role in institutionalizing a certain common and unitary legal language for the Americas within the golden period of Pan-Americanism around advancing continental legal declarations, relying on the notions of rights and duties as mutually inter-linked with one another. Indeed, it is not coincidence that the first institutional meeting of the AIIL was held in 1915 in Washington shortly after the outbreak of the First World War and that the organization adopted a "Declaration of the Rights and Duties of Nations" drafted by Scott. This declaration was to inform the projects for the codification of American International Law advanced by the AIIL later in the 1920s. More importantly, these declarations and projects central precedents for the formulation of the "American Declaration of the Rights and Duties of Man" conceived in 1945, but adopted only in 1948 as part of the OAS Charter. When presenting the Declaration of the Rights and Duties of Nations in the first official meeting of the AIIL and formulating Pan-American legal designs for the Americas, Scott maintained an ethnocentric and US-led legal vision.[13] He explicitly drew on the US Declaration of Independence to advance the notion of "sovereign equality" and the "natural rights of individuals" for the Americas as a whole, stressing that "the Government of the United States not only recognizes these rights, in so far as its citizens are concerned, but that it insists that governments in American countries in which the United States has influence shall secure to the people thereof the protection and enjoyment of these rights."[14] Scott was clear in that in order to safeguard these individual rights, it was fundamental for the US to maintain the right of intervention. He drew on the example of the US right to intervene in Cuba under the Platt Amendment, which "reserved the right to intervene in Cuba not only for the preservation of Cuban independence but for the maintenance of these specified rights," that is, the individual rights of the human person.[15] Article 3 of the AIIL declaration cited the US Declaration of Independence, and it thus read:

> Every nation is in law and before law the equal of every other nation belonging to the society of nations, and all nations have the right to claim and, according to the Declaration of Independence of the United States, "to assume, among the Powers of the earth, the separate and equal station to which the laws of nature and of nature's God entitle them."[16]

Moreover, Scott was convinced that the Supreme Court of the United States was in form and procedure the "prototype" of the Court for the Society of Nations. Although his approach to Pan-Americanism was rather ethnocentric and tended to dissolve the differences between the US and Latin America legal traditions into a US-led unitary worldview for the Americas, he placed a great emphasis on Pan-Americanism and solidarity as inter-connected hemispheric doctrines, in particular on the contribution of Álvarez. He argued that international solidarity was more marked among the nations of the American continent than anywhere else. As such, it was a specific doctrine of the Americas. Drawing explicitly on the writings of Álvarez, who was certainly the most fervent advocate of Pan-Americanism solidarity among the jurists of the Americas, Scott linked the principle of solidarity to Pan-Americanism. Indeed, he regarded Pan-Americanism as "a fact," rather than a "sentiment" as "its opponent would call it."[17] Scott believed it was worth relying on a Latin American source to defend Pan-American solidarity, in particular he did refer to "the admirable statement of American solidarity made by Mr. Alejandro Álvarez, with whom Pan Americanism is at once a religion and a reality."[18] The AIIL Declaration was a source of inspiration for the elaboration of the projects for the codification of international law prepared by Álvarez and advanced by the AIIL in the 1920s. Both the AIIL Declaration and its codification projects contributed to constructing the first body of legal principles for the Americas. As such, it set up the standard of rights and duties as a continental parameter for building legal doctrines in the Americas in the years to come. Rights were thus originally envisioned in the Western Hemisphere legal tradition as mutually inter-dependent from and inter-linked to duties. More importantly, the AIIL manifested a high regard for the natural rights of individuals and formal sovereign equality among nations, that is, early human rights ideas, on the one hand, and state sovereignty and non-intervention, on the other. Álvarez maintained these two aspirations presented by Scott in the AIIL Declaration, but he gave to them a different twist, offering a combination grounded in a Pan-American solidarist approach, which was to have perdurable resonances in the years to come.

The context of the First World War and the fact that European nations were involved in imperial competition and war, contributed to consolidating and legitimizing the project of Scott and Álvarez of creating of the AIIL in 1915 and reinforcing the worldview promoted by both, especially Álvarez. The aftermath of the First World War created the conditions for a significant revision of the fundamental tenets of European universalism and especially Eurocentric conceptions of international law. Writing from Paris, Álvarez was convinced that European conceptions of international law needed to be significantly redefined in the aftermath of the First World War, and thus the international law of the future could be renovated from the Americas as a new model to be delivered to international society. Therefore, the First World War stimulated a new faith in Pan-Americanism and prospects for its renovation. It presented a window of opportunity to move away from European influences and to look inward to the Western Hemisphere projecting a continental approach to international society and American international law.[19]

Álvarez famously contrasted American international law, as based on the principles of continental solidarity, peace, and republicanism, to a European international law, rooted instead on the balance of power, imperial competition, war and armed piece and monarchical regimes.[20] In a study sponsored by the AIIL and published in 1916 the context of the Great War, Álvarez presented the Americas as a fertile soil for forging what he termed the international law of the future. He projected the standards of American international law as a series of lessons to be delivered to the Old World.[21] Ironically, the perspective of Álvarez was inspired by the French solidarist and sociological approach to international law according to which the social transformations of international society and international life paved the way and were the guiding force of legal transformations. Indeed, Álvarez, who spent most of his academic career in Paris, was a renowned jurist associated to the French solidarist approach.[22] As such, he sought to consolidate a Pan-American school of international law in the Americas to be projected as a model for the (re)construction of European international law following the Great War. His pioneering conceptions of the individual rights of the human person were profoundly grounded in his own particular approach to solidarism, since he believed that "the traditional emphasis of the law on the rights of individuals should give way to" and be complemented with "the recognition of the *duties* of persons to assist fellow members of society in cases of need."[23] Indeed, Álvarez placed a strong emphasis on interdependence as the basis to safeguard and protect those individual rights through social and collective mechanisms of solidarity among the members of the international community, which could potentially involve collective interventions for humanitarian reasons.[24]

The optimism of Álvarez in the Americas as a model for the international law of the future was rooted in an ideal of hemispheric exceptionalism. American international law and the evolution of international life in the Americas proved to be rooted, according to Álvarez, in an exceptional hemispheric disposition towards cooperation, solidarity and the promotion of peace. Yet like Pan-Americanism, the hemispheric exceptionalism advocated by Álvarez was US-led in that the US was the guiding and exceptional leader of the Western Hemisphere in the promotion of neutrality, peace, and solidarity. Indeed, in order to safeguard the Americas from European interventions, Álvarez was convinced that the US Monroe Doctrine, redefined in terms of a multilateral Pan-American principle of international law, was a perfectly suitable tool. Moreover, he went as far as to believe that US hegemony was beneficial for Latin America.[25] Therefore, Latin American nations, so Álvarez considered, had to follow the path initially advanced by the US in the promotion of neutrality and peace. He affirmed:

> While the United States formulated those protests [in defense of the rights of neutral countries] in their own name, they have become once again, as they were a hundred years ago—in the times of President Monroe— the country that ostensibly speaks for the overall feelings of the New World; and all the nations that composed it have formulated along with them [the United States] a common cause.[26]

As a pioneering advocate of Pan-American liberal internationalism and a legal thinker of the twenty years crisis, Álvarez became in turn an intellectual ideologue for the emerging US-led LIO of 1945 and the Inter-American Human Rights System. He believed that Latin America and the US were performing an exceptional and reformist task with global effects as promoters of Pan-Americanism and thus progenitors of "the international law of the future." He envisioned this idea in the context of the First World War and maintained this conviction in almost the same terms twenty years later in the context of the Second World War. As it will be shown in the next section, Álvarez was to insist on this conviction once again by 1940. By 1916, he believed that it was the duty of the Americas to study and "prepare the reconstruction of international society" and "the law that will govern its future" and according to him, the countries of the New World were to conduct this study through these two important hemispheric institutions, the "Pan-American Union and the American Institute of International Law."[27] He asserted:

> once the ideas that this latter body seeks to unify have been approved and ratified by the former, the New World as a whole, motivated by one single hope for peace, inspired by the ideas of liberty and fraternity that have always safeguard its action could present to the world assembly following the War, its own body of conceptions and aspirations as regards the reorganization of the international life of the future.[28]

Álvarez considered that the recent renovation and progress of Pan-Americanism offered in itself a testimony that the Americas could assume the important task of reconstructing the international law of the future. As it emerged in the last century, "Pan-Americanism has reached nowadays great proportions, assuming a diverse set of positive aspects, in historical, political, economic, juridical, scientific and intellectual terms."[29] The critical situation of the First World War and the success and popularity of Pan-Americanism could create grounds, according to Álvarez, for a certain degree of optimism in the future of international society, for it offered an opportunity for consolidating a Pan-American continental legal tradition and projecting it globally so that it could potentially "exert a great influence in the development of international law in the continent and all over the world."[30]

Álvarez created grounds for the emerging Pan-American liberal internationalist aspiration of advancing pioneering human rights ideals for the Americas in the inter-war period, which led in turn to the so-called Inter-American Human Rights System, as well as to consolidating the OAS Charter and a US-led multilateral Inter-American System in the early Cold War period.[31] Álvarez played a pioneering role promoting early notions of the individual rights of the human person through an international legal language and proposing that they had to be recognized by international law.[32] His precursor human rights advocacy was certainly in line with the broader Latin American legal tradition.[33] In the context of the second meeting of the AIIL held in Cuba in 1917, Álvarez presented early notions of human rights under the name of "international rights of individuals and international associations." These included certain individual rights, such as, the inviolability of property, the right to enter to and reside in any part of the territorial jurisdiction of the state, the right to associate and meet, the rights to liberty of press, consciousness, cults, commerce, navigation, and industry, the rights of foreigners to be protected by the national tribunals of their country of residence, and the rights of states to protect their nationals when their rights have been affected.[34] These notions were part of the first preliminary draft he presented as a "Project on the Fundamental Basis of International Law" and were then incorporated into the projects for the codification of American international law prepared and drafted by Álvarez himself in 1923 and revised in 1926 by the Executive Committee of the AIIL.[35] The new conceptions of the individual rights of the human person, as well as "the new problems that would emerge following this war," were at the core of the new agenda that Álvarez envisioned for this emerging "Pan-American school of international law." This school was to become, according to him, hegemonic not only in the Western Hemisphere, but also in the international community as a whole. He thus affirmed "this last stage of Pan-Americanism [was] destined to take the initiative in the reconstruction of international law over the basis of well-understood notions of liberty, democracy, equality and solidarity among all the members of the society of nations."[36]

In order to safeguard the individual rights of the human person and international persons in the international community, Álvarez made a case for exceptional and collective interventions. He believed that when the rights of individuals and the interest of the international community were at stake it, certain forms of collective interventions and even interventions in exceptional circumstances were admissible. The justification for legitimizing these interventions was presented in collective and societal terms in tone with his solidarist approach. In other words, it had to be done in the name of the ideals of solidarity and interdependence towards the international community. This approach of Álvarez could be also considered somehow condescending with regards to the regular practice of US interventions in Latin America, in particular with the Platt Amendment.[37] In 1917, Álvarez maintained a moderate approach to non-intervention, creating certain exceptions for "friendly" and "conciliatory" interventions on the part of one state in the internal affairs of another one.[38] Indeed, one of the exceptions was the case "when one State concedes to another one the faculty of intervening," that is, a situation similar to that of the Platt Amendment, which conceded the US the right to intervene in Cuba on a regular basis as part of the Cuban Constitution.[39]

When Álvarez prepared the projects for the codification of international law for the AIIL in the 1920s, he adopted a more robust but still a moderate approach, which gave room for collective, multilateral and non-violent interventions. The declaration he formulated on non-intervention read: "No State may intervene in the external or internal affairs of another American State, against its own will. The only interference that these could exert is amicable and conciliatory, without any character of imposition."[40] This specific declaration and the AIIL projects on codification, created a great deal of controversy over the principle of intervention and non-intervention at Rio de Janeiro Commission of Jurists (1927) and the Sixth Pan-American Conference held in Havana (1928). Following the polemical debate over intervention at Havana, where it was not possible to institutionalize the principle of absolute non-intervention, Álvarez regarded his own moderate version of non-intervention with exceptions as a principle of "American international law."[41] Carlos Saavedra Lamas's South American Anti-War Treaty of Non-Aggression and Conciliation proved to be a strategic tool for consolidating the principle of non-intervention in absolute terms at the Seventh Pan-American Conference held in Montevideo, for the Treaty was presented there as a "fait accompli."[42] Once this robust and absolute notion of non-intervention was adopted in 1933 at Montevideo, it became a core principle of American international law. While Álvarez played a central role in its doctrinal inception, promoting a moderate version in tone with his solidarist approach and his advocacy for the rights of the human person, Saavedra Lamas proved to be a central figure in the practical and diplomatic consolidation of non-intervention as an absolute principle at Montevideo.[43]

The Second World War, the Legacy of Pan-Americanism and the AIIL, and Ideological Origins of Inter-American Human Rights and the Liberal International Order

Pan-Americanism—and even American international law—remained for a long time until at least the 1940s as an influential worldview among international lawyers, diplomats, and politicians across the Americas, especially in Latin America.[44] It was to be progressively replaced by inter-American multilateralism in the late 1930s and 1940s and this transformation coincided with the progressive US turn to globalism, that is, from hemispheric to global hegemony. Human rights ideals were consolidated and institutionalized in the context of the projection of the US as a global hegemon and leader in the promotion of global governance and the so-called LIO, following the Bretton Woods and San Francisco Conferences with the creation of the United Nations in the aftermath of the Second World War, and the transformation of the Pan-American Union into the Organization of American States (OAS).[45] Human rights ideas and the institutions of global governance that were created to enforce them were at the core of the so-called US-led LIO that emerged in 1945.[46] Yet the US promotion of Pan-Americanism and hemispheric governance in previous decades played a central role as a continental laboratory for advancing early human rights ideals in the Americas before the US contributed to institutionalize the LIO and global governance by 1945. By the early 1940s Pan-Americanism, which emerged in the 1880s and 1890s in US circles in connection to the rise of US hemispheric hegemony, began to be replaced by the term inter-Americanism, which had clear multilateral implications. Yet Álvarez and other jurists and diplomats continued to hold a great appeal for the traditional notion of Pan-Americanism.

In the context of the beginning of the Second World War, Álvarez maintained great hopes in the mission of the Americas as progenitors of the international law of the future and the (re)construction of the new international order. If we consider Álvarez as a legal thinker of the twenty years crisis, he might well be regarded as a liberal internationalist and legal idealist who remained confident from 1916 up to the 1940s that international law principles, and codification projects were enough for re-establishing world peace and thus there was no need of advancing geopolitical and strategic realist considerations of hard power politics. Yet by 1940, in the context of the fifty years anniversary of the founding of the Pan-American Union, Álvarez was perfectly conscious that Europe and Asia were central strategic concerns for consolidating world peace, as was to be the case for the US foreign policy elite when it projected a geopolitical vision a few years later and projected to intervene in Europe and Asia, moving away from legalistic approaches.[47] According to Álvarez, the great powers of these two continents "have been often at war" but more importantly they were "animated by antisocial sentiments—hatred, envy, desire of revenge" and thus international law "has frequently been violated."[48] The Americas were moving in the opposite direction, according to Álvarez, that is, towards peace, solidarity and cooperation, so they have important international legal lessons to deliver to Euroasia.

Like in 1916 and 1917, by 1940 Álvarez still regarded Pan-Americanism as a vital feature in the reconstruction of the new international order of the aftermath of the Second World War. Unlike Europe and Asia, thanks to the prevalence of Pan-Americanism, in the Americas peace, solidarity and cooperation prevailed and thus international law was highly regarded. Pan-Americanism, in the view of Álvarez, had long rested on a spirit of cooperation, unity and harmony, but Franklin Delano Roosevelt's expressed renunciation to the policy of US supremacy with the Good Neighbor Policy provided the context for a new orientation and "new phase of Pan Americanism."[49] Historian Arthur P. Whitaker has placed the decline of Pan-Americanism within this very same context, a time when a series of influential figures of the US foreign policy elite, such as Henry L. Stimson, Eugene Staley, Nicholas J. Spykman, and Walter Lippmann began to promote a globalist approach, departing from Pan American continentalism.[50] This controversy was structured around a debate between the advocates of continental isolationism and a broader geopolitical and globalist vision to promote US intervention in Europe and Asia.[51] This emerging geopolitical, globalist and interventionist vision emerged as a social and ideological construction within US foreign policy circles and US public opinion, rather than as a response to real threats to US global hegemony, based on hard political evidence. It emphasized geographical proximities, security concerns, potential threats and the strategic planning of foreign policy.[52] One could well interpret the approach of Álvarez as simply out of date, which might or might not be the case, but in any case he remained all through the

1940s convinced that there was a legacy and heritage from the development of international law and international life in the Americas that could be effectively deployed for the construction of a new international order after the Second World War. Álvarez sought to project that legacy towards the future. In his retrospective overview of what could be learned and effectively used from the efforts displayed by the AIIL, the Pan-American Union and Pan American conferences, Álvarez portrayed himself as a progenitor of American international law and key protagonist of the Pan American movement, especially regarding the formation of the ideals of American international law, the continental projects for its codification and the promotion of early notions of the individual rights of the human person in international law.

Álvarez presented himself as progenitor of the idea of American international law to the extent that he affirmed that before him "nothing was written on the development and the particularities of international law in America."[53] When tracing the development of international law in the Americas, Álvarez identified certain specific continental attitudes and principles that emerged throughout the nineteenth century, but these matters had not been explores by Latin American publicists. They were only examined for the first time, he contended, in his work *Le droit international américain* (1909) and only a few years later in 1912 his own ideals of American international law were put into practice when the AIIL was founded and began to operate in the context of the European catastrophe of the First World War. With the aim of recovering once again in the 1940s the mission performed by the AIIL and the Pan-American Union, Álvarez traced a sharp contrast between European wars and the achievements of the AIIL. He thus affirmed that "in 1916, while all Europe was at war," the AIIL "met in Washington and approved a Declaration of Rights and Duties of Nations, presented by Dr. Scott, the President of the Institute."[54] He went on to suggest that his work *Le droit international d l'avenir* (1916) was another important contribution of the AIIL to recover the European continent from its own catastrophe and reconstruct the fundamentals of a new international order following the First World War.

In a rather teleological and evolutionist overview of the trajectory of international law in the Americas, Álvarez also portrayed himself as the architect and promoter of the projects for the codification of American international law, officially advanced by the AIIL and supported by the Pan-American Union in 1925. A preliminary draft of such projects was first presented in 1917 for the second meeting of the AIIL and later at the Fifth Pan American Conference held in Santiago de Chile in 1923.[55] It was through successive versions of these projects that Álvarez began to put forward certain notions of the rights of the human person in international law. He proposed and incepted them as early as in 1917, as has been already shown, in the context of the second meeting of the AIIL. The projects for the codification of American international law were one of the most important achievements and legacies of the AIIL.[56] The efforts of codification undertaken by the AIIL were recovered by Álvarez as a cornerstone of the contributions of the Americas and the AIIL to international law, but he did not hesitate to show that his proposed method of "gradual and progressive work" in the codification of public international law prevailed.[57] In order to legitimize his role as an intermediator between the codification efforts undertaken in Europe and the Americas in the 1940s, Álvarez also presented himself as a legitimate voice in the promotion of the new Pan American international law of the future. He thus placed a great emphasis on his own efforts for coordinating the codification projects advanced in the Americas by the Pan-American Union and the AIIL with those of the League of Nations in the 1930s. After all, Álvarez was legitimizing Pan-Americanism not only as a hemispheric legal movement for the Americas, but also as a civilizing legal mission to extend and globalize the values and traditions of the Americas towards the world.

Álvarez persistent obsession with projecting the evolution of international law in the Americas as a model for the future should not be regarded simply as an idealized vision of Western Hemisphere international law in the face of the two great European wars of the twentieth century. It is also a testimony of how a leading and foundational figure in the hemispheric tradition of American international law saw the contribution of the region to the construction of the LIO, especially to its core ideals of human rights and international organizations. As such, it merits to be taken very seriously. In recent years, a new body of scholarship has shown persuasively that the contribution of Latin American jurists to the UN and OAS human rights declarations was decisive to the extent that the "American Declaration of the Rights and Duties of Man," the first inter-governmental human rights declaration preceded and inspired the Universal Declaration of Human Rights drafted in the General Assembly of the UN in 1948.[58] If one groups together and compares the previous and pioneering contribution of the AIIL, especially its "Declaration on the Rights and Duties of Nations" drafted by Scott in 1916, as well as the pioneering declarations on the individual rights of the human person promoted by Álvarez in 1917, it becomes clear that the AIIL, the Pan American movement, Scott and Álvarez played a key role in the construction and consolidation of a hemispheric legal and humanitarian tradition that was to have a significant impact in the construction of the LIO.

In the early 1940s, Álvarez sought to revive and amplify further the arguments he advanced in the context of the First World War for the construction of the international law of the future. He insisted on the need to reconstruct and reconstitute the basis of international law and adapted it to what was then a current crisis of traditional approaches to international law and of European civilization as a whole introduced by the Second World War. It was imperative to construct a new international law in order to overcome classic individualistic conceptions and forge a new international order based on the ideals of solidarity, interdependence and a social and collective approach to law.[59] The quest for this disciplinary renovation was, according to him, a fundamental task in the aftermath of the Second World War. So he affirmed in a series of conferences he delivered in 1941 at the University of Buenos Aires in Argentina when he was awarded a doctorate honorary degree. These conferences focused primarily on disciplinary transformations, but Álvarez approached this question emphasizing, like in most of his writings, the contribution of the Americas to the new international order.[60] By 1945 he went as far as to refer to this question as the "American genius."[61] the Second World War had produced very concrete effects in the field of international law in times of war or laws of war. These questions, according to Álvarez, gained particular relevance in the Americas. Therefore, American international law as a hemispheric tradition offered concrete responses and solutions to these new challenges. In practical terms, this challenge led to the formation of a series of new inter-American institutions, some of which proved to be eventually crucial for the advancement of the OAS Charter in 1948. These included the Consultant Economic and Finance Committee, the Executive Committee on post-War problems, the Inter-American Juridical Committee and the Consultant Committee of Emergency for the Political Defense of the Continent.[62] Moreover, a new set of conferences of Ministers of Foreign Affairs of the Americas were also held in order to reinforce the autonomy of American international law and they generated a number of resolutions that strengthened the rights of neutral countries.[63] In doctrinal terms, these institutions and meetings led to a new set of principles and resolutions that were contributing to reconstructing and reconstituting international law in a new key. Indeed, Álvarez identified new tendencies in the field that were acquiring particular prominence in the Americas. For instance, one of his tendencies was to "grant international character to the rights of individuals" and "to give to individuals a personality so that they could become a proper subject of international law."[64]

The tradition of the AIIL contributed to forging some of the core institutions of the LIO, especially the OAS Charter. Indeed, the projects and contributions advanced by Álvarez played a central role in this regard to the extent that he was a member of the juridical commission of the Chilean government for the study of post-War problems. More importantly, Álvarez presented himself as a main legal and intellectual architect of the post-the Second World War order and the LIO. He framed all his ideas about the reconstruction of international law in the 1940s around a "Declaration on the Fundamental Basis and Great Principles of Modern International Law" he himself presented back in 1931 before the International Diplomatic Academy, the International Juridical Union, the International Law Association, the *Institut de droit international* and AIIL.[65] As this Declaration acquired international recognition worldwide, Álvarez still deployed it in 1945 as a model for reconstituting the international of the future. He affirmed that all the central principles of American international law were incorporated to it so that they adopted a universal character.[66] More importantly, according to Álvarez, the Declaration introduced a series of important legal innovations. These included the notions of interdependence, solidarity and social and collective law, an emphasis on international duties, as well as rights; the adherence to the principle of non-intervention providing scope for certain exceptions for collective interventions; and the promotion of the international rights of the individual.[67] Álvarez made clear that in the preliminary version of the Declaration he delivered a much wider and detailed project in support of the international rights of the human person, but it encountered a great deal of resistance, and thus it was shortened. In its shortened version, it recognized the international rights of individuals, including the right to life, liberty, and property without any distinction of sex, race, language or religion.[68] Yet he was to insist on the importance of granting recognition to these international rights of the human person, presenting once again in 1945 a much wider declaration on this matter. Indeed, in October 1945 Álvarez presented before the IV Inter-American Conference of Lawyers a "Project on the Fundamental Charter for the American Continent."[69] As part of this broader and ambitious project, which certainly informed the OAS Charter, Álvarez presented a new Declaration on the international rights of the human person, which was renamed as "Declaration of the International Rights and Duties of Men and International Persons" with the aim in mind of enhancing and modernizing existing notions of democracy.[70] The similarities between these final versions of the projects advanced and revised once again by Álvarez in 1945 on the individual rights of the human person and those included a few years as part of the OAS Charter in 1948, are certainly striking, in particular as regards its Resolution number 30, widely known as "American Declaration of the Rights and Duties of Man."

At a time when human rights ideals and the international rights of the human person began to reach wider appeal among the international community in the 1940s, Álvarez was astute in presenting himself as a pioneering and long-standing Pan American advocate of this notion. In 1945, Álvarez was perfectly aware of the wider global implications that the advocacy for international human rights ideals began to adopt since the outbreak of the Second World War. He asserted: "since long ago and especially since the outbreak of the war of 1939, it has been developing, above all in the countries of the Americas, a great movement to proclaim the rights of the individual, human rights, with an international character."[71] According to Álvarez, the rights of individuals had been granted and recognized in national legislation and the Americas were more advanced than Europe in this regard, but they had not been recognized yet in international law. He thus regarded his own project presented before the AIIL in its second meeting of 1917 as the "first tentative to proclaim internationally the rights of men," which he presented once again in 1923 at the Fifth Pan-American Conference along with the draft projects for the codification of public

American international law.[72] In the new revised version presented at the fourth Inter-American Conference of Lawyers, along with the "Project on the Fundamental Charter for the American Continent," Álvarez added to the original projects of 1917 some important social rights which were consistent with the more robust notions of social and collective rights that he began to promote since the 1930s. These included "equality between nationals and foreigners in their civil rights, access to justice and juridical institutions, the right to elementary education, the right to work and to be paid for that labour, the right to social security" and "the right to protection from misery."[73] These declarations were precedents that were to inform the foundations of the OAS Charter and its "American Declaration of the Rights and Duties of Man" drafted in 1945, but proclaimed a few years later in 1948.

The self-celebratory overview presented by Álvarez of his pioneering historical advocacy within the AIIL and the Pan American movement for the proclamation of the international rights of the human person was perfectly consistent with the testimonies of his fellow colleagues of the AIIL. Ricardo Alfaro, who, like Álvarez, acted as General Secretary of the AIIL before its final dissolution in 1942, acknowledged that Álvarez was the one who "for the first time, suggested in 1917 that the rights of the individual be internationally recognized."[74] According to Alfaro, a few years later, in 1921, Albert Jouffre de Lapradelle, who founded jointly with Álvarez the *Institute des hautes etudes internationales* in Paris and was closely connected to him, drew on this project and presented over the European *Institut de droit international* a new draft declaration of the rights of individuals, inspired in the original project of Álvarez. These early ideas of human rights emerged out from the AIIL projects for the codification of international law in the Americas advanced and supported by the Pan-American Union, but they were to have an important impact on a European legal audience. Once the projects for codification, including the ideas on the individual rights of the human person proposed by Álvarez, began to reach an audience outside the Western Hemisphere and thus they were projected as an achievement of the Americas and an ideal model to reconstruct the European international law and order of the future, they began to be truly Pan-American. Pan-Americanism after all was a US-led policy of hemispheric solidarity and cooperation towards Latin America that gained popularity and reached its highest peak in the context of the world wars. In this context of the twenty years crisis, as shown in this chapter, Pan-Americanism began to be deployed as an orientational model for (re)constructing a new international order, in which Europe was condemned to lose its primacy in the hands of the US. The latter could recover and gained inspiration from its past continental hegemonic experiences of Pan-American governance in order to project a new US-led model of global governance, known as the LIO.

Conclusion: The Resonances of Pan-American Human Rights after 1948 and the Institutionalization of the Inter-American Human Rights System

One of the most important legacies of Pan-Americanism and the AIIL and their early human rights ideals and declarations was the OAS Charter of 1948, which incorporated and framed a human rights declaration in the language of rights and duties pioneeringly promoted by the AIIL. The Inter-American Commission of Human Rights created in 1959 and even the Inter-American Court of Human Rights created much later in the 1970s were also legacies of the continental principles, norms, and codification projects of the AIIL and the Pan-American movement, especially the early ideas of human rights and the notions of rights and duties promoted by Álvarez and Scott. The objectives and projects of the AIIL of codifying a set of continental norms and principles and creating an Inter-American Court of Justice to sort out disputes through legal means, informed the creation of a more solid legal and institutional architecture for the Americas with the institutionalization of the Inter-American Commission of Human Rights and the Inter-American Court of Human Rights in the 1960s and 1970s.[75]

In the context of the creation of the Inter-American Commission of Human Rights in 1959, following the Cuban Revolution, a controversial debate emerged over the tensions between the effective exercise of representative democracy and the respect for human rights, on the one hand, and the principle of non-intervention, on the other hand. All these principles were still regarded in 1959 as "fundamental principles of American international law."[76] Some of these tensions, especially that between the respect for the international rights of the human person and non-intervention certainly captured the attention and was thus anticipated by Álvarez in the 1920s. Álvarez sought to create grounds for collective and multilateral interventions to protect these rights through social and collective mechanisms of solidarity and interdependence among the members of the international community. Álvarez could thus be regarded as a pioneering advocate of early human rights ideas, that is, Pan-American human rights. For he was perfectly aware, since the 1920s at least, that certain collective and multilateral mechanisms were necessary for safeguarding human rights and condemning their violation through a solid institutional and legal framework. This question began to be discussed consistently only later since the creation of the Inter-American Commission of Human Rights in 1959 until the present day.

This chapter does not seek to discuss or revise whether human rights in the Americas were or were not a pioneering regional initiative that predated the UN Declaration, neither does it aim to show that it was a precursor notion advocated in Latin America for a long time. It has shown rather that the notion of the international rights of the human person emerged out in the Americas from a broader missionary and exceptional hemispheric project devoted to promote Pan-Americanism as the most suitable worldview and framework for the international organization of the Americas and especially for reconstructing the European international law of the future after the two great wars of 1914 and 1939. Some preliminary notions of the international rights of the human person were envisioned by Álvarez and proposed by the AIIL alongside a series of projects for the codification of American international law, which were advanced through the Pan-American Union as a truly Pan American legal project. Before human rights began to be deployed as an international doctrine, it could be affirmed that they were Pan American ideals and aspirations, at least in the original formulation of Álvarez.

This chapter has shown that human rights, as they were originally envisioned in the Americas, were an essential part of the Pan-American movement. Pan-Americanism as such was not only an internal phenomena of the Western Hemisphere to project and develop through the leadership of the US common institutions and the practice of cooperation within the Americas, but it also became a policy to be projected as an exceptional example and model for (European) international society. In the context of the First and Second World Wars, when international law had been violated by European powers, the AIIL and Álvarez devoted their efforts to extract lessons and experiences from the emerging Pan-American school of international law with the missionary aim of projecting them to reconstruct the international law of the future in the aftermath of the two great European catastrophes.

Finally, human rights had an important inception in international society through the pioneering Pan-American quest of forging a specific body of legal principles for the Americas, as it was advanced by one of its most eloquent legal advocates, Alejandro Álvarez. In the course of the twenty years crisis, Álvarez sought to project two waves of solutions and renovations for a new international order firstly in 1917 and later in the 1940s.

As shown throughout this chapter, the legal and intellectual spirit of these two waves presented important similarities. Firstly, as shown in the first section of the chapter, the first wave of human rights aspirations alongside the AIIL projects for the codification of international law, promoted mainly by Álvarez, emerged as an attempt to promote and project Pan-Americanism and American international law as the international law of the future following World War 1. In this context, Pan-Americanism and Pan American human rights in particular, were deployed by Álvarez very much in an idealist Hegelian language. Indeed, Álvarez presented the "Pan-American school of international law" as a synthesis of the US Anglo-Saxon and the Latin America continental ones and thus as a model for the international law of the future to be projected to European international society in order to overcome the catastrophe of the Great War. It was more of an idealist vision for the reconstruction of the new international order than a concrete project or declaration for international organization and the creation of international institutions. Secondly, as shown in the second section of the chapter, the second wave of human rights ideals and projects for

156 *Juan Pablo Scarfi*

international organization were grounded on concrete projects elaborated by Álvarez that were supported by both European and Western Hemisphere legal and diplomatic audiences, as was the case of his "Declaration on the Fundamental Basis and Great Principles of Modern International Law" presented in 1931. Álvarez sought to act as an intermediator between Europe and the Americas. In October 1945, on the grounds of a still idealized vision of the hemispheric superiority of American international law and Pan-Americanism, Álvarez went as far as to present a "Project on the Fundamental Charter for the American Continent" alongside a "Declaration of the International Rights and Duties of Men and International Persons," which contributed to shaping the OAS Charter, its human rights declarations and the LIO. These projects and institutions provided the legal and institutional framework for the construction of the Inter-American Human Rights System.

Acknowledgments

A preliminary version of this chapter was delivered at the Conference "Paradoxes of Universalism" held at the University of Helsinki, Finland on November 4–6, 2020. I am grateful to Paolo Amorosa and Jacob Giltaij for comments and suggestions on that previous version of this chapter.

Notes

1. See Juan Pablo Scarfi, *The Hidden History of International Law in the Americas: Empire and Legal Networks* (New York: Oxford University Press, 2017), 1–30; and Scarfi, *El imperio de la ley: James Brown Scott y la construcción de un orden jurídico interamericano* (Buenos Aires: Fondo de Cultura Económica, 2014), 47–85.
2. Alejandro Álvarez, *El derecho internacional del porvenir* (Madrid: Editorial-América, 1916); and Álvarez, *La reconstrucción del derecho de gentes: El nuevo orden y la renovación social* (Santiago: Editorial Nascimento, 1945).
3. These conferences were published three years later as a book. See Alejandro Álvarez, *Después de la guerra* (Buenos Aires: Imprenta de la Universidad, 1943). See also Alejandro Álvarez, "International Life and International Law in America: Their Development during the Last Fifty Years," *Bulletin of the Pan-American Union* 74 (1940): 232–62.
4. E. H. Carr, *The Twenty Years Crisis, 1919–1939: An Introduction to the Study of International Relations* (New York: Harper, 1964). See also David Long and Peter Wilson, eds., *Thinkers of the Twenty Years' Crisis: Inter-War Idealism Reassessed* (Oxford: Oxford University Press, 1995).
5. Ricardo D. Salvatore, *Disciplinary Conquest: US Scholars in South America, 1900–1945* (Durham, NC: Duke University Press, 2016); Katherine Marino, *Feminism for the Americas: The Making of an International Human Rights Movement* (Chapel Hill, NC: University of North Carolina Press, 2019); Mark Petersen, "Argentine and Chilean Approaches to Modern Pan-Americanism, 1888–1930" (Ph.D. Dissertation, University of Oxford, 2014); Mark Petersen, "The 'Vanguard of Pan-Americanism': Inter-American Multilateralism in the Early Twentieth Century," *Cooperation and Hegemony in US–Latin American Relations: Revisiting the Western Hemisphere Idea*, ed. Juan Pablo Scarfi and Andrew Tillman (New York: Palgrave Macmillan, 2016), 111–37; Juliette

Dumont, *Diplomatie culturelle et fabrique des identités. Argentine, Brésil, Chili (1919–1946)* (Rennes, Presses Universitaires de Rennes/IDA, 2018); Dumont, "Latin America at the Crossroads: The Inter-American Institute of Intellectual Cooperation, the League of Nations and the Pan-American Union," *Beyond Geopolitics: New Histories of Latin America at the League of Nations*, ed. Alan McPherson and Yannick Wehrli (Albuquerque, University of New Mexico Press, 2015), 155–67; Scarfi, *Hidden History*; Juan Pablo Scarfi and Andrew Tillman, eds., *Cooperation and Hegemony in US–Latin American Relations: Revisiting the Western Hemisphere Idea* (New York: Palgrave Macmillan, 2016); and Richard Cándida Smith, *Improvised Continent: Pan-Americanism and Cultural Exchange* (Philadelphia: University of Pennsylvania Press, 2017). For an excellent overview of the recent transformations in the historiography of US–Latin American relations, see Tanya Harmer, "Commonality, Specificity and Difference: Histories and Historiography of the Americas," *Cooperation and Hegemony*, ed. Juan Pablo Scarfi and Andrew Tillman, 71–108.

6 See, for example, Kathryn Sikkink, "Latin American Countries as Norm Protagonists of the Idea of International Human Rights," *Global Governance* 20 (2014): 389–404; Paolo G. Carozza, "From Conquest to Constitutions: Retrieving a Latin American Tradition of Human Rights," *Human Rights Quarterly* 25 (2003): 281–313; Patrick Willam Kelly, *Sovereign Emergencies: Latin America and the Making of Global Human Rights Politics* (Cambridge: Cambridge University Press, 2018); and Fernando J. Rosenberg, *After Human Rights: Literature, Visual Arts, and Film in Latin America, 1990–2010* (Pittsburgh: University of Pittsburgh Press, 2016).

7 A pioneering book in this new wave of revisionist history of human rights is Samuel Moyn, *The Last Utopia: Human Rights in History* (Cambridge, MA: Harvard University Press, 2010). See also Stefan-Ludwig Hoffmann ed., *Human Rights in the Twentieth Century* (Cambridge: Cambridge University Press, 2011); Hoffmann, Stefan-Ludwig, "Human Rights and History," *Past and Present* 232, no. 1 (2016): 279–310; and Samuel Moyn, "The End of Human Rights History," *Past and Present* 233, no. 1 (2016): 307–22. For a brief overview of this new historiography, see Juan Pablo Scarfi, "Del giro ético al historicista: El potencial y los límites de la perspectiva histórica en los derechos humanos y el derecho internacional," *Revista Latinoamericana de Derecho Internacional* 6 (2017): 1–14.

8 David K. Adams and Cornelis A. van Minnen, eds., *Reflections on American Exceptionalism* (Newcastle: Keele University Press, 1994).

9 David Sheinin, "Rethinking Pan Americanism: An Introduction," *Beyond the Ideal: Pan Americanism in Inter-American Affairs*, ed. David Sheinin (Westport: Praeger, 2000), 1.

10 Scarfi, *Hidden History*, 33.

11 Ibid., 31–85.

12 Juan Pablo Scarfi, "In the Name of the Americas: The Pan-American Redefinition of the Monroe Doctrine and the Emerging Language of American International Law in the Western Hemisphere, 1898–1933," *Diplomatic History* 40, no. 2 (2016): 189–218.

13 Juan Pablo Scarfi, "Pan-American Legal Designs: The Rise and Decline of American International Law in the Western Hemisphere," *Cooperation and Hegemony in US–Latin American Relations: Revisiting the Western Hemisphere Idea*, ed. Juan Pablo Scarfi and Andrew Tillman (New York: Palgrave Macmillan, 2016), 171–208.

14 James Brown Scott, *The American Institute of International Law: Its Declaration of Rights and Duties of Nations* (Washington, DC: The American Institute of International Law, 1916), 26.

15 Ibid., 26.

16 Ibid., 88.
17 Ibid., 41.
18 Ibid., 43.
19 Juan Pablo Scarfi, "El pensamiento legal internacional latinoamericano ante la Primera Guerra Mundial: el panamericanismo legal, el nuevo derecho internacional, y el renacimiento del latinoamericanismo defensivo," *La Gran Guerra en América Latina: Una historia conectada*, ed. Olivier Compagnon, Camille Foulard, Guillemette Martin and María Inés Tato (Mexico City: Centro de Estudios Mexicanos y Centroamericanos (CEMCA) and Institut des Hautes Études de l'Amérique Latine (IHEAL), 2018), 203–20. See also Olivier Compagnon, *América Latina y la Gran Guerra: El adiós a Europa (Argentina y Brasil, 1914–1939)*, (Buenos Aires: Crítica, 2014) and Stefan Rinke, *Latin America and the First World War* (New York: Cambridge University Press, 2017).
20 See Álvarez, "Latin America," and Álvarez, *Le droit international américain: son fondement, sa nature* (Paris: A. Pedone Éditeur, 1910).
21 Alejandro Álvarez, *El derecho internacional del porvenir* (Madrid: Editorial-América, 1916).
22 Martti Koskenniemi, *The Gentle Civilizer of Nations: The Rise and Fall of International Law, 1870–1960* (Cambridge: Cambridge University Press, 2001), 302–5; and Carl Launder, "A Latin American in Paris: Alejandro Álvarez's Le droit international américain," *Leiden Journal of International Law* 19, no. 4 (2006): 957–81.
23 Stephen C. Neff, *Justice Among Nations: A History of International Law* (Cambridge, MA: Harvard University Press, 2014), 292.
24 For a more detailed analysis of the solidarist approach of Álvarez, see Neff, *Justice among Nations*, 290–97, and Scarfi, *Hidden History*, 54–8.
25 Scarfi, "In the Name of the Americas."
26 Álvarez, *El derecho internacional del porvenir*, 14.
27 Ibid., 15.
28 Ibid., 15–16.
29 Ibid., 21.
30 Ibid., 222–3.
31 Ibid., 94–7; and Alejandro Álvarez, "Declaración de los derechos y deberes internacionales del hombre y de las personas internacionales," *La reconstrucción del derecho de gentes. El nuevo orden y la renovación social* (Santiago: Editorial Nascimento, 1945), 462–3.
32 Álvarez, "Declaración de los derechos," 458.
33 Kathryn Sikkink, *Evidence for Hope: Making Human Rights Work in the 21st Century* (Princeton: Princeton University Press, 2017), 62–3.
34 Alejandro Álvarez, "Sección Séptima: Derechos internacionales del individuo y de las asociaciones internacionales," Instituto Americano de Derecho Internacional, *Actas, memorias y proyectos de las sesiones de la Habana (Segunda reunión del Instituto) 22 a 27 de enero de 1917* (New York: Oxford University Press, 1918), 346–47.
35 Álvarez, "Proyecto sobre bases fundamentales del derecho internacional," Instituto Americano, *Actas, memorias y proyectos*, 340–50; and Alejandro Álvarez, *La codificación del derecho internacional en América: trabajos de la tercera Comisión de la Asamblea de Jurisconsultos reunida en Santiago de Chile* (Santiago: Imprenta Universitaria, 1923), 99–101. See also "American Institute of International Law: Texts of Projects," Supplement: Collaboration of the American Institute of International Law with the Pan-American Union, *American Journal of International Law* 20, no. 4 (1926): 326–7.
36 Alejandro Álvarez, "La futura sociedad de las naciones," Instituto Americano de Derecho Internacional, *Actas, memorias y proyectos*, 305. These statements are

also stressed almost in similar terms in the concluding paragraphs and sections of Álvarez, *El derecho internacional del porvenir*, 222–3.
37 Scarfi, *Hidden History*, 53–5.
38 Álvarez, *El derecho internacional del porvenir*, 94; and Álvarez, "Apéndice Número VII: Derechos fundamentales de los Estados," Instituto Americano de Derecho Internacional, *Actas, memorias y proyectos*, 378–9. See also Scarfi, *Hidden History*, 54.
39 Álvarez, "Sección Séptima," 379.
40 Álvarez, *La codificación*, 98.
41 Alejandro Álvarez, *Le panaméricanisme et la Sixième Conférence Panaméricaine, tenue à La Havane en 1928* (Paris: Les Éditions Internationales, 1928), 72.
42 Greg Grandin, "Your Americanism and Mine: Americanism and Anti-Americanism in the Americas," *American Historical Review* 111, no. 4 (2006): 1055, and Stephen C. Neff, *War and the Law of Nations: A General History* (Cambridge: Cambridge University Press, 2005), 296.
43 See Scarfi, *Hidden History*, 147–74.
44 Arnulf Becker Lorca, "International Law in Latin America or Latin American International Law? Rise, Fall, and Retrieval of a Tradition of Legal Thinking and Political Imagination," *Harvard International Law Journal* 47, no. 1 (2006): 283–305; and Scarfi, *Hidden History*, 175–89.
45 See Mark Mazower, *No Enchanted Palace: The End of Empire and the Ideological Origins of the United Nations* (Princeton: Princeton University Press, 2009); and Mark Mazower, *Governing the World: The History of an Idea* (London: Allen Lane, 2012), 116–213.
46 Daniel Deudney and G. John Ikenberry, "The Nature and Sources of Liberal International Order," *Review of International Studies* 25, no. 2 (1999): 179–96.
47 John A. Thompson, "The Geopolitical Vision: The Myth of an Outmatched USA," *Uncertain Empire: American History and the Idea of the Cold War*, ed. Joel Isaac and Duncan Bell (New York: Oxford University Press, 2012), 91–114.
48 Álvarez, "International Life," 232.
49 Ibid., 233, 262.
50 Arthur P. Whitaker, *The Western Hemisphere Idea: Its Rise and Decline* (Ithaca, NY: Cornell University Press, 1954), 154–71.
51 Thompson, "The Geopolitical Vision."
52 Ibid.
53 Álvarez, "International Life," 240.
54 Ibid., 242.
55 Ibid., 255.
56 See Scarfi, *Hidden History*.
57 Álvarez, "International Life," 255.
58 See Kathryn Sikkink, "Latin American Countries as Norm Protagonists of the Idea of International Human Rights," *Global Governance* 20 (2014): 389–404; and Paolo G. Carozza, "From Conquest to Constitutions: Retrieving a Latin American Tradition of Human Rights," *Human Rights Quarterly* 25 (2003): 281–313.
59 Álvarez, *La reconstrucción del derecho de gentes*, 67.
60 Álvarez, *Después de la guerra*, 23–105.
61 Álvarez, *La reconstrucción del derecho de gentes*, 3
62 Ibid., 44.
63 Ibid., 41–4.
64 Ibid., 46–7.
65 Álvarez, "Declaración sobre las bases fundamentales y los grandes principios del derecho internacional moderno," *La reconstrucción del derecho de gentes*, 85–93.
66 Álvarez, *La reconstrucción del derecho de gentes*, 59.
67 Ibid., 60–63.

160 Juan Pablo Scarfi

68 Ibid., 91.
69 Ibid., 309–34.
70 Ibid., 311.
71 Ibid., 457.
72 Ibid., 458.
73 Alejandro Álvarez, "Declaración de los derechos y deberes internacionales del hombre y de las personas internacionales," *La reconstrucción del derecho de gentes. El nuevo orden y la renovación social* (Santiago: Editorial Nascimento, 1945), 457–63.
74 Ricardo J. Alfaro and the United Nations Conference on International Organization, *Derechos y libertades fundamentales del hombre* (Panama: Imprenta Nacional, 1946), cited in Sikkink, *Evidence for Hope*, 62.
75 See Scarfi, *El imperio de la ley*, 57–85; and Scarfi, *Hidden History*.
76 Quinta Reunión de Consulta de Ministros de Relaciones Exteriores, Santiago de Chile, 12–18 de August 1959 (Washington, DC: Unión Panamericana, 1960), 3, 6. See also C. Neale Ronnning, *Law and Politics in Inter-American Diplomacy* (New York: John Wiley & Sons, 1963), 69–85.

Bibliography

Adams, David K. and Cornelis A. van Minnen, eds., *Reflections on American Exceptionalism*. Newcastle: Keele University Press, 1994.
Bell, Duncan. "The Dream Machine: On Liberalism and Empire," In *Reordering the World: Essays on Liberalism and Empire*, edited by Duncan Bell, 19–61. Princeton: Princeton University Press, 2016.
Cándida Smith, Richard. *Improvised Continent: Pan-Americanism and Cultural Exchange*. Philadelphia: University of Pennsylvania Press, 2017.
Carozza, Paolo G. "From Conquest to Constitutions: Retrieving a Latin American Tradition of Human Rights." *Human Rights Quarterly* 25 (2003): 281–313.
Carr, E. H. *The Twenty Years Crisis, 1919–1939: An Introduction to the Study of International Relations*. New York: Harper, 1964.
Compagnon, Olivier. *América Latina y la Gran Guerra: El adiós a Europa (Argentina y Brasil, 1914–1939)*. Buenos Aires: Crítica, 2014.
Deudney, Daniel and G. John Ikenberry. "The Nature and Sources of Liberal International Order," *Review of International Studies* 25, no. 2 (1999):179–196.
Dumont, Juliette. *Diplomatie culturelle et fabrique des identités. Argentine, Brésil, Chili (1919–1946)*. Rennes: Presses Universitaires de Rennes/IDA, 2018.
Dumont, Juliette. "Latin America at the Crossroads: The Inter-American Institute of Intellectual Cooperation, the League of Nations and the Pan-American Union." In *Beyond Geopolitics: New Histories of Latin America at the League of Nations*, edited by Alan McPherson and Yannick Wehrli, 155–167. Albuquerque: University of New Mexico Press, 2015.
Grandin, Greg. "Your Americanism and Mine: Americanism and Anti-Americanism in the Americas." *American Historical Review* 111, no. 4 (2006): 1042–1066.
Harmer, Tanya. "Commonality, Specificity and Difference: Histories and Historiography of the Americas." In *Cooperation and Hegemony*, edited by Juan Pablo Scarfi and Andrew Tillman, 71–108. New York: Palgrave Macmillan, 2016.
Hoffmann, Stefan-Ludwig. "Human Rights and History." *Past and Present* 232, no. 1 (2016): 279–310.

Hoffmann, Stefan-Ludwig, ed. *Human Rights in the Twentieth Century*. Cambridge: Cambridge University Press, 2011.

Kelly, Patrick William. *Sovereign Emergencies: Latin America and the Making of Global Human Rights Politics*. Cambridge: Cambridge University Press, 2018.

Koskenniemi, Martti. *The Gentle Civilizer of Nations: The Rise and Fall of International Law, 1870–1960*. Cambridge: Cambridge University Press, 2001.

Launder, Carl. "A Latin American in Paris: Alejandro Álvarez's Le droit international américain." *Leiden Journal of International Law* 19, no. 4 (2006): 957–981.

Long, David and Peter Wilson, eds. *Thinkers of the Twenty Years' Crisis: Inter-War Idealism Reassessed*. Oxford: Oxford University Press, 1995.

Lorca, Arnulf Becker. "International Law in Latin America or Latin American International Law? Rise, Fall, and Retrieval of a Tradition of Legal Thinking and Political Imagination." *Harvard International Law Journal* 47, no. 1 (2006): 283–305.

Marino, Katherine. *Feminism for the Americas: The Making of an International Human Rights Movement*. Chapel Hill, NC: University of North Carolina Press, 2019.

Mazower, Mark. *Governing the World: The History of an Idea*. London: Allen Lane, 2012.

Mazower, Mark. *No Enchanted Palace: The End of Empire and the Ideological Origins of the United Nations*. Princeton: Princeton University Press, 2009.

Moyn, Samuel. "The End of Human Rights History." *Past and Present* 233, no. 1 (2016): 307–322.

Moyn, Samuel. *The Last Utopia: Human Rights in History*. Cambridge, MA: Harvard University Press, 2010.

Neff, Stephen C. *Justice Among Nations: A History of International Law*. Cambridge, MA: Harvard University Press, 2014.

Neff, Stephen C. *War and the Law of Nations: A General History*. Cambridge: Cambridge University Press, 2005.

Petersen, Mark. "Argentine and Chilean Approaches to Modern Pan-Americanism, 1888–1930." PhD dissertation, University of Oxford, 2014.

Petersen, Mark. "The 'Vanguard of Pan-Americanism': Inter-American Multilateralism in the Early Twentieth Century," *Cooperation and Hegemony in US–Latin American Relations: Revisiting the Western Hemisphere Idea*, edited by Juan Pablo Scarfi and Andrew Tillman, 111–137. New York: Palgrave Macmillan, 2016.

Rinke, Stefan. *Latin America and the First World War*. New York: Cambridge University Press, 2017.

Rosenberg, Fernando J. *After Human Rights: Literature, Visual Arts, and Film in Latin America, 1990–2010*. Pittsburgh: University of Pittsburgh Press, 2016.

Salvatore, Ricardo D. *Disciplinary Conquest: US Scholars in South America, 1900–1945*. Durham: Duke University Press, 2016.

Scarfi, Juan Pablo. "Del giro ético al historicista: El potencial y los límites de la perspectiva histórica en los derechos humanos y el derecho internacional." *Revista Latinoamericana de Derecho Internacional* 6 (2017): 1–14.

Scarfi, Juan Pablo. *El imperio de la ley: James Brown Scott y la construcción de un orden jurídico interamericano*. Buenos Aires: Fondo de Cultura Económica, 2014.

Scarfi, Juan Pablo. *The Hidden History of International Law in the Americas: Empire and Legal Networks*. New York: Oxford University Press, 2017.

Scarfi, Juan Pablo. "In the Name of the Americas: The Pan-American Redefinition of the Monroe Doctrine and the Emerging Language of American International Law in the Western Hemisphere, 1898–1933." *Diplomatic History* 40, no. 2 (2016): 189–218.

Scarfi, Juan Pablo. "Pan-American Legal Designs: The Rise and Decline of American International Law in the Western Hemisphere." In *Cooperation and Hegemony in US–Latin American Relations: Revisiting the Western Hemisphere Idea*, edited by Juan Pablo Scarfi and Andrew Tillman, 171–208. New York: Palgrave Macmillan, 2016.

Scarfi, Juan Pablo. "El pensamiento legal internacional latinoamericano ante la Primera Guerra Mundial: el panamericanismo legal, el nuevo derecho internacional, y el renacimiento del latinoamericanismo defensivo." In *La Gran Guerra en América Latina: Una historia conectada*, edited by Olivier Compagnon, Camille Foulard, Guillemette Martin, and María Inés Tato, 203–220. Mexico City: Centro de Estudios Mexicanos y Centroamericanos and Institut des Hautes Études de l'Amérique Latine, 2018.

Scarfi, Juan Pablo and Andrew Tillman, eds. *Cooperation and Hegemony in US–Latin American Relations: Revisiting the Western Hemisphere Idea*. New York: Palgrave Macmillan, 2016.

Sheinin, David. "Rethinking Pan Americanism: An Introduction." In *Beyond the Ideal: Pan Americanism in Inter-American Affairs*, ed. David Sheinin, 1–8. Westport: Praeger, 2000.

Sikkink, Kathryn. *Evidence for Hope: Making Human Rights Work in the 21st Century*. Princeton: Princeton University Press, 2017.

Sikkink, Kathryn. "Latin American Countries as Norm Protagonists of the Idea of International Human Rights." *Global Governance* 20 (2014): 389–404.

Thompson, John A. "The Geopolitical Vision: The Myth of an Outmatched USA." In *Uncertain Empire: American History and the Idea of the Cold War*, edited by Joel Isaac and Duncan Bell, 91–114. New York: Oxford University Press, 2012.

Whitaker, Arthur P. *The Western Hemisphere Idea: Its Rise and Decline*. Ithaca: Cornell University Press, 1954.

8 Epilogue
Pan-Americanism and the Changing Nature of US Hegemony

Ricardo D. Salvatore

Much has been said already in the Introduction about the nature and motivation of this volume. The essays could be classified into three types: some examine Pan-Americanism as an arena where different Latin American actors (architects and economists, in this case) were able to project internationally their own agenda; others follow the mass impact and support that the Good Neighbor Policy had on the US civil society; and a third group presents two contrasting agents (the Argentine military and a Chilean jurist) trying to accommodate their agendas (the struggle against left-wing guerrillas and the internationalization of Human Rights) to the new scenario of the Cold War period. In my view, these contributions deepen our understanding of Pan-Americanism while following the line of research opened by *Close Encounters of Empire* (1998), a volume that invited scholars to extend the study of inter-American relations to a multiplicity of actors and to a variety of texts, outside the three realms that have occupied the attention of historians for many decades: the economy, the armed forces, and diplomacy.[1]

Reading this impressive and valuable collection of essays, I was impelled to re-think my own views of Pan-Americanism in relation to the question of US Hegemony, a Gramscian term that has been used and misused for more than sixty years. In the first section of this chapter, I try to understand US interventions and US promotion of Pan-Americanism within the framework of Hegemony, as redefined by Ranajit Guha in 1997. In the second section, I briefly summarize my research interest in US Pan-Americanism and my own changing characterizations of the phenomenon over time. From a "representational machine" my view evolved into the "imperiality" and usefulness of disciplinary knowledge, and lately into back again into the combination of hard and soft machines to impress South Americans, within the context of an organization apparatus built to export the American-way-of-life while importing the "representative cultures" of Latin American nations.

I

What was Pan-Americanism? Was it an ideal, a continental alliance, a bureaucratic organization, a social movement, a mask for US imperialism?

DOI: 10.4324/9781003252672-9

My answer to this broad question is that Pan-Americanism was an alliance forged between diplomats and politicians in the United States and in Latin America; yet it was also an organization, at first dominated by the United States, that after 1933 gradually moved into a multilateral project of cooperation with a more plural leadership. In the post-war period, *circa* 1945–48, as the American hegemon projected itself as a Global Power in contention with the USS.R., the force of Pan-Americanism into decline and the State Department paid much less attention to the region. Within the context of a new global confrontation between Capitalism and Communism, the Organization of American State (the new inter-American organization that replaced the Pan America Union) had a minor role to play.

Yet, Pan-Americanism was more than this. First, before 1933, within and without the Pan America Union (PAU) there were Latin American voices that contested the dominant view of a US-led inter-American alliance, demanding an end to US interventions in the circum-Caribbean region and claiming a more democratic representation of Latin American nations in the direction of the organization. Second, Pan-Americanism was also a movement, to the extent that its ideals generated massive support within the United States, made evident in street parades, music concerts, radio programs, student clubs, and high-school and university classrooms. Small and big organizations joined President Franklin D. Roosevelt's campaign to make the Americas a region governed by relations of good-neighborhood, rather than a fragmented territory permeated by old (European) antinomies and rivalries. Third, the actions and policies of the PAU did not represent the whole extent of Pan-American initiatives. From Latin American nations diverse agents and civic organizations (lawyers, medical doctors, defenders of the environment, and feminists) raised new questions and policy initiatives that were later debated in specialized Pan-American conferences. Speaking softly but with solid arguments, Latin American physicians, feminists, sport promoters, architects and economists used the Pan-American conferences to build transnational alliances and promote ideals and policy goals in quite important areas of social life and human welfare. Aside of these ventures, were the literary currents for and against Pan-Americanism, concerned more with issues of modernism, language, and ideology.

Was Pan-Americanism also an ideology? To the extent that it contained major policy objectives relating to peace, commerce, security, and rights, it was at least a set of propositions that could function as organizing principles on a continental space, however different were the populations, languages, and ways-of-life of the countries belonging to the PAU. In areas such as education, childcare, financial institutions, transportation, and public health there was effective cooperation and exchange, whether promoted by the PAU, by professional associations, or leaders of social movements. In this regard, there was a two-way circulation of ideas and technologies across the continent the Pan-American institutions contributed to generate. In similar ways, we can think that Latin America ideologies—whether we refer to republicanism, anarchism, Indigenismo, nationalism, cooperativism, or Krausism—entered in dialogue with movements and ideologies earlier developed in the United States and Europe, though with a different modality and rhetoric. The existence of an inter-American organization helped to intensify this transfer of ideologies, movements, and technology. What about the ideals of consumer sovereignty, imitation of preferences, and the fantasy of abundance? These were also ideologies, yet propagated mostly by the US private sector. Even in this area, the organizational machinery of Pan-Americanism served to facilitate the flow of ideologies of consumerism as a path to development and social welfare.[2]

When Leo S. Rowe assumed the chair of the Pan-American Union (1920), the organization was already a bureaucracy with specialized departments and clear set of objectives. Its goal was to make Latin American representatives accept or join the United States in a series of predetermined objectives. The Americas would be a hemisphere of peace and open commerce, not involved in Europe's militarism and protectionist policies; a set of political national communities united by a long experience in Republicanism, taking steps towards Democracy; and the inter-American system would be governed by general rules, the most important of which was the peaceful resolution of disputes through arbitration. The PAU was a bureaucracy with clearly defined objectives, and Latin American representatives saw in it both the constant insinuation of the Big Brother and a series of opportunities for progress in a variety of fields.

If as an organization, its change was slow, as an ideal, it kept changing. Each director gave the organization its own imprint. John Barrett, the first PAU director, imbued the organization with a business mentality and oriented it towards the solution of practical problems. Representatives of Latin America and the United States, Barrett thought, should get together to solve common problems as US businessmen saw them. For him, integration was a matter of solving practical things (banks, railroads, postal protocols, trademarks, and so forth). That is why he called his mission "practical Pan-Americanism." The second director of the organization, Leo S. Rowe, had a quite different view: for him, there two things that would unite the Americas: intellectual cooperation and cultural exchange. For him, the United States and the Latin American intelligentsias had a crucial role to play in the building of inter-American cooperation. That is why he proposed a vast program of student exchanges at the university level. In addition, he expected to bring to the United States the "representative" folklore, music, dance, literature, and theatre from each Latin American nation, in order to acquaint the US public with the cultural richness of the lands south of the Rio Grande. Rowe's "constructive Pan-Americanism" put a premium on building social connections among intellectuals and other educated people across the continent, while encouraging authorities and institutions in the two Americas to engage in a widespread exchange of culture.

We also know by now what Pan-Americanism was not. It was not a doctrine of cooperation based on the imperatives of history or geography. Although the notion of a "hemisphere apart" was repeated as a mantra by proponents of a continental brotherhood since Jefferson's times, geography was not determinant in uniting the three parts of the continent—quite to the contrary. The historical argument was equally flimsy. That the United States and the Spanish American republics had been colonies in the past and had later rebelled against their colonial masters opting for the republican form of government were similarities that said nothing about their impulse to cooperate internationally. Nothing could be inferred from geography or history to compel North, Central, and South American nations to unite their destinies into a common organization. While the ex-colonies of the Spanish empire (viceroyalties and captaincies general) divided into multiple nations; the Thirteen Colonies remained united (during most of the time) and expanded its territory to reach the Atlantic coast.

In 1889–90 when US Pan-Americanism appeared as an emergent continental force, there started a narrative that continued over time. This argument stated that early efforts to unite the continent promoted by Latin American leaders—started by Bolivar in 1826 and followed by various international conferences—had been a failure and that the wisdom and practicality of US Americans made possible a successful truly inter-American conference in 1890. Parallel to this, promoted by intellectuals from Cuba, New York, Nicaragua, and various South American cities, run a second argument that affirmed that in the South scholars and the people had embraced a trans-national patriotism for "Nuestra América." This sort of expanded motherland was to be rooted on the criollo or mestizo race, which in turn would abolish race in the construction of a more democratic and egalitarian nationhood. This distinction between an Anglo-Saxon Pan-Americanism and a mestizo or racially mixed Latino-Americanism never entered into the house of the Pan-American Union, and obviously could not serve as an argument for union and cooperation, for it worked in the opposite direction: for the separation between the United States and Our America. This sort of ideological confrontation was treated by the key enunciators of Pan-Americanism as a remora of the past, as innocuous and empty rhetoric, with little to add to the discussion about cooperation in matters of trade, governance, internal security, mutual defense and cultural interactions.

II

In the years of the Good Neighbor Policy, "Pan-America" as an imagined community, yet one that required a light and occasional "patriotism." In the United States, Pan-American Day (February 14) was the day chosen to celebrate this hemispheric-wide imagined community. From school children to university students, from farmers to business associations, from Spanish Clubs to the National Federation of Pan-American Societies, from the US presidents to majors of middle and large cities, all contributed to represent –in their speeches, parades, music concerts, or school acts—the aspiration of good-will and mutual understanding among the American republics. Tons of government publicity and the effective participation of civil society made of these celebrations a success, at least until the Second World War (the war effort) shifted completed the attention of the American public.

At the end of the Second World War this ephemeral imagined commonwealth started to weaken, while Pan-American Day became a small ritual, kept mostly within US government offices. In 1946 the *New York Times* lamented the closing of the Office of Inter-American Affairs and a year later, the same newspaper noted that after the war, the United States government started to pay much less attention to Central and South America than before. Between 1947 and 1952, Pan-American Day faded away from US public memory, while the State Department and US diplomats engaged fully the problems of global security and the expansion of Communism, leaving behind the dreams of an American commonwealth.

When it closed its offices (1948) to give way to the new Organization of American States, the Pan-American Union had promoted for more than thirty-seven years the construction of a hemisphere of peace and commerce, united by common ideals about republican government, individual rights, social welfare, and the resolution of disputes through arbitration. Did this ideal or imagined community exist in reality, outside of official circles and more specifically in Central and South America? Judging by the celebration of Pan-American Day, even in the times of the Good Neighbor Policy, there was much less enthusiasm for a hemispheric federation in Latin America than in the United States. The countries that celebrated with enthusiasm Pan-American Day were those with closer (colonial or neo-colonial) ties to the United States, not the Andean nations, nor the Southern Cone.

Was Pan-Americanism itself an imperial force? At the beginning (c. 1890–1926), hemispheric institutions gave disproportionate weight to US policies and initiatives, including those coming not only from government, but also those stemming from the business community, professional associations, universities and scientific societies. Yet the encounter of US diplomats and scholars with their South American peers led to a more collaborative exchange, particularly within the ambit of Pan American conferences, gave room to an increasing number of issues of public policy in which Latin American diplomats and scholars were interested. And with time, between 1927 and 1933, Latin American representatives forced the United States to accept a weak version of the doctrine of non-intervention, later ratified in a speech by President Franklin D. Roosevelt. It appears then, that Latin American representatives gained some terrain in the discussion with its more powerful northern sister-nation and ultimately achieved the promise the have been demanding from the Hegemon: non-intervention in national policies and the respect for national sovereignty. This was then, a peculiar Hegemon, one that retracted from its earlier claim to its absolute right to intervene in the Western

Hemisphere to solve problems of debts created by "chronic wrongdoing" or uncontrolled social or political disorder.

Elsewhere I have claimed that what was "imperial" was the disciplinary knowledge created by the expansion of US scholarship and investment over South America, a knowledge-power that was envisioned as centralized, dominant, and superior to existing national knowledge formations in the sub-continent. The vision of an all-encompassing will-to-know that could generate truths in different realms of South American life was imperial. Yet in matters of inter-American policy, I tend to agree with the notion of cooperation and hegemony or, more precisely with the existence of a weakening hegemony in the period 1890–1945. Let us explore this proposition.

As conceived by Subalternist historian Ranajit Guha (1997), power relations are made up of two forces: Domination (D) and Resistance (R). Domination itself could be achieved by the combination of Coercion (C) and Persuasion (P). Within this scheme, Hegemony is a condition in which Persuasion overweighs Coercion in the practice and process of domination. That is:

There is Hegemony when P > C in D.

Let us apply this scheme to the history of Inter-American relations in the period examined in this volume. In the Americas, we recognize three phases in the US construction of Hegemony: 1890–1933, 1934–1947, and 1948–1989.

- **1890–1933**: During this period two different forms of relationship between the United States and Latin America coexisted. On the one hand, the US built a colonial rule in the Caribbean, influencing in a quite visible manner Central American governments. On the hand, it maintained cooperative and non-interventionist relations with regard to South American nations.[3] US policy toward Mexico can be described as a reluctant interventionism that geared over time to a conflictive yet cooperative relationship. Hence in the Caribbean and Central America, Coercion prevailed over Persuasion, to the extent that these territories at times occupied and at other times bombarded by the US Navy. US relations with South America on the other hand were characterized by an attempt to achieve cooperation with resort to persuasion rather than gunboat diplomacy. In the 1920s, there was a bit of Dollar Diplomacy, but since Elihu Root's visit to the region (1906) there was a persistent effort in persuasion on the similar paths of North and South America. More importantly, US scholars "discovered" progress and civility in the nations of the Southern Cone, while finding only social and economic backwardness in the Andean nations.
- **1934–1947**: as a result of the US declaration of the Good Neighbor Policy, and in particular its respect for the sovereignty of Latin American nations, there was a rapid and effective withdrawal from countries in the Caribbean basin that had been occupied or bombarded for a

variety of reasons. To gain the admiration and respect of its southern neighbors, the United States was ready to disarm or relocate its military forces and stop further interventions in the region. That is, the hemisphere entered a period of Hegemonic engagement (Persuasion outweighing Coercion) in most of the Americas. And after 1933, there was an effort to coopt Latin American politicians and elites into a large circle of friendship and respect (the respect that a Neighbor deserves). Underneath these crucial decisions (the withdrawal from the American Mediterranean and the respect for the sovereignty of Latin American nations) were the Nazi threat to Democracy in the continent and the need to gain allies for the war in Europe. The years of the Good Neighbor Policy were marked a dramatic decline in US interventionist impulses in the rest of the Americas. This was a period where cooperative efforts clearly outweighed the politics of economic or political pressure.

- **1953–1989**: From the end of the Korean War, the peculiar conflict between the United States and the USSR intensified. The following year, the CIA orchestrated a coup to overthrow President Jacobo Arbenz in Guatemala. This was the first intervention motivated by the alleged infiltration of Communists in government, that event marked the start of the Cold War in Latin America. To the extent that the Cold War represented an increase in the number of US interventions in Latin America, sometimes to sustain anti-Communist dictators, other times to overthrow governments too friendly to Communism or the Left, Coercion increased and Persuasion remained stable, producing a more forceful type of hegemony, one animated again by the fear of intervention. However, the United States was not supposed to openly challenge existing treaties of commerce and friendship with Latin American nations, hence, most interventions took the form of covert actions.

During the Cold War, the Policy of the Good Neighbor was abandoned as the US Department of State deployed a new strategy to contain Communism and organized indirect world governance through multilateral agencies. Naturally, the combination of Coercion and Persuasion changed. The United States supported dictators wherever they showed to be allies in the fight against communist infiltration; it provided intelligence to identify and prevent the activities of Left guerrillas; it trained elite military men in the doctrine of National Security to help them fight these guerrillas; it conducted and financed covered operations to overthrow left-win popular leaders. This was indirect government using coercive actions. Together with this The Alliance for Progress and various programs of assistance by the World Bank and the Inter-American Bank presented the US as a progressive power helping the Latin American republics join the road of development. This constituted the most visible form of Persuasion under the new Cold War hegemony.

III

To fragment a problem is an efficient way to understand the problem, if at the end of the road, one returns to a re-conceptualization that incorporates the fragments, if one attains a new synthesis by placing the findings of the fragmentation into a wider theoretical framework. The process of fragmenting United States' hegemony in Latin America into its multiple components opened up with a brilliant essay by Gilbert Joseph in *Close Encounters of Empire*.[4] There Joseph called scholars in inter-American relations to consider all possible encounters between US-Americans and Latin Americans, not just the activities of those involved in diplomacy, the armed forces, of the economy. His call included examining the multiple dimensions of these relationships: domination, cooperation, mutual recognition, disavowal, appropriation, negotiation, subalternization, and resistance. This project entailed placing in the same plane of relevance activities, travels, discoveries, and encounters by individuals, institutions, and associations from the United States in Latin America, in the process of discovering, "conquering," coopting, or negotiating positions of influence in Latin America. And, in reciprocal manner, it implied studying the discoveries, encounters, and negotiations by Latin Americans in the United States.

This Great Fragmentation would not only incorporate new agencies to the process of hegemony and contention—a process that was already in the way—but also make use of all the new approaches that had changed the humanities and the social sciences (gender, racial, and postcolonial studies) to better understand the nature of US imperialism historically and regionally. To the extent that this approach intended to examine a multiplicity of micro-encounters between a variety of "outsiders" and "insiders," the new narrative of inter-American relations would be dramatically altered, reducing the explicatory power of military, diplomatic, and economic factors in the making of imperiality and hegemony.

Joseph's call emphasized the multiplicity of agencies in the making of the neo-colonial or post-colonial forms of engagement, and at the same time embraced the cultural turn. In particular, there was to be an emphasis in the study of discourse, texts, and rhetoric, in the way they were used in literary and gender studies. I was commissioned to write about the question of representation and empire. In my contribution to the volume[5] I tried to deal with this important question, arguing that each micro-encounter of US-Americans in Latin America had left some sort of representation, and that these representations composed a great machinery for understanding the Latin American Other. Thought many forces motivated this micro-encounters, Gain and Knowledge were central to most of them and, in my opinion, at least for the US "rediscovery of South America" in 1890–1930, the will to know seem to be dominant in all of them. If this was so, the exploration of South America in this period should coincide with an explosion of representations about the region (travelers' memoirs, illustrated articles, guides and handbooks, maps, sketches, photographs, and silent films).

This 1998 article contained two main propositions. First, that each micro-encounter had to build a representation that made readable and understandable what was being reported and done on a particular field. Each US observer represented its own mission as well as the territory, government and societies under scrutiny, and imagined them in relationship to a larger engagement between US American forces (economic progress, science, technology, republican government, consumer modernity, Protestant religion, law and regulations, universities, etc.) and the diverse totality called Spanish America. That is, in each traveler's memoir or scientific report one could detect fragments of a discussion about the possible engagement of a modern, informal, non-imperialist hegemon. The second key proposition was that all representations product of these micro-encounters were constructed under the impulse and binding force of knowledge. Each representational product of the neo-colonial encounter was itself the product of the will to know, culturally defined on US American soil, under US institutions of knowledge.[6] So, I call this vast collection of initiatives, texts, and ideologies "The Enterprise of Knowledge." This was my way of saying that the study of US hegemony had to shift towards the analysis of representations and knowledge projects, rather than follow the paths of US capital, diplomacy or the Navy. Neo-colonizing a country in South America implied the construction of knowledge about the population, its territory, and forms of government, a project only tangentially related to the establishment of hard power (military, economy, and diplomacy).

After that I continued to study the issue of empire and representations of South America, publishing various papers and a short book, titled *Imágenes de un imperio* (2006).[7] I repeated here the proposition that the US presence in South America was accompanied by an "avalanche" or "explosion" of representations about the subcontinent, and explored the diversity, nature, and the content of these representations. In this short book I tried to deal with a vast enterprise of re-discovery (pioneered by US prospectors, scientists, churchmen, investors, merchants, and professionals) that is still useful to think of neo-colonization as a collective and massive act of representation, motorized by the will-to-know.

In my book *Disciplinary Conquest: US Scholars in South America, 1900–1945*, I studied the efforts made by five US scholars (a historian; an archaeologist; a geographer; a sociologist; and a political scientist) to apprehend, classify and synthesized the realities of South America.[8] The book argues that these scholars, guided by the methods of inquiry of their own disciplines and motivated by their personal interests and academic curiosity, tried to produce the most accurate description of the sub-continent. These disciplinary renderings contained interesting revelations and insights. Scholars went south to discover the situation and potentialities of a continent that to most US people remained dormant and unknown since the fall of the Spanish empire. At times, the propositions and conclusions of these scholars at times contradicted each other, yet interestingly, some of them imagined natural limits to the advance of American capital and technology, while others underscored the continuity of poverty and pre-modern social relations among Indigenous peoples.

Anticipating Latin American critics of the 1960s and 1970s, US scholars divided South America into progressive and backward (undeveloped) nations. While in the Southern Cone (Argentina, Brazil, Uruguay, and Chile) were progressive nations, that have adopted contracts and wage labor and developed individual liberties and rights, the rest of South America was a sea of widespread poverty and ignorance. In the Andean nations, the Republican experiments have not transformed labor and property relations in the countryside and, as a result, have failed to elevate the standards of life of the indigenous masses. *Disciplinary Conquest* deals with the relationship between knowledge, imperial visibility, and US foreign policy in ways that I consider novel. The discoveries made by scholars, in addition to opening new lines of investigation, presented questions and dilemmas about the "Lands South of Panama" that were transmitted to the State Department and discussed by diplomats, navy commanders, and key investors.

More recently, I have been trying to put together a collection of old and new essays that would be titled *Imperial Mechanics: Essays on the Cultural Politics of US Pan-Americanism*. Some of these essays insist on the idea that US Pan-Americanism was an organized mechanism of cooperation. The US hegemonic project consisted of the building of a cooperative alliance and organization that would promote peace, multilateral commerce, the arbitration of disputes, and cultural exchange with Latin America. This was a sort of organizational machine based probably on the experience of businessmen or mainstream politicians. This machine promoted a modern, persuasive way of imperial engagement. The key proposition was: if you invited partners to cooperate and did sufficient work of persuasion, you could build a supra-national form of governance in which nobody would feel invaded or intervened. The Pan-American Union and its heir, the Organization of American States, were the legacies of such a thought and efforts of disseminating US Pan-Americanism.

The book contains essays on Practical versus Cultural Pan-Americanism, the Panama Canal and the Pan American Railway, Pan-American Day, Libraries collections of Latino-Americana, the teaching of Spanish in the United States, J. W. Thompson's advertising techniques, and a discussion of US American democracy in Buenos Aires. In a certain way, this book responds more closely to research agenda proposed in *Close Encounters of Empire* bringing under examination engineering marvels, book collecting, advertising techniques, the promotion of US American government, and the massive teaching of Spanish as if they were distinct types of machines brought together by a collective impulse to accumulate knowledge, reach distant territories, sell modern goods, and impress the souls and minds of South Americans.

Notes

1 Gilbert M. Joseph, Catherine C. LeGrand, and Ricardo D. Salvatore, eds, *Close Encounters of Empire* (Durham: Duke University Press, 1998).
2 Some scholars have argued that the US films and advertising that inundated the Latin American households with imagery of consumer dreams and consequently were the most powerful instruments for the penetration of the "American way of life," and in their way redefined the concepts of development and human welfare towards the elusive notion of consumer satisfaction.
3 Ricardo D. Salvatore, *Disciplinary Conquest: US Scholars in South America, 1900–1945* (Durham: Duke University Press, 2016).
4 Gilbert Joseph, "Close Encounters: Toward a New Cultural History of US–Latin American Relations," in Joseph et al., *Close Encounters of Empire*, 3–46.
5 Ricardo D. Salvatore, "The Enterprise of Knowledge: Representational Machines of Informal Empire," in Joseph et al., *Close Encounters of Empire*, 69–104.
6 This inexhaustible curiosity produced millions of representations that accumulated in US libraries, archives, exhibits, university classrooms, and Spanish clubs.
7 Ricardo D. Salvatore, *Imágenes de un imperio* (Buenos Aires: Sudamericana, 2006).
8 Salvatore, *Disciplinary Conquest*.

Contributors

Teresa Davis is Postdoctoral Fellow in Transnational Latin American History at Emory University. Her research focuses on the entangled histories of law and capitalism, especially on the origins and fate of efforts to legally manage the globalization of capital. She is working on *jus soli* citizenship in Latin America and conducting research on the transnational legal battle over the creation of Argentina's state-owned oil company in 1922.

Juliette Dumont is an Associate Professor of Contemporary History at the Institute of Higher Studies on Latin America (Université Sorbonne Nouvelle—Paris 3) and a researcher at the Center for Research and Documentation of the Americas (CREDA). She is currently developing a research project focused on academic exchanges within the framework of Pan-Americanism during the first half of the twentieth century.

Mark J. Petersen is Associate Professor of History at the University of Dallas. His research has focused on the history of inter-American cooperation and Chilean foreign policy. He is the author of *The Southern Cone and the Origins of Pan America, 1888–1933* (University of Notre Dame Press, 2022).

Aida Rodríguez holds a PhD in Contemporary History from the Universidad Autónoma de Madrid. Her research concerns international relations between the United States and Europe, and inter-American connections. She has participated in numerous international conferences and is editor of the journal *Revista Historia Autónoma*.

Ricardo D. Salvatore is Professor of History at the Universidad Torcuato Di Tella in Buenos Aires. His books include *Close Encounters of Empire* (co-edited with Catherine LeGrand and Gilbert Joseph, Duke University Press, 2016); *Disciplinary Conquest: US Scholars in South America, 1900–1945* (Duke University Press, 2016); *Los lugares del saber* (Beatriz Viterbo, 2008); *Culturas Imperiales* (Beatriz Viterbo, 2005); and *Bibliotecas y Cultura Letrada en America* (co-edited with Carlos Aguirre, PUCP, 2018).

Ricardo is currently writing a book entitled *Imperial Mechanics* that will deal with the cultural politics of Pan-Americanism in the twentieth century.

Juan Pablo Scarfi is Research Associate at the Argentine National Scientific and Technical Research Council (CONICET) and Lecturer in Global History & International Relations, University of San Andres, Argentina. His books include *The Hidden History of International Law in the Americas: Empire and Legal Networks* (Oxford University Press, 2017); *Cooperation and Hegemony in US–Latin American Relations: Reconsidering the Idea of the Western Hemisphere* (co-edited with Andrew Tillman, Palgrave Macmillan, 2016); and *El imperio de la ley: James Brown Scott y la construcción de un orden jurídico interamericano* (Fondo de Cultura Económica, 2014). He has held a Fulbright Postdoctoral Fellowship (George Washington University, 2019–20) and Visiting Research Fellowship at the Institut des Hautes Études de l'Amérique Latine (IHEAL), Université Paris 3, Sorbonne Nouvelle (2019).

David M. K. Sheinin is Professor of History at Trent University and Director of the Trent University History Graduate Program. He is the winner of the Trent University Distinguished Research Award (2017) and served as the university's Social Sciences and Humanities Research Council of Canada mentor from 2015 to 2020. A member of the Argentine National Academy of History, David has held the J. Franklin Jameson Fellowship in American History (Library of Congress/American Historical Association), and in 2008–9, the Edward Larocque Tinker Visiting Professorship in Latin American History at the University of Wisconsin-Madison. He has published sixteen books, the most recent of which are *Race and Transnationalism in the Americas* (co-edited with Benjamin Bryce, University of Pittsburgh Press, 2021) and *Armed Jews in the Americas* (co-edited with Raanan Rein, Brill, 2021).

Lisa Ubelaker teaches history at the University of San Andrés in Buenos Aires. She holds a PhD from Yale University (2013) and has held a Social Sciences Research Council Doctoral Fellowship. She is the author of multiple articles on Pan-American cultural histories.

Index

Acción Argentina 104
Aguirre, Juan E. 122
Alessandri, Arturo 35
Alfaro, Ricardo 153
Alliance for Progress 116, 125, 128, 169
Álvarez, Adolfo Teodoro 122
Álvarez, Alejandro 48, 58, 70–1, 138–56
Amadeo, Mario 126
American Code of Private International Law (Bustamante Code) 16
American Institute of International Law (AIIL) 46, 138–56
American School Peace League 68
American Society of International Law 139
Arbenz, Jacobo 4, 17, 120, 169

Baroffio, Eugenio 32
Barrett, John 14–15, 52, 165
Bemis, Samuel Flagg 3
Blaine, James G. 47, 58
Boffi, Jorge Alberto 127
Brainerd, Eloise 78
Brandao, Pimentel 126
Brum Doctrine 34–6
Bunge, Alejandro 54–5, 58–60

Calvo, Carlos 48–9, 117, 119, 122–3
Carnegie Endowment for International Peace (CEIP) 55, 68, 76, 139, 141
Casal Castel, Alberto 102–3
Casasús, Joaquín 54
Castello Branco, Humberto 122
Castro, Guillermo 122
Castro Ossandón, Hernán 70, 73
Catalán, Arenales 126
Claridad 103–5
Clark, John Bates 54

Colombo, Ricardo 117, 119, 122–3, 125, 127–30
Commercial Bureau of American Republics 22
Coppola, A. E. 30
Cuban Missile Crisis (1962) 121
Curtis, William E. 12
Congress of Panama 11–12
Costa Méndez, Nicanor 125
Customs Union of the South 59–61

De Alverar, Carlos 117
De Oliveira, Xavier 79–80
Defense Advisory Committee (DAC) 120–1
Del Brazo con los Varela 106–8
Del Mar, Roland 122
Division for International Cooperation (DIC) 76–8
Drago, Luis María 13, 49, 117, 119
Dulles, John Foster 17

El Fortín 104
El Hogar 102–4
El Mundo 104
El Pampero 104

Federal Reserve Act (United States, 1913) 52
Fisher, Irving 54
Fuerzas Armadas de la Liberación Nacional (FALN) 123, 124

Gallardo, Ángel 35
Gálvez, Gabriel 126–7
Good Neighbor Policy 2, 17, 70, 90–106, 108–9, 116, 118, 148, 163–9
Grassi, Italo Luis 57
Guggenheim Foundation 76

Guha, Ranajit 163, 168
Gunther, John 103

Hanke, Lewis 104
Hispanic American Historical Review 68
Hollander, Jacob 54
Hoover, Herbert 45, 53, 56–7

Illia, Arturo 120, 123
Inman, Samuel Guy 72
Inter-America 68
Inter-American Commission on Human Rights 116, 119
Inter-American Defense Board (IADB) 120–9
Inter-American Defense College 119
Inter-American Institute of Intellectual Cooperation (IAIIC) 79
Inter-American Institute of Musicology (IAIM) 80
Inter-American Judicial Committee 123
Inter-American Peace Force 124, 128
Inter-American Treaty for Reciprocal Assistance (TIAR) 117, 120–1, 125–7
International Committee on Intellectual Cooperation 66–7
International High Commission 49
Iricibar, Manuel 122

Jenks, Jeremiah 54
Jouffre de Lapradelle, Albert 153

Kemmerer, Edwin 52–4
Klein, Julius 45, 52–3
Krausism 165

La Prensa 104
Ladies' Home Journal 96, 101
Lanusse, Alejandro Agustín 117, 119, 123, 127–30
Latin American Free Trade Association (LAFTA) 128
Le May, Curtis E. 120
League of United Latin American Citizens (LULAC) 100
Letelier, Orlando 130
Liberal International Order (LIO) 138–40, 144, 147, 150–1, 153–4
Lippman, Walter 148

Magalhaes, Juraci 124–5
Malvinas War 117
Marianno, José 33
McAdoo, William G. 55

McNamara, Robert 125
Mezzera, Rodolfo 34–5
Miranda, Carmen 96
Miss Pan America 97
Monge Gordillo, Carlos 122
Monroe Doctrine 4, 17, 49, 79, 117, 141, 144
Montoneros 119

Naón, Rómulo S. 52
non-intervention 3

Office of the Coordinator of Inter-American Affairs (CIAA) 93–7, 101–6, 167
Oliver, Maria Rosa 104
Onganía, Juan Carlos 128–9
Operation Condor 117, 128, 130
Ortiz, Roberto M 35

Pan-American Conferences: First International Conference of American States (1889–90) 4, 12–13, 47, 73; Pan-American Medical Congress (1893) 22; First Latin American Scientific Congress (1898) 69, 70; Pan-American Exposition (1901) 24–25, 29; Second Pan-American Conference (1902) 13–14, 22, 70, 72, 73; Third Pan-American Conference (1906) 13, 73; First Pan-American Scientific Congress (1908) 52; Fourth Pan-American Conference (1910) 14, 73; First Pan-American Financial Conference (1915) 54–5; Second Pan-American Scientific Conference (1915–16) 54, 72, 75; Second Pan-American Financial Conference (1920) 54; Fifth Pan-American Conference (1923) 15, 35, 73, 118, 149, 152; Rio de Janeiro Commission of Jurists (1927) 147; Sixth Pan-American Conference (1928) 16, 73, 118, 147; Seventh Pan-American Conference (1933) 17, 30, 37, 70, 74, 147; Inter-American Conference for the Maintenance of Peace (1936) 70, 74, 78; Eighth Pan-American Conference (1938) 17, 70, 74, 78, 80; Pan-American Congress on Popular Housing (1939) 32; Inter-American Conference on War and Peace (1945) 120; Ninth Pan-American Conference (1948) 17, 120; Tenth Inter-American Conference (1954),

Index

3–4; Second Extraordinary Inter-American Conference (1965) 122–3; Eleventh Meeting of Consultation of Ministers of Foreign Affairs (1967) 124–6; Thirteenth Meeting of Consultation of Ministers of Foreign Affairs (1969) 128
Pan-American Day 17–18, 97–9, 167
Pan-American Games 116
Pan-American Health Organization 70, 72, 116
Pan-American Railroad 22
Pan-American Student Forum 99–100
Pan-American Union Building 24–5, 28, 29
Pearson, Samuel Hale 55
Pistarini, Pascual A. 125–6
Platt Amendment 116, 142, 146
Portela, Epifanio 117
Presser Bello, Ary 121–2
Pueyrredón, Honório 16, 118

Quesada, Vicente 117

Radio Belgrano 105–6
Radio Spendid 105–6
Radiolandia 103, 107
Ramos, Constantino 120
Rockefeller Foundation 73, 76
Root, Elihu 47, 70, 168
Rowe, Leo S. 3, 65–6, 70, 72, 165
Ruiz Moreno, Isidoro 51

Saavedra Lamas, Carlos 50–1, 147
Saénz Peña, Roque 48
San Martín, José de 122
Santander, Francisco de Paula 122
Scott, James Brown 138–45, 149, 154
Selecciones del Reader's Digest 106–9
Seligman, Edwin 54
Sherwell, Guillermo 52
Sintonía 106
Simson, Henry L. 148
Suárez, Leopoldo 120
Subercaseaux, Guillermo 54, 59

Tornquist, Carlos Alfredo 55
Torres Rioseco, Arturo 66
Tupamaros 119

Vieyra, Enrique Benjamín 121

Warburg, Paul 45, 52–3
Welles, Sumner 101
Whitaker, Arthur P. 1–3, 66, 148
Wilson, Woodrow 28, 49, 52, 72
Women's Wear Daily 94–5
World Peace Foundation 68

Yrigoyen, Hipólito 49

Zamora, Antonio 104
Zavala Ortiz, Miguel Angel 121, 123
Zeballos, Estanislao 49

Printed in the United States
by Baker & Taylor Publisher Services